THE VIENNESE CAFÉ AND FIN-DE-SIÈCLE CULTURE

AUSTRIAN AND HABSBURG STUDIES
General Editor: Gary B. Cohen

Published in Association with the Center for Austrian Studies, University of Minnesota

THE VIENNESE CAFÉ AND FIN-DE-SIÈCLE CULTURE

Edited by

Charlotte Ashby
Tag Gronberg
and
Simon Shaw-Miller

berghahn
NEW YORK · OXFORD
www.berghahnbooks.com

First edition published in 2013 by

Berghahn Books

www.berghahnbooks.com

© 2013, 2015 Charlotte Ashby, Tag Gronberg and Simon Shaw-Miller
First paperback edition published in 2015

Library of Congress Cataloging-in-Publication Data

The Viennese cafe and fin-de-siecle culture / edited by Charlotte Ashby ... [et al.] -- 1st ed.
    p. cm. -- (Austrian and Habsburg studies)
    Includes bibliographical references and index.
    ISBN 978-0-85745-764-6 (hbk. : alk. paper) -- ISBN 978-1-78238-926-2 (pbk. : alk.
paper) -- ISBN 978-0-85745-765-3 (ebook)
    1. Coffeehouses--Austria--Vienna. 2. Coffeehouses--Social aspects. 3. Vienna (Austria)--
Intellectual life--19th century. 4. Vienna (Austria)--Intellectual life--20th century. 5. Jews--
Austria--Vienna--Intellectual life. 6. Vienna (Austria)--Civilization. I. Ashby, Charlotte.
    TX907.5.A92V5488 2013
    647.95436'13--dc23

                                                                2012033447

British Library Cataloguing in Publication Data
A catalogue record for this book is available from the British Library

Printed on acid-free paper

ISBN: 978-0-85745-764-6 hardback
ISBN: 978-1-78238-926-2 paperback
ISBN: 978-0-85745-765-3 ebook

CONTENTS

LIST OF ILLUSTRATIONS

PREFACE

This volume is the result of three years' work undertaken by the team of the Vienna Café Project, as led by Professor Jeremy Aynsley at the Royal College of Art and Dr Tag Gronberg and Professor Simon Shaw-Miller at Birkbeck, University of London. Also on the team were Dr Charlotte Ashby at the Royal College of Art and the doctoral students, Diane Silverthorne, at the Royal College of Art, and Sara Ayres, at Birkbeck. The project was most ably administered by Angela Waplington. The team would like to thank the Royal College of Art and Birkbeck, University of London, for the support given to the project. We are especially grateful for the generous funding awarded by the Arts and Humanities Research Council of Great Britain without which much of the work of the project could not have been undertaken.

The early stages of conception and planning of the project benefitted from the encouragement of Dr Markus Kristan at the Albertina, Dr Eva B. Ottlinger at the Hofmobiliendepot and Dr Michael Zimmermann during his tenure as director of the Austrian Cultural Forum, London. The assistance of Reingard Witzman and Dr Ulrike Spring at the Wien Museum was also most valuable during the research stages of the project.

The exhibition, *Vienna Café 1900*, the accompanying festival of events and the conference, *The Viennese Café as an Urban Site of Cultural Exchange*, held in 2008, involved the participation of a number of partners. The Austrian Cultural Forum in London continued its support of the project. In particular we would like to thank the then director, Dr Johannes Wimmer, as well as Andrea Rauter and Vanessa Fewster. Their enthusiasm for our work was a constant source of encouragement. The Austrian Trade Commission and Austrian Tourism, in particular Gerhard Müller and Oskar Hinteregger, helped the project greatly. We would also like to thank the then Austrian Ambassador to London, Dr Gabriele Matzner-Holzer. The Anglo-Austrian Society, the Coffeehouse Owners Association of Vienna, Hotel Das Triest, the Vienna Tourist Office and the Wien Museum all contributed funds towards the exhibition and public events. The exhibition and conference were beautifully catered for by the pop-up Viennese café run by Demel of Vienna. Events accompanying the exhibition were co-hosted at the Royal College of Art, the Austrian Cultural Forum, the Royal Academy of Music and Birkbeck Cinema.

Additionally, throughout the AHRC project we were grateful for the advice and support of our Academic Advisory Group made up of Dr David Crowley, from the Royal College of Art, Dr Leslie Topp from Birkbeck, Professor Amanda Glauert from the Royal College of Music, and Dr Johannes Wimmer of the Austrian Cultural Forum.

Finally we would like to thank all the contributors to this volume for their enthusiastic participation in the project conference and all their work in preparing the essays for this collection. Many thanks also to Ann Przyzycki and Marion Berghahn at Berghahn Books for their help in the production of this volume.

Special thanks are due to the late Paul Overy, to whose memory this volume is dedicated.

THE VIENNESE CAFÉ AND FIN-DE-SIÈCLE CULTURE

Charlotte Ashby

The café is a space intimately associated with the development of modern urban culture: a site of spectacle, consumption and sexual licence on the one hand, and on the other a site for the gestation of new political, social and creative ideas. From Jürgen Habermas' *The Structural Transformation of the Public Sphere*, in 1962, the link between the coffeehouse and the development of modern public discourse was established.[1] Despite the recognised significance of the café space, the informal, haphazard and ephemeral nature of café life has made it relatively resistant to scholarly enquiry.

In recent years there have been a number of works that have sought to address the coffeehouse and its contribution to European culture more directly. Ulla Heise's *Coffee and Coffee-houses* is a wide-ranging study exploring the evolution of the coffeehouse as a social and cultural institution across the cities of Europe.[2] The coffeehouse as the site for the birth of urban modernity in eighteenth-century England has been explored in Markman Ellis's *The Coffee House: A Cultural History* and Brian William Cowan, *The Social Life of Coffee: The Emergence of the British Coffeehouse*.[3] Both these works trace in detail the social circles and the formal and informal institutions established in these venues, marked as they were by freedom of speech and association. Giving an alternative picture of the social life of the café, W. Scott Haine presents a fascinating insight into the role played by the café in communities of the working classes in Paris through the course of the nineteenth century.[4] The coffeehouse as a designed space has been closely analysed in Christoph Grafe and Franziska Bollerey's *Cafés and Bars: The Architecture of Public Display*.[5] These titles represent just a fraction of the books that have sought to commemorate and capture the coffeehouse as a space in the social and cultural lives of our cities.

In relation to Vienna, the central importance of the coffeehouse to Viennese culture is an established part of the city's history. The role of the coffeehouse in the lives of many of the key figures within Viennese modernism is a recurring theme in the literature devoted to Vienna 1900 studies. Formative works in the field of Vienna 1900 studies, such as Carl Schorske's *Fin-de-siècle Vienna: Politics and Culture* and William M. Johnston's *The Austrian Mind: An Intellectual and Social History, 1848–1938*, conveyed the importance of the coffeehouse in relation to the intellectual and cultural life of the city.[6]

The coffeehouse as a recurring theme in the literature of the period has also made its mark on German literary studies. As this arena of scholarship expanded in various disciplines over the proceeding decades, the presence of the coffeehouse remained ubiquitous.[7] Newer works have added to our understanding of the social make-up of the city and its impact on the development of the distinct modern culture of the city. Steve Beller's *Vienna and the Jews, 1867–1938: A Cultural History* raised the important issue of the centrality of Vienna's Jewish communities to this history.[8] Edward Timms' *Karl Kraus, Apocalyptic Satirist: Culture and Catastrophe in Habsburg Vienna*, and his explanation of the importance of the social and professional networks determining the circulation of ideas in Vienna, raised understanding of the importance of such personal contacts.[9] The international dimensions of coffeehouse culture have been explored in Klaus Thiele-Dohrmann's *Europäische Kaffeehauskultur* and Michael Rössner's anthology of essays, *Literarische Kaffeehäuser*.[10]

The exhibition hosted in 1980 by the Wien Museum, then the Historisches Museum der Stadt Wien, on the Viennese Coffeehouse was important in presenting the first synthesis of the coffeehouse as a physical space in the city, its history and its association with the development of Viennese modernism.[11] The fame of the Viennese café has also resulted in a host of publications intended for the general public which largely depend on the uncritical recycling of the same anecdotes and sayings.

Though the coffeehouse has, therefore, long been recognised as a site of importance in Vienna at the turn of the century, there has as yet been little scholarly investigation into how this site really functioned in relation to the broader culture and society of the city. In recent years there has been a great deal of active research in relation to the literature of the Jung Wien group and their peers, Jewish Vienna and the art and design innovations of the Secession. The essays collected within this volume are drawn from a number of different disciplines: art history, design history and cultural history, German literature and Jewish studies. The theme of the café occurs in all these areas, but often with relatively little cross-disciplinary contact and this is something our 2008 conference and this collection seeks to remedy. By bringing the varied methodologies and concerns of these disciplines to bear on the question of the coffeehouse, this volume provides a point of contact between these different fields of research and allows them to mutually inform one another. Considering the theme of the coffeehouse as a site for the fruitful transgression of established boundaries, this book attempts to provide a comparable meeting place of ideas, finding new points of contact between different fields of research. This way of relating physical space and design with intellectual, social and cultural trends within a specific historical context has potential implications for research and the development of appropriate methodologies in the broader field of histories of metropolitan culture.

Our thematic concern with the coffeehouse as a site of urban modernity and cultural exchange has resulted in a focus that is primarily oriented towards the large, bourgeois coffeehouses of the city centre. This focus on these coffeehouses, patronised by a broad range of Vienna's professional, intellectual and artistic classes, nonetheless excludes a great many smaller cafés and inns that provided comparable services for Vienna's lower-middle and working classes out in the suburbs. This exclusion is also in large part a reflection of the comparative richness of available source material in relation to the grander coffeehouses, documented as they are in contemporary literature, guidebooks and journalism, postcards, photographs, design journals and so on. A detailed social history of the coffeehouse across all strata of Viennese society would be greatly welcomed, but lies outside the scope of this present volume.

The Viennese Café and Fin-de-siècle Culture represents both the final outcome of a three-year Arts and Humanities Research Council research project and a conference entitled *The Viennese Café as an Urban Site of Cultural Exchange* held in 2008. The research project, launched jointly in 2006 by Professor Jeremy Aynsley at the Royal College of Art and Dr Tag Gronberg and Professor Simon Shaw-Miller at Birkbeck, University of London, was constituted with the intention of exploring the Viennese café as a key site of turn-of-twentieth-century modernity. With a focus on an interior urban space, rather than 'the street' which usually serves as a metonym for the city, the project showed how the café offers a slower paced, but no less complex lens through which to understand urban modernity.

The challenge of editing this volume reflects the complexity of attempting to adequately address the many issues bound up in Viennese modernism and urban modernity at the turn of the century. The very fluidity and interrelatedness of the issues raised defies a simple, linear overview. A number of key themes arose repeatedly during the conference and reappear among the essays presented here, as outlined below. This repetition illuminates the points of convergence between different disciplines through the contrasts in the ways in which these ideas are handled, as imagery, as text and as historical source. Certain key texts, such as Habermas' and Fredrich Torberg's recollections of the coffeehouse, are referenced in a number of the essays.[12] The editors have decided to let this repetition stand as in each case these texts are used by different writers from different disciplines to make different points.

*

The café offers a site where different perspectives can be tried against one another. Its place in the city exemplified the shifting ground of Viennese urban modernity, as it provided a key location for the blurring or breaking down of time-honoured hierarchies and social frameworks of exclusion and inclusion. In Vienna, where in many spheres archaic and restrictive social mores prevailed, the café stood out as an institution at the heart of the city in which such rules could be bent. This was, in part, a manifestation of the café's identity as a casual site of recreation. Though far from free of regimentation, tradition and the observance of class, race and gender boundaries, the perceived informality and triviality of coffeehouse life allowed it to become a space within the city where such boundaries could be temporarily transgressed. This is one explanation for why the coffeehouse became a 'home' for more marginalised groups within the city.

The relative inclusiveness and informality of coffeehouse life contributed to its importance for a number of groups. The coffeehouse as a 'home from home' is one of the recurring themes in discussions of the Viennese café. One of the aims of this collection is to subject such well-established ideas relating to the café to critical enquiry. Charlotte Ashby and Richard Kurdiovsky's essays both call on visual and textural evidence to explore how socially accessible and home-like the café really was. Steven Beller and Shachar Pinsker also examine this perceived homeliness in relation to the café as a space in which both the assimilated and newly-arrived Jewish communities in Vienna might 'belong'.

The Viennese café as a Jewish space in the city constitutes another strand of enquiry running through this volume. The café was constructed, often antisemitically, as Jewish in contemporary journalism. Subsequently, post-Second World War accounts of the Viennese café are often coloured by the traumatic destruction of pre-war café life, brought about by the forced aryanisation of cafés and the expulsion or murder of Vienna's Jewish inhabitants.[13] The tourist culture of Vienna today is frequently at pains to gloss over this rupture and emphasise instead continuity with the pre-war tradition.[14] The image of the Viennese café as the social hub of Viennese life is not a new one. The Viennese café was the subject of nostalgic myth-making and civic pride from the nineteenth century onward, as Ashby and Gilbert Carr explore.

The idea of the café as a fertile ground for literary innovation, based on its role as a site where young writers can meet and be encouraged by their older colleagues and connections between like-minded people can be forged and maintained, is also explored across the collection. In the essays by Ashby, Carr and Edward Timms, this is looked at in connection with Viennese literary modernism. Pinsker, Katarzyna Murawska-Muthesius and Ines Sabotič approach the same question from the perspective of Hebrew and Yiddish writers in Lemberg, Vienna and Berlin, Polish writers in Kraków and Croatian writers in Zagreb.

Murawska-Muthesius, Ashby and Mary Costello examine the perception and realities of the accessibility of the café for women and the idea of the gendering of public space, also considered in Tag Gronberg's essay. By analysing these recurring themes from different perspectives the collection is able to get closer to understanding the mechanisms behind the myth that fostered the renowned creativity of the café.

In many ways the café encapsulated the complexity of urban life and the construction of urban modernity at the beginning of the twentieth century. While nineteenth-century cultural commentators, such as Baudelaire, were captivated by the pace and mutability of life on the streets of the city, the café provided an essential counterpoint to it. The anonymity of the pedestrian provided a certain kind of freedom. Anonymity within the Viennese café was up for negotiation: one could become a *Stammgast* (regular) and make oneself at home or remain a passing stranger. This extra level of complexity and individual agency provides an alternative manifestation of the modern urban experience, in which the desire for community is in conflict with the desire for personal freedom. Withdrawn from the pace of the street, but not wholly removed from it, the café provided a place for reflection and thus a potentially productive venue for the forging of new identities.

The book opens with Ashby's essay, which introduces the subject of the café and its relationship to the social and cultural life of Vienna. The famous role of the café as a centre of masculine intellectual life is set alongside its multifarious identities as a site of leisure and frivolity deeply rooted in the social life of the city. The reality of the limited accessibility of the café in terms of class and gender is nuanced by an exploration of the conventions and permitted transgressions hallowed by the café's long-established traditions. That the Viennese café did not quite achieve the heights of free and vigorous political debate idealised in Habermas' theory of the bourgeois public sphere is shown to be comparatively unimportant in relation to its versatility in embracing the richness and contradictions of public life in the city.

Carr's essay in turn introduces the intellectual space of the coffeehouse, examining the representation and construction of the legend of the Viennese café in contemporary journalism, nostalgic autobiography and fictional form. The fluidity of the identity of the café, in terms of time and space, presented here parallels the development of the literary modernism practised by its habitués. A fragmented, facetted picture of the café emerges, confirming the essential intangibility of the creative legacy of the coffeehouse. Carr observes that relatively few writers engaged with the café as a subject despite its purported importance to them and much of what he has uncovered reveals more about the memoir genre's realm of self-deconstructive myth-making than it does of the realities of café life.

This is followed by three essays which variously consider the café in relationship to the figure of the outsider. Beller's essay explores the question of the Viennese café as a Jewish space within the city. The nature of the coffeehouse – at the heart of the city, but outside the formal institutional framework of the city's hierarchies – is suggested as one of the factors that made it a congenial environment for Vienna's Jews who, although prominent within the city, were also often regarded as outsiders. Gronberg's essay explores the close association between the founding legend of the Viennese coffeehouse and the Viennese victory over the Turks in the 1683 siege in relation to the articulation of identities, for individuals as well as for the city itself. The ideas of progress and decline and the modernist or modernising perspective of the outsider that concerned many Viennese thinkers at the turn of the century can also be considered as part of this Orientalist discourse, which offers a new perspective on the cultural position of the café within the city. Pinsker's essay further explores the Jewish identity of the coffeehouses of Vienna. He shifts the focus from the highly acculturated Jewish figures of the Jung Wien group and Vienna's assimilated Jews to the emergent literary circles of the Hebrew and Yiddish-speaking communities. In this story of a far less well-known literary modernism, the coffeehouses again appear as vital locations providing a physical space in which communities could be constructed and fruitful networks established. Pinsker's essay expands beyond the boundaries of Vienna, to look at the comparable role played by cafés in other centres, notably Lemberg and Berlin.

This departure from Vienna is continued in the following two essays, which explore the parallel developments of café life elsewhere in the Dual Monarchy of Austria-Hungary. Murawska-Muthesius' study of a particular Krakówian café, Michalik's Den, presents a space in which modernity in the visual arts was explored alongside the emergence of a modern Polish identity. The medium of caricature was one which allowed artists to transgress conventional boundaries and engage in contemporary social and political debates. This transgression was literally played out on the walls and furnishings of the café and in the cabaret performances given there. Again the theme of the outsider recurs, as Murawska-Muthesius examines how Jews and women were represented within the imagery of Polish modernism. Ines Sabotič's essay presenting the development of the café as an institution in Zagreb in the late nineteenth and early twentieth centuries provides a valuable alternative paradigm against which to re-examine the institution of the Viennese café. The development of café culture in Zagreb was a reflection of its relationship to Vienna as the cultural centre of the lands of Austria-Hungary and the existence of a pan-Central European, German-speaking bourgeois culture. The importance of the coffeehouses for the emergence of literary modernism in Zagreb paralleled that of the coffeehouses of Vienna. At the same time, the emergence of

Croatian nationalism in the early twentieth century challenged the hegemony of German-speaking culture in favour of both localism and an internationalism oriented towards cultural centres, such as Paris, beyond Austria-Hungary. The dominance of the issue of national identity in Zagreb highlights conversely the cosmopolitan nature of Viennese café society in which the individual and not the nation dominated intellectual enquiry.

The similarities and differences between the café cultures of these different cities provide different perspectives which are mutually illuminating. Mary Costello's essay examines the gendering of the space of the café, through the case study of a noted alternative to the café, Adolf Loos's Kärntner Bar, and its reproduction as a space in the Senior Common Room of Trinity College, Dublin. Again, different perspectives are drawn on as Costello investigates the established opposition between Loos's modern, masculine bar and the Viennese café. The Trinity Bar provides a reflection upon the original and on how social spaces can be both mythologised and loaded with cultural values. The role of design in gendering space and the complexities and inconsistencies in the gendering of modernism and the city in the early twentieth century reveal a picture which is far more complex than the simple image of the coffeehouse as a site of masculine sociability.

The relationship of the cafés to design modernism is also the subject of the following two essays by Jeremy Aynsley and Richard Kurdiovsky. Aynsley's essay considers the Viennese café from a history of design perspective, through an examination of the visual representation of the café in print culture and signage. This essay provides a visual counterpoint to the question of the construction of the coffeehouse in journalistic and literary sources. Here the visual identity of the café, represented in advertisements, posters and as interiors in journals such as *Das Interieur*, is explored to examine the construction of expectations of a modern, urban café. Kurdiovsky's essay considers the interior design of Viennese cafés in order to interrogate their association with the home or living room. The points of similarity and difference to domestic interior design that he reveals are illuminating in relation to both the development of interior design in Vienna and the construction and performance of public and private identities in the city. Edward Timms' essay takes a reflective step back to consider the Viennese café in the light of a comparison to an alternative scene of urban, modernist, literary endeavour. He presents the role of coffeehouses, as public spaces, in the intellectual life of Vienna in contrast to the Bloomsbury group and the private, domestic space of the tea party. Alongside the dichotomy set up between Vienna's urban dynamism and Bloomsbury's domestic cosiness, Timms also presents parallels between these two discursive worlds in the way in which they relied on the cross-fertilisation of ideas across disciplines and on personal networks. Discussing both the theme of sexuality and the impact of Freud's psychoanalytic theory, through the translations published by the Hogarth Press, Timms offers a case study of both the differences and the intellectual connections forged between these two famous sites of early twentieth-century modernity.

Notes

1. Jürgen Habermas, *The Structural Transformation of the Public Sphere: An Inquiry into a Category of Bourgeois Society* (1962), trans. Thomas Burger et al., Cambridge 1989. Habermas' theory of the public sphere in relation to the Viennese café is examined in more detail in Charlotte Ashby, 'The Cafés of Vienna: Space and Sociability' in this volume (Chapter 1).
2. Ulla Heise, *Coffee and Coffee-houses*, West Chester, Penn. 1987. Also published as *Kaffee und Kaffeehaus*, Leipzig 1987.
3. Markman Ellis, *The Coffee House: A Cultural History*, London 2005 and Brian William Cowan, *The Social Life of Coffee: The Emergence of the British Coffeehouse*, Yale 2005.
4. W. Scott Haine, *The World of the Paris Café: Sociability among the French Working Class, 1789–1914*, Baltimore and London 1996.
5. Christoph Grafe and Franziska Bollerey, *Cafés and Bars: The Architecture of Public Display*, Abingdon 2007.
6. Carl E. Schorske, *Fin-de-siècle Vienna: Politics and Culture*, London 1980 and William M. Johnston, *The Austrian Mind: An Intellectual and Social History, 1848–1938*, Berkley and Los Angeles 1972 (2nd edition 2000).
7. The emergence of the field of Vienna 1900 scholarship is mapped out in detail in the introduction and first chapter of Steven Beller (ed.), *Rethinking Vienna 1900*, New York and Oxford 2001.
8. Steve Beller, *Vienna and the Jews, 1867–1938: A Cultural History*, Cambridge 1991.
9. Edward Timms, *Karl Kraus, Apocalyptic Satirist: Culture and Catastrophe in Habsburg Vienna*, Yale 1989.
10. Klaus Thiele-Dohrmann, *Europäische Kaffeehauskultur*, Düsseldorf 1997 and Michael Rössner (ed.), *Literarische Kaffeehäuser*, Wien 1999.
11. *Das Wiener Kaffeehaus: Von den Anfängen bis zur Zwischenkriegzeit*, Historisches Museum der Stadt Wien, Vienna 1980.
12. Friedrich Torberg, *Die Tante Jolesch oder Der Untergang des Abendlandes in Anekdoten*, Munich 1977.
13. The image of pre-Second World War café life was created by Viennese émigré writers in the post-war period. Notable works include Stefan Zweig, *The World of Yesterday: An Autobiography*, London 1943; Hilde Spiel, *The Dark and the Bright: Memoirs 1911–1989*, trans. Christine Shuttleworth, Riverside, California 2007; and Torberg, *Die Tante Jolesch.* The story of the Viennese café has resulted in a slew of popular histories and guides, which repeat largely similar information and anecdotes, and which are still regularly being produced. See for example, Helfried Seemann und Christian Lunzer (eds), *Das Wiener Kaffeehaus 1870–1930: Das Wiener Kaffeehaus in Zeitgenössischen Photographien*, Vienna 2000; Birgit Schwaner, *Das Wiener Kaffeehaus: Legende, Kultur, Atmosphäre*, Vienna 2007; Christopher Wurmdobler, *Kaffeehäuser in Wien: Ein Führer durch eine Wiener Institution: Klassiker, moderne Cafés, Konditorien, Coffeeshops*, Vienna 2005.
14. See, for example, the web pages of the Vienna Coffeehouse Owners' Club: http://www.kaffeesieder.at [accessed on 7 May 2009].

Chapter 1

THE CAFÉS OF VIENNA
Space and Sociability

Charlotte Ashby

In every large or small town throughout the Habsburg lands there is a Viennese coffeehouse. In it can be found marble tables, bentwood chairs and seating booths with leather covers and plush upholstery. In bent-cane newspaper-holders the *Neue Freie Presse* hangs among the local papers on the wall ... Behind the counter sits the voluptuous and coiffured cashier. Near her looms the expressionless face of the head waiter, who as soon as the call 'Herr Ober, the bill!' is issued, will vanish from the guest's field of vision. The barman lurks casually, but jumps to attention readily enough, though at no time giving the impression of hurried bustle. All in good time, the junior waiter brings the quietly clinking metal tray with its full glass of water to your table. One orders the coffee by means of a secret language that no one from outside the country understands: 'eine Melange mehr licht', 'eine Teeschale Braun', 'eine Schale Geld passiert'.[1]

This evocative picture of the classic Viennese café can be found replicated in multiple histories, memoirs, biographies and works of fiction that focus on Vienna of the late nineteenth century. This quotation captures the affection and nostalgia which has long coloured any consideration, academic or otherwise, of the Viennese café. The image evoked, of the marble table tops, bent-wood chairs, multiple newspapers and idiosyncratic staff, is one that has become something of a legend. The distillation of the one thousand or so coffeehouses there were in Vienna around 1900 into a single image obscures the multiplicity and complexity of this particular space-type within the city.[2] This chapter will introduce the cafés of Vienna as a social space in the city and the role they played in the city's social and cultural life. A historical account of the role of the cafés is difficult to establish because, for the most part, it requires delving into the ephemeral realm of the everyday life and habits of the people of Vienna. This life was essentially transitory and casual in nature and as such proves resistant to recording and documentation. Various opportunities for excavating the ephemeral do however exist. A number of the cafés themselves survive, in a more or less altered state, as a material record of these spaces. Visual records – photographs, drawings, paintings and postcards – can also offer a window onto the nature of these spaces and the society within. In addition, literary sources, such as fiction, travel writing, biography and autobiography, provide another perspective on how the cafés of Vienna were used and regarded by contemporaries.

The importance of the cafés as part of the 'story' of Vienna 1900 is not simply a nostalgic construction following the Second World War. The café was the foremost public social institution within the city. Unlike the theatre or the opera house, the café could be visited every day and at virtually any time of day. The proliferation of cafés through the city indicates that they were a regular feature in the lives of many Viennese. The café appeared as a location in novels and other literary works of the period.[3] Guide books in both English and German all make particular reference to the cafés of the city, exclaiming on their numerousness and the quality of the service.[4] As a ubiquitous feature of city life, the café was multifarious in its provision of services to people of different classes and genders. The ephemeral nature of the sociability it played host to continues to make it difficult to categorise, in its close relation to the complex identity of the city at the dawn of the twentieth century.

The Café and its Relation to High and Low Culture

The relationship of cafés to the development of cultural life is well established. Jürgen Habermas presented the coffeehouses of eighteenth-century London as the crucibles for the formation of a bourgeois public sphere in England.[5] These cafés provided a space for an active public of private individuals with shared concerns to come together and create shared discourse. The printed word made a vital contribution to the establishment, through the practices of criticism and critical debate, of the realm of public discourse:

> The predominance of the 'town' was strengthened by new institutions that, for all their variety, in Great Britain and France took over the same social functions: the coffeehouses in their golden age between 1680 and 1730 and the salons in the period between the regency and the revolution. In both countries they were centres of criticism – literary at first, then also political – in which began to emerge, between aristocratic society and bourgeois intellectuals, a certain parity of the educated.[6]

Habermas' thesis maintained that this public sphere declined in the late nineteenth and early twentieth centuries into a passive culture of mass consumption rather than public discourse. This decline was engendered by the growth in the number of people who constituted the public until its unity, as a single public, was impossible to sustain.[7] Within Habermas' thesis the development of the practice of voicing public opinion spread from the arena of literature naturally into matters of political and public interest, engendering the development of a sphere in which all matters of public interest could be discussed and new ideas formulated.

Habermas' theory cannot be applied seamlessly to the role of the café in Vienna. For one thing, prior to 1848, prohibitions on the expression of political opinions, together with the lack of a democratic framework of any kind in which such opinions could carry weight, made the development of a public sphere of the kind evoked by Habermas largely impossible. By the late nineteenth century, when the cafés of Vienna had become sites of intense public discourse, both literary and political, the onset of mass culture, presented by Habermas as the antithesis of the public sphere, was also well under way. The Viennese café is thus a site in which the development of a public sphere is both delayed and complicated by its chronological compression. By looking at the points at which the Viennese café does and does not conform to the outline of public space and public sphere developed by Habermas, we can build a clearer picture of the way in which the café contributed to the life of the city.

The Café as a Site of Leisure

Habermas' assessment of the rise of popular mass culture at the end of the nineteenth century was couched in terms of the fracturing and decline of the public sphere, as culture and ideas were packaged for consumption rather than evolving through rational debate. This view, however, sets up an artificial dichotomy between high and low culture, the serious and the frivolous, which obscures the essence of the cafés as institutions straddling both professional and recreational spheres. The café's function as leisure venue was an established part of its identity as a public space. The link between recreation and café culture in the city of Vienna goes back to the eighteenth century. The Prater Park had been opened to the people of Vienna by Josef II in 1766 and the first café, the Erste Café, opened in the Prater in 1787. The Zweite Café followed in 1799 (Figure 1.1). Lithographic topographies of the city in the eighteenth and early nineteenth centuries frequently show such outdoor cafés, either those on the Prater or overlooking the city bastions. Such scenes indicate the ubiquity of these cafés as social spaces around the city. The stroll in the park, the promenade on the bastion and later the Ringstrasse, and the visit to the

Figure 1.1 *The Zweite Café on the Prater,* c.1820. Courtesy of the Wien Museum.

café were intimately woven into the pattern of Viennese leisure habits from the late eighteenth century onwards. Though the majority of cafés did not provide elaborate entertainments until the late nineteenth century, their offerings of refreshments, relaxed ambiance and table-top games were enough of a draw to make them prime sites for recreation in the city. For the bourgeoisie in particular, the cafés of the city centre and wealthy suburbs provided a well-loved and regularly used space outside of the home for informal, primarily but not exclusively masculine socialising and private relaxation. The precise nature of this sociability will be discussed further on in this essay.

The café's function as a place where people went to relax and as a site of urban leisure is not an aspect that can be filtered out of any discussion of its role. By the late nineteenth century the growth of mass media, the entertainment industry and the advent of party politics, all of which Habermas viewed as sounding the death knell to true public discourse, was well under way even in Vienna. Within the supposed decline of the public sphere the only roles left for cafés to play would have been either as venues of popular entertainment or as retreats for an elite intellectual culture, divorced from public relevance. The growth of the large-scale entertainment cafés in Vienna from the 1870s confirms the idea of the rise of mass culture. From relatively simple establishments serving coffee and various other beverages, tobacco, simple snacks and table-top games, cafés expanded in the nineteenth century to take advantage of the growing wealth of the urban middle classes and the entertainment industry was born. Grand entertainment establishments in new hotels, in city parks and new bourgeois suburbs took the basic idea of a café and extended it to include more elaborate forms of entertainment.

The new hotels built in expectation of the crowds attending the 1873 World's Fair in Vienna all included extensive café spaces on the ground floor of their premises. Prasch's Café and Billiard Hall, on the Wienzeile, which first opened in 1851, offered extensive recreational facilities, including multiple games rooms, a concert hall, a reading room, a refreshment room and conservatories.[8] Café Volksgarten, in the city centre, offered a fine restaurant and outdoor concerts in the smartest park in the city. The Prater Park, with its long history as a centre for recreation, developed to include various amusements, such as the 'Venice in Vienna' attraction, opened in 1895, and the Ferris wheel completed in 1897. The Café Dritte, originally established in the Prater Park in 1802, was refurbished in time for the World's Fair, expanding on the idea of the concert-café to become a café and variety theatre with a capacity for 5000.[9] Although the World's Fair proved to be something of a flop, the café was bought up by Anton Ronacher and became a huge success, showing musical comedies, operettas and other stage acts (Figure 1.2). Much of the expansion of the entertainment industry in the late nineteenth century was undertaken under the auspices of the café, as an established leisure-venue type. The large entertainment cafés did not, therefore, represent an overturning of a more worthy, intellectual and politicised café space, but rather an elaboration on one ongoing aspect of the identity of the Viennese café.

The Biedermeier Café

Alongside the identity of the Viennese café as a leisure destination, its role as a centre of cultural life was also a well-established facet of its popular identity. In the late nineteenth century in particular, the café society of the early nineteenth century was celebrated nostalgically as an emblem of the past cultural and intellectual achievements of the city. This so-called 'Biedermeier period' was regarded by many as the pinnacle of good taste and authentic Viennese brilliance, from which modern culture had sadly declined.[10] Adolf Loos's design for the Café Museum of 1899 was a conscious attempt to revive the atmosphere and ambience of a Biedermeier café. The image of the Biedermeier café incorporated within it a suggestion of vibrant intellectual and creative discourse followed by the city at large, and is analogous with Habermas' bourgeois public sphere.

Figure 1.2 Laszlo Frecskay, *Ronacher's Grand Café in the Prater*, 1879. Courtesy of the Wien Museum.

The Biedermeier café was a public sphere in the sense that
centre for the communication and propagation of new ideas. F
purview was limited to the arena of culture and aesthetics, it:
was stunted in relation to the development from a cultural discourse of literary
criticism to a broader, politicised public discourse. The idea of the decline of
the café into a mere venue for mass consumer culture has been shown to be
too limited, setting leisure and public discourse in opposition to one another,
rather than accepting that the recreational side of café life has always existed
alongside any more serious functions. The fact that the cafés of Vienna played
a significant role in the developing mass entertainment industry at the end
of the nineteenth century did not preclude their continued contribution to
Viennese culture. Habermas' notion of the disintegration of the public sphere
dealt with any lingering manifestations of public creativity and vibrancy by
relegating them to the province of elite intellectual circles, marooned and ever
more irrelevant to the wider public. This dismissal underplays the importance
of cafés as public venues for the development of literary and artistic modernism
later in the nineteenth century. It exaggerates both the degree to which the
earlier café had been inclusive and the later café exclusive in its attitude to
public engagement with culture.

The essence of the Biedermeier café was encapsulated in the popular
imagination by the 'silver coffeehouse'. This celebrated café, which operated
between 1824 and 1846, was nicknamed 'silver' on account of its glamorous
interior design, which included luxurious details such as silver tableware and
other fittings.[11] A suitably illustrious clientele, including the writer Franz
Grillparzer, the actor Ferdinand Raimund, the theatre director Ignaz Schuster
and the musicians Josef Lanner and Johann Strauss, were drawn to the café as it
became a well-known meeting place for Vienna's cultural elite.[12] The nostalgia
felt for this lost brilliance is encapsulated in a print by Vinzenz Katzler, *Die
Kassierin vom Silbernen Kaffeehaus* (The Cashier from the Silver Coffeehouse),
purporting to illustrate a scene in the café in 1826, which was circulated as
a picture supplement in the conservative political journal *Hans Jörgl* in 1871
(Figure 1.3). A circle of cultural luminaries are depicted gesticulating and
conversing, grouped in an admiring circle around the cashier.

The Viennese 'literary café' of the Biedermeier era remained crucially
different from the English model celebrated by Habermas, however, in
that the cultural life associated with it remained un-politicised. The strict
regulation of all forms of expression within the Habsburg Empire prohibited
the development of a mature politicised public discourse. The music of Strauss
and the stage performances of Nestroy remained light-hearted and popular in
character. Grillparzer was fundamentally frustrated by the restrictions placed
upon him. Prior to 1848, Vienna had only three daily newspapers, all either
government controlled or heavily censored. A tax on newspapers, not repealed

Die Kassierin vom silbernen Kaffehaus.

Figure 1.3 Vinzenz Katzler, *The Cashier from the Silver Coffeehouse*, 1871. Courtesy of the Wien Museum.

until 1900, inhibited the development of mass circulation newspapers, although a vigorous print culture did emerge.[13] These constrictions in the printed realm prevented the effective mobilisation of individual public opinion necessary for the creation of a politically engaged public sphere.

The Viennese café at the turn of the twentieth century was both a delayed example of the role of the café in the development of public discourse and a compression of the evolution of this role. In terms of politics, the café provided a venue for the development of advanced political discourse, with Victor Adler and the circle of early Austrian Social Democratic movement meeting in the Café Griensteidl and foreign political activists, such as Trotsky, meeting their fellow socialists in the Café Central.[14] The development of this semi-private discourse largely coincided with, rather than preceded, the birth of mass party politics and the commercial mass circulation press, which Habermas presented as antithetical to the survival of the bourgeois public sphere.[15] Similarly, the café continued to play an important role as a venue for advanced cultural discourse at the same time as playing a central role in the city's social life and the development of mass entertainment culture.

Class and Gender Barriers and the Café

A number of writers have pointed out the exclusions, particularly on the basis of class and gender, which compromised the supposed unity of the public sphere.[16] Any exploration of the role of the café in Viennese society also needs to take such exclusions into account. In relation to sociability, issues of class and gender in Vienna are indivisibly intertwined. In general, different cafés throughout the city catered for people of different social classes, with the upper and lower middle classes making up the primary constituency of patrons. Although male members of the aristocracy would occasionally attend the smarter town-centre cafés, rigid social codes dictated that their socialising took place primarily in the private houses of the elite circles in which they moved.

For the working classes there existed *Wirtshäuser*, or taverns. In 1902 there were approximately 4000 of these, in comparison to the city's 1100 cafés, the majority located in the outer districts of the city.[17] These taverns and restaurants provided venues for working-class sociability, with an emphasis on alcohol and food. W. Scott Haine, in his study of the working-class cafés of Paris, described the communities that formed around the different local cafés as providing crucial support networks for newly arrived young urban workers attempting to negotiate the transition to life in the big city.[18] It is likely that the *Wirtshäuser* of Vienna performed a similar function for new workers flooding into the city from across the Dual Monarchy of Austria-Hungary. Shaschar Pinsker's essay in this volume observes that the cafés of Vienna and other large cities within Austria-Hungary provided similar points of orientation and adoptive communities for newly arrived Jews from the East. Haine's study does not discriminate between cafés and taverns. The distinction maintained in Vienna between the two types of venues, *Kaffeehäuser* and *Wirtshäuser*, was primarily a reflection of the class demographic of the clientele, rather than a reflection of any fundamental distinction in the sociability and services provided. The social institution of the *Stammtisch* (Regulars' Table) was maintained in both and the popularity of table-top games was also common.[19] The role of the *Stammtisch* in coffeehouse sociability will be explored further later on. Just as a number of cafés were expanded into large entertainment venues, so various large entertainment facilities for the working classes were also developed at the end of the nineteenth century. Weigl's Dreher-Park, set up by the Dreher brewery, offered daily concerts and variety performances and had a capacity of 20,000.[20]

The café itself remained primarily a bourgeois institution, with multiple gradations between the finest haute-bourgeoisie establishments and the lower-middle-class cafés of the outer districts. Suburban coffeehouses catered primarily for local residents, so their nature reflected the demographics of different neighbourhoods. The coffeehouses of the first district tended towards the most elegant, but even cafés out in the less affluent suburbs maintained similar core features: a grand counter as a centrepiece, clusters of tables, billiard tables, newspapers and so on.

The regulation of social class and the question of which cafés it was appropriate to patronise were governed by the unwritten rules that are maintained in all class conscious societies. The prominent figure of the head waiter, who oversaw every aspect of each guest's visit, no doubt played a role in who was welcomed and who was not, but the system primarily ran by self-regulation. For example, in his autobiography Stefan Zweig noted that his father, a wealthy Jewish businessman, 'avoided dining at Sachers' (a grand Hotel and Café) and that this was 'not for reasons of economy, but because of a natural feeling of respect; it would have been distressing or unbecoming to him to sit at a table next to a Prince Schwarzenberg or a Lobkowitz'.[21]

Despite the undoubted social divisions that regulated socialising even within the upper middle class, the idea of the accessibility of the public space of the café continued to have important currency. Habermas highlighted the importance of the emergence of the idea of the public and public sphere as, in principle at least, inclusive:

> However exclusive the public might be in any given instance, it could never close itself off entirely and become consolidated as a clique; for it always understood and found itself immersed within a more inclusive public of all private people, persons who – insofar as they were propertied and educated – as readers, listeners and spectators could avail themselves via the market of the objects that were subject to discussion. The issues discussed became 'general' not merely in their significance, but also in their accessibility: everyone had to be able to participate.[22]

Zweig's often quoted statement that 'the Viennese coffeehouse was a sort of democratic club to which one bought admittance for the price of a cup of coffee',[23] is one that, even if not strictly true, reflects through its frequent repetition the importance of the principle of the accessibility of coffeehouse discourse. At the very least, it suggests that within the coffeehouses a certain relaxation of the otherwise draconian observation of social propriety governing the bourgeois Viennese could be witnessed. The truth in Zweig's statement lies in the comparative accessibility of the coffeehouses, particularly within the general spectrum of the educated bourgeoisie. While he was still a schoolboy, Zweig and his contemporaries enjoyed the facilities of the coffeehouses. The biographies of many of Vienna's intellectuals include reference to the contacts they made in coffeehouses with established figures in their field, who served as mentors for their early careers. The schoolboy Hugo von Hofmannsthal's meeting with Herman Bahr in the Café Griensteidl and his subsequent inclusion in the Jung Wien circle is one of the most famous examples.[24] The recurrent myth-making by writers recounting events like this is explored further in Gilbert Carr's essay in this volume, and a similar theme of coffeehouses as a location for important meetings between young and established writers and between insiders and outsiders appears in the essays of Shachar Pinsker, Ines Sabotič and Katarzyna Murawska-Muthesius.

The accessibility of the cafés for women was, in the first instance, governed by class. The entertainment establishments and fairground cafés offered a space where both men and women, primarily of the working classes and lower middle classes, could socialise together. Towards the bottom of the social scale, where both men and women had to work in order to keep their households going, the social niceties of who could patronise cafés and taverns were not so closely observed. Women of the lower classes, taken up as girlfriends by members of the bourgeoisie, were also welcome to accompany them to the grander cafés. Altenberg's series, 'Rules for my Stammtisch', include various references to female companions.[25] The line between girlfriends and prostitution was frequently blurred and certain cafés were also known as places where one could make the acquaintance of the *demi-monde*.[26] However, as the waiting staff in the Viennese cafés were male, rather than female, the direct overlap of café and bordello that occurred frequently in Paris was not common in Vienna. The only consistent female presence in most cafés was the *Sitzkassiererin* (cashier). She corresponded to the role played by *La Belle Limondière* in the Parisian café: an attractive hostess, whose charms encouraged customer loyalty:

> Enthroned behind the bar, among the bottles and glasses is that ambassador of the fairer sex, the cashier. She is always a very sweet-tempered, accommodating representative of her sex. … However cold-hearted you are, to be in the presence of her warm heart will melt yours. Indeed, many have gone to the café to win a game and end up losing their hearts to the cashier![27]

Haine comments that attractive or even famous young women were hired to lend lustre to the cafés of Paris. Alternatively, in the case of couples who ran cafés, the wife often took the role of cashier and accountant.[28] The city directories of 1891 and 1902 reveal that around 24 per cent of cafés were listed under the name of a female proprietor.[29] Haine notes the common practice in Paris of the ownership of cafés being passed on and maintained by wives following the death of the husband and it is possible that there is a similar explanation for the comparatively large numbers of female proprietors in Vienna. Despite these female incursions into the male domain of the café, they remained primarily masculine spaces and as such were allowed to relax the rigid observance of social hierarchies and of public morality. It is not surprising therefore that for middle-class women, for whom reputation was everything, they were largely prohibited spaces.

Alma Mahler Werfel's diaries record the daily social life of a young middle-class woman who moved in advanced cultural and artistic circles. Despite her relative freedom to attend concerts and galleries and private parties in mixed company, Mahler Werfel was not included in the café-based social life of her Secession friends and admirers. The only visits to cafés she records were a number of occasions on which she met with female friends in Demel's, the Imperial confectioners and chocolatiers. The *Café-Konditorei* that grew up within such cake shops were crucially different in a number of ways from regular coffeehouses. The waiting staff were female rather than male and the atmosphere remained closer to that of an elite shop. The cafés within the central parks of the city that hosted café-concerts were the only other type of café that a middle-class woman might commonly visit without the company of a man. For example, Frau Matzner, the ex-brothel-keeper in Joseph Roth's *The String of Pearls*, is deeply concerned with her respectability, but is happy to attend concerts in the Stadtpark and Volksgarten cafés.[30] This supports the visual evidence of prints and drawings depicting the elegant men and women who attended such concerts.

Visibility played a large role in what differentiated the spectrum of respectability between different cafés. The open-air, high visibility of the café-concerts in particular made them sufficiently respectable spaces for bourgeois women to visit unaccompanied as their conduct there was implicitly open to monitoring. The *Café-Konditorei* shared with the concert cafés a greater degree of public visibility, as they had shop display windows and as retail premises they entreated passers by to look in. In most Viennese coffeehouses, however, the relationship between the interior and the street was more ambivalent. Unlike the broad plate-glass windows and richly illuminated interiors of the Parisian cafés that made café visitors highly visible from the street, Viennese café interiors were not so immediately permeable. Windows were furnished with short curtains which guests could draw to keep out the sun or conceal themselves from the street without obscuring their own view out, making the visibility of guests optional. The division of the café interior into separate rooms for reading, billiards or card games, and the arrangement of booths with intimate seating, facilitated the free use of the space by men who could choose what activity they wanted to pursue and whether they wanted to be seen or remain concealed from anyone poking their head in the door. However, this division of space contributed to the maintenance of the café as a masculine space, as there was not enough visibility to guarantee respectability for female visitors.

The café was, therefore, primarily a masculine space, albeit one that was penetrated by women under certain conditions. A survey of the rich visual record of the cafés of Vienna amassed in the collections of the Wien Museum reinforces this perception.[31] A number of the interiors reveal scenes of solely masculine sociability. Here and there, women appear, conforming to the exceptions outlined above. Ladies are shown being escorted to outdoor concerts, or taken for coffee in the high-ceilinged, glittering halls of the grander city-centre cafés. Families enjoy Sunday outings to grand Ringstrasse cafés. There are bawdier tavern scenes, where waitresses resist being pulled into the laps of male café patrons. There is also an ambiguous class of female coffeehouse patron, whose position is impossible to deduce from visual sources and who is also absent from the existing literature on the coffeehouse. Many a predominantly masculine crowd is shown to contain a handful of female figures. Some may indeed be the *demi-mondaines* or girlfriends alluded to above, but a number of matronly figures who appear to exude respectability can also be seen (Figure 1.4). In the absence of further evidence, one can only speculate over the grounds on which they secured their dispensation to partake in male coffeehouse life. It must also be noted that the period spanning the nineteenth to the twentieth century was one of uncertainty and contestation in relation to both class and gender norms. As Mary Costello's essay later in this volume explores, the café as a masculine space epitomised in Adolf Loos's Café Museum design of 1899 had been so eroded by 1908 that he designed his American Bar as an explicit alternative to the overly feminised world of the coffeehouse. Murawska-Muthesius' essay similarly notes Tadeusz Boy-Żeleński's dismissive attitude to Viennese-style cafés that catered to families and ladies in contrast to the more robust, masculine cafés he favoured.

Figure 1.4 Café Dobner, c.1900. Courtesy of the Österreichische Nationalbibliothek.

Literary Circles and the Creative Space

The association of the café with culture and the literary realm, established in the Biedermeier period, persisted into the twentieth century. The multiple dimensions and guises of the literary café are explored in a number of the essays within this book. After the closure of the 'silver coffeehouse', Café Griensteidl became the favoured home for the writers of Vienna. For a detailed exploration of the literary circles of the Café Griensteidl, see the following chapter by Gilbert Carr. This sense of being part of a great Viennese tradition may in itself be an element of what the café contributed to culture – imparting a particular flavour to the experience of people frequenting the café – encouraging them, lending gravitas to their activities there. One of the many things the café offered writers and thinkers of all kinds was a place that was partially secluded, safe and home-like (private), as well as being integrated into the life of the city (public). The tensions between all these different aspects of the café played a major role in the vitality of the space.

The café challenges the established binaries commonly used for understanding space. It is a public space, and yet spaces within it, the table of the solitary habitué or of the established group of regulars, is rendered private or semi-private. It is an informal space, in that socialising between figures from different social backgrounds and the bending of rules in regards to extra-marital or pre-marital relationships with women are condoned. But at the same time it is a space governed by its own formalities and institutions: the formal dress and internal hierarchy of the waiting staff; the opaque lexicon of the different coffee preparation names of the Viennese café tradition; the ritual of service, with the coffee brought upon a metal tray, accompanied by a dish of sugar and a glass of water with the coffee spoon balanced on top of it. These formalities mirror, but do not match, the formalities that governed the world outside, in the manner of a Foucauldian heterotopia.[32]

Foucault coined the term 'heterotopia' to describe spaces that were the same, but different from the real spaces of the world. These sites allowed for reflection on the real world and the enactment of many different kinds of difference:

> There are also, probably in every culture, in every civilization, real places – places that do exist and that are formed in the very founding of society – which are something like counter-sites, a kind of effectively enacted utopia in which the real sites, all the other real sites that can be found within the culture, are simultaneously represented, contested, and inverted. Places of this kind are outside of all places, even though it may be possible to indicate their location in reality. Because these places are absolutely different from all the sites that they reflect and speak about, I shall call them, by way of contrast to utopias, heterotopias.[33]

Such counter-sites offer us another potential model for understanding the complex relationship of the café to the social and cultural life of Vienna. The ambiguity of the café as a space was reflected in the attitudes of the writers who frequented them: café life was both celebrated and derided. Rather than embracing the idea of the Viennese café as a 'literary institution', many writers focused instead on the café as a frivolous place, thereby challenging the distinction between serious high culture and careless, trivial, low culture. The *Kleinkunst* developed by the Jung Wien was an explicit challenge to such notions of serious versus trivial endeavour and the frequenting of cafés was a real-life enactment of this challenge. By working in the café, these writers were able to associate with each other and with the everyday informal life of the city with which the cafés were so intrinsically bound. The Viennese café as a site of leisure, outlined above, had led to an established image of its habitués as timewasters and lay-abouts, an association at least as strong as that of the celebrated Biedermeier café circles. The café was not a serious place. It was a place of idleness that contrasted with the real world of work. In Stephan Zweig's *Ungeduld des Herzens* (Beware of Pity, 1938), the young Second-Lieutenant Hofmiller resolves to reform his life:

> How stupid then, to idle away one's leisure time day after day at the café playing boring games of cards with dull-witted companions, or strolling up and down the promenade. No, from now on no more of this torpid existence, this beastly lounging about. ... I would go less often to the café, would give up playing billiards and that wretched Tarock, would have done once and for all with all those efforts to kill time that were of no earthly use to anyone and only blunted my own intelligence.[34]

Its value as a site for productive creativity was frequently criticised by writers:

> Seriousness and thoroughness do not thrive in the atmosphere of the coffeehouse. This smoke impregnated air, tainted by gas jets and polluted by the sitting together of many people, this whirring of people coming and going, jabbering of guests and bustling waiters, this tangle of shadowy apparitions and indeterminable sounds, makes any quiet reflection, and collected thought impossible.[35]

And yet, despite this disdain, they all continued to spend significant portions of time there. The revolt against tradition witnessed in their writing, the subjective, self-reflective, ambiguous, paradoxical and transitory shifts they played with were well suited to this association with the café as a site of frivolity, play and fecklessness. The link between the café and the rise of Modernism in the late nineteenth century is also well established. Max Nordau, the influential Austro-Hungarian cultural critic and Zionist, presented the café as the natural habitat for the activities of the cultural 'degenerates' he derided. In his famous book, *Entartung* (*Degeneration*, 1892), his discussion of the origins of the Symbolist movement in Paris tied the group closely to the cafés they frequented:

Shortly after 1880 there was, in the Quartier Latin in Paris, a group of literary aspirants, all about the same age, who used to meet in an underground café at the Quai St Michel, and, while drinking beer, smoking and quibbling late into the night, or early hours of the morning, abused in a scurrilous manner the well-known and successful authors of the day, while boasting of their own capacity, as yet unrevealed to the world.

... About 1884 the society left their paternal pot-house, and pitched their tent in the Café Francois I., Boulevard St Michel. This café attained a high renown. It was the cradle of Symbolism. It is still the temple of a few ambitious youths who hope, by joining the Symbolist school, to acquire that advancement which they could not expect from their own abilities. It is, too, the Kaaba to which all foreign imbeciles make pilgrimage.[36]

Although derisive in tone, the quotation gives an indication of what the café as an institution offered young aspiring writers: companionship, the solidarity of like-minded individuals and a space apart from the main institutions of culture where new ideas could be gestated. Additionally, once its reputation is established, the café becomes a destination, drawing others of a similar caste of mind and providing a crucial hub for the growth and nourishment of a new movement. Nordau characterises this scathingly as the refuge of the talentless. His attitude is similar in many ways to that expressed by Karl Kraus in his satirical essay *Die demolirte Literatur* (A Literature Demolished, 1897), in which he mock-lamented the closure of the Café Griensteidl and the blow this would strike to the, in his opinion, effete literary circles who met there.[37] The many criticisms of the café, as asylums where the hopeless and idle found mutual empty assurance of their worth, carry within them evidence of the role of cafés as venues for important support networks for new cultural movements.

The café provided a place where those who did not fit comfortably into the established public institutions of culture – the universities and academies – felt they belonged. Andrew Barker, in his study of the ultimate café habitué and outsider figure, Peter Altenberg, sums up the value of the café environment:

An organisation for the disorganised, where young aesthetes renowned for their sensitivity felt safe from the threatening world outside. It was however, an institution where they could not only socialise, but also read and write. In addition, they could read about themselves: Vienna had long been famed for its capacity to produce and consume art, and public fascination with artists meant that their doings regularly made the newspaper headlines of the popular press, as they still do in a city neurotically aware of and sensitive to its artistic traditions.[38]

This quotation highlights both the community role played by the café and also its role as a site of communication and exchange. The practice of the majority of Viennese cafés in taking a selection of newspapers and journals for the use of patrons was well established. Newspaper hawkers in the streets were forbidden, making the cafés important locations in which to access printed news.[39] Cafés that catered to literary circles, such as Café Griensteidl, took a huge range of national and international newspapers and periodicals.

Altenberg's career encapsulated in many ways the nature of the relationship between the Viennese café and the city's modern literary culture. The written form he specialised in, the prose poem or sketch, captured the transience and immediacy of everyday life. The ephemeral character of this form, easily dismissed as insubstantial, corresponded with general perceptions of the inadequacy of the modern literary movement. Much of Altenberg's work was first published in literary journals or newspapers so the café would have been a key venue for the consumption as well as the production of his work. In addition to his published work, he was a prolific letter-writer, with many of his letters written and received in the Café Central.

The legend of Altenberg's initiation into the literary scene of Vienna also indicates yet another way in which the café, as an informal environment, facilitated the permeability of the groups that met there. In his own version of the story, Altenberg presented himself sitting in the Café Central, reading a newspaper that carried a cover story of a missing girl, 'Joanna W'.[40] His emotional response to her plight moved him to write the sketch 'Lokale Chronik'.[41] While he was writing at the table, Schnitzler, Hofmannsthal, Salten, Beer-Hofmann and Bahr, whom he knew as fellow regulars of the café, came in, noticed him writing and took up his sketch; their admiration of it prompted them to propel him into a literary career. In Salten's version of the same story he comments on the amazement of the Jung Wien circle when they found out that the author of this literary gem was none other than Richard Engländer, the cigarette salesman from the night café.[42] Altenberg's contacts with café regulars helped him, as a thirty-four-year-old cigarette salesman, to establish himself as a writer. The café remained a place where the elite of Vienna's art and culture could position themselves in a way that made them accessible to each other and to the wider city, while at the same time carving out a space apart for themselves.

Sociability and the Inner World of the Café

For all its importance in the world of cultural production, the café was primarily a social space. It was sufficiently respectable to be openly frequented by the most august burgers of the city, but not so respectable as to prohibit a certain relaxation of social and moral mores. What was the nature of the sociability practised within the cafés that enabled such a relaxed attitude? Time in the café was composed of a myriad of fleeting moments: moments of private contemplation and moments of connection between old friends and casual acquaintances. Its very looseness was a striking counterpoint to the rigidity of the rest of Viennese life and customs. The café's identity as a site of urban leisure, as already mentioned, is an important factor in explaining the temporary suspension of strict codes of behaviour. At the same time, the café was not an anarchic site of hectic pleasure but remained bound up with respectable, bourgeois city life. A closer look at behaviour within the café can help us to understand its ambiguous nature.

The cafés of Vienna provided spaces throughout the city where men could withdraw from the street, without going home, and spend a few pleasant hours in solitary contemplation or group conviviality (Figure 1.5). They provided an important venue for peer-group socialising for groups of bohemian artists and writers as well as for more respectable and professional circles. A German guide to Vienna from the 1860s indicated that each café had its noted regulars. The guide outlined in which cafés visitors could find different types of groups congregating: students, bureaucrats, foreigners, financiers, Jews, grocers, fops, the *demi-monde* etc.[43] These established social circles are linked to the already mentioned idea of the *Stammtisch*. The *Stammtisch* was a time-honoured social institution in German and Central European culture. *Stammtische* ranged from formally constituted clubs to the informal social practice of it simply being known that certain groups of friends frequented certain café tables on certain

Figure 1.5 Felician Myrbach, *A Suburban Coffeehouse*, 1892. Courtesy of the Wien Museum.

days. An article in the illustrated paper *Illustrierte Wiener Zeitung* in 1912 focused on the Viennese institution of the café *Stammtisch*.[44] The article was largely nostalgic, recalling the great days of the Biedermeier *Stammtische* and the luminaries who met there, but it was accompanied by a series of photographs of contemporary *Stammtische*, revealing the range of groups who met under this heading. These groups revolved around shared interests, such as the *Wintersport-Klub* that met at the Café Kremser, or professional ties, such as the *Stammtisch* of actors and actresses at the Café Weghuber (Figure 1.6) or the *Stammtische* of painters or of military men.

The major contribution that the cafés made to Viennese social and cultural life was the hosting of such *Stammtische*. These groups were vital, for both writers and many other professional and social circles, for the exchange of informal news, gossip and so on, as well as for the dissemination and discussion of printed news. In a city in which much of the management of government, academia, the economy and the arts were bound in interminable observance of protocol and elaborate established procedure, the ability to exchange knowledge informally and establish networks behind the scenes played a vital role in keeping the system moving. The *Stammtisch* groups, though not inherently inclusive, were at least more permeable than the more strictly observed hierarchies governing professional associations and familial

Stammtisch im Café Weghuber: 1. Schauspieler Ruffel. 2. Schauspielerin Waldow. 3. Schauspielerin Ullerich. 4. Schauspielerin Ferry. 5. Frau Dunjesty. 6. Frau Martinelli. 7. Schauspieler Martinelli. 8. Schauspieler Ethofer. 9. Schauspieler Ziegler. 10. Schauspieler Pick. 11. Direktor R. v. Wazlawicek. 12. Schauspieler Weiß. 13. Schauspielerin Jaro-Fürth.

Figure 1.6 *Stammtisch of Actors and Actresses at the Café Weghuber* from 'Wiener Stammtische', *Österreichs Illustrierte Zeitung*, December 1912, 329.

social circles. *Stammtisch* groups had to be formed at some point and their membership, though regular, could evolve over time.

It would certainly be easier to effect an introduction to a new social circle at a café table than if that group met in the privacy of one or other of the members' houses. The contrasting sociability of the Viennese café and the domestic circles of the Bloomsbury group is explored in Edward Timm's essay in this volume. The niches in which many of the *Stammtische* were situated, illustrated for example in Figure 1.6, were still part of the wider space of the café interior. The common arrangement of café tables, with niches fitted with upholstered benches running around the edges of the room and free-standing tables surrounded by bentwood chairs scattered across the middle of the space, did not allow for impermeable privacy. The greater visibility of the groups who met there would have made it easier for a would-be member to identify with the group they would like to join. Memoirs and autobiographies indicate that these *Stammtishe* were more or less permeable. Groups evolved and coalesced around key cultural figures and transformed over time as new contacts were made or old ties were broken. Lina Loos was drawn into the Altenberg circle through her sister, who was a writer, and became a key figure in this group, also meeting her husband Adolf Loos there.[45] The Jung Wien literary movement operated in many ways like a *Stammtisch* in the Café Griensteidl, and later the Café Central, and was flexible enough to admit new members, such as Peter Altenberg, into the circle.

Another of the striking aspects about café sociability is the extent to which unsociable behaviour was an established norm. The solitary coffeehouse habitué, who had minimal contact with the staff and even less with the other guests, is a common figure in accounts of the coffeehouse:

> Judge Reiter appeared each day – for decades – at the Café Colosseum at four o'clock in the afternoon, sat down at the same table, was served a Mélange with whipped cream and two horn-shaped shortbreads, received the evening papers first and then successively all other national and international papers, read them, paid and did not have to utter a single word during this entire procedure.[46]

The role of the café as the home of the vital new modern movement in culture, needs to be set against the background of the café as a staple element in conventional, bourgeois, male existence across Austria-Hungary:

> Yes, it's the District Commissioner – and what's so strange about that? He comes here every day between five and seven, to read the newspaper and the official digest and to smoke a Virginia. The whole town knows that, it's what he's been doing for thirty years.[47]

The café was associated with both cultural productivity, in the form of the literary cafés of the Biedermeier era, and with fecklessness and indolent loungers. It was patronised by the most upstanding city fathers, but was also a place where you could take your girlfriend without attracting undue censure. The writers of the Jung Wien movement and the other practitioners of early modernism embraced these contradictions, finding in the café the perfect venue for an exploration of the tensions between art and life. Café life is characterised by professional and semi-professional networking, in-depth literary discussion and frivolous play. The café was a vital part of life within the city, but at the same time had a marginal quality. It was a place that could be found at the heart of both conservative and bohemian male sociability, without any apparent resentment between the two groups because, after all, café life was not a matter to be taken too seriously. The society that went on within it was both vital to the smooth running of the city and the flourishing of its cultural life, but was also inconsequential and trivial, thereby escaping excessive social regulation. The ambiguities of café life allowed urban modernity to creep into a city that preferred to look back to a glorious past rather than forwards towards an uncertain future.

Notes

1. Hilde Spiel, 'Das Kaffeehaus als Weltanschauung' in *Wien: Spektrum einer Stadt*, Munich 1971, 124.
2. Information derived from the number of directory entries under 'coffeehouse' in Adolph Lehmann, *Lehmann's Allgemeiner Wohnungs-Anzeiger nebst Handels- und Gewerbe-Adressbuch für Wien*, Vienna 1902.
3. Harold B. Segel (ed.), *The Vienna Coffeehouse Wits, 1890–1938*, West Lafayette, Indiana 1993, presents a selection of essays and shorter literary works known as *Kleinkunst* that revolve around the café in Viennese life. The novels of Arthur Schnitzler, Stefan Zweig and Joseph Roth include cafés as locations, as is indicated by the literary quotations included in this chapter.
4. Bruno Bucher and Carl Weiss, *Wiener Baedeker: Wanderungen durch Wien und Umgebungen*, Vienna 1868, 13–14; Charles Mcarmor, *The New Handbook of Vienna, Including a Guide for the Danube, the Austrian Alps and their Chief Watering-places*, Vienna 1879, 98–99; Julius Meurer, *A Handy Illustrated Guide to Vienna and Environs*, Vienna and Leipzig, 1906, 6–7; Ludwig Hirschfeld, *Das Buch von Wien: Was nicht im Baedeker Steht*, Munich 1927, 31–48.
5. Jürgen Habermas, *The Structural Transformation of the Public Sphere: An Inquiry into a Category of Bourgeois Society* (1962), trans. Thomas Burger et al., Cambridge 1989.
6. Ibid., 32.
7. Ibid., 181–195.
8. J.G. Grünwald, *The Ground Plan of Leander Prasch's Caffee- und Billard-Halle in Wien*, 1861. Wien Museum Collection, 15.512/2.
9. Gerhard Eberstaller, *Ronacher: Ein Theater in seiner Zeit*, Vienna 1993, 8.
10. This thinking was particularly prevalent at the turn of the twentieth century, with architects and architectural theorists such as Otto Wagner, Adolf Loos, Josef Hoffmann and Joseph August Lux all extolling the virtues of the design of the period.
11. *Das Wiener Kaffeehaus: von den Anfängen bis zur Zwischenkriegszeit*, Historisches Museum der Stadt Wien, Vienna 1980, 79.

12. Ibid., 79.
13. Daniel M. Vyleta, *Crime, Jews and News: Vienna, 1895–1914*, Oxford 2007, 71.
14. Leon Trotsky, *My Life*, London 2004, 262.
15. Habermas, *Structural Transformation*, 202–207.
16. For example see Nancy Fraser, 'Rethinking the Public Sphere: A Contribution to the Critique of Actually Existing Democracy', Mary P. Ryan, 'Gender and Public Access: Women's Politics in Nineteenth-Century America', and Geoff Eley, 'Nations, Publics, and Political Cultures: Placing Habermas in the Nineteenth Century', all in Craig Calhoun (ed.), *Habermas and the Public Sphere*, Cambridge, Mass., 1992, 289–339. See also Joan Landes, *Women and the Public Sphere in the Age of the French Revolution*, Ithaca 1988.
17. Lehmann, *Lehmann's Allgemeiner Wohnungs-Anzeiger* – entries for *Gastwirthe*, not including guesthouses and hotels.
18. W. Scott Haine, *The World of the Paris Café: Sociability among the French Working Class, 1789–1914*, Baltimore and London 1996, ix.
19. *Im Wirtshaus. Eine Geschichte der Wiener Geselligkeit*, Wien Museum, Vienna 2007.
20. Lehmann, *Lehmann's Allgemeiner Wohnungs-Anzeiger*, 1550.
21. Stefan Zweig, *The World of Yesterday: An Autobiography*, London 1943 (1987 edition), 28.
22. Habermas, *Structural Transformation*, 37.
23. Zweig, *The World of Yesterday*, 41.
24. Bahr's own account of the meeting was recorded in Herman Bahr 'Loris', in *Das Hermann-Bahr-Buch*, Berlin 1913, 253–260, while Stefan Zweig's account of the meeting can be found in Zweig, *The World of Yesterday*, 46.
25. Peter Altenberg, 'Rules for my Reserved Table', in Segel (ed.), *The Vienna Coffeehouse Wits*, 134–135.
26. Travel guides sometimes contained such useful information. See for example *Die Kaiserstadt an der Donau: Wiener Photographien*, Zürich and Stuttgart c.1868, 203.
27. Ibid., 205.
28. Haine, *The World of the Paris Café*, 184–185.
29. *Kaufmännisches Adressbuch für Industrie, Handel und Gewerbe der Österreichisch-Ungarischen Monarchie*, Vienna 1891: 25 per cent of cafés registered under a female name. Lehmann, *Lehmann's Allgemeiner Wohnungs-Anzeiger*: 23 per cent of cafés registered under a female name.
30. Joseph Roth, *The String of Pearls*, trans. Michael Hofmann, London 1998, 102–103.
31. A partial record of this portion of the Wien Museum's collection can be found in the catalogue to the exhibition on the Viennese coffeehouse held in 1980. See note 11.
32. Michael Foucault, Of Other Spaces: Heterotopias, 1967. http://foucault.info/documents/heteroTopia/foucault.heteroTopia.en.html [accessed on 19 August 2009].
33. Ibid.
34. Stefan Zweig, *Beware of Pity*, trans. Phyllis and Trevor Blewitt, London 2003, 61.
35. Edmund Wengraf, 'Kaffeehaus und Literatur' (1891), in Segel (ed.), *The Vienna Coffeehouse Wits*, 385–386.
36. Max Simon Nordau, *Degeneration*, Lincoln, Neb. and London 1993, 100–101.
37. Karl Kraus, 'The Demolition of Literature' in Segel (ed.), *The Vienna Coffeehouse Wits*, 65–86.
38. Andrew W. Barker, *Telegrams from the Soul: Peter Altenberg and the Culture of Fin-de-siècle Vienna*, Columbia, S.C. 1996, 23.
39. Mark Twain, 'Stirring Times in Austria' (1897), reproduced in Horst and Lois Jarke (eds), *The Other's Austria: Impressions of American and British Travellers*, vol. 1: 1814–1914, Riverside, California 2006, 353.
40. Peter Altenberg, 'Wie ich Schriftsteller wurde', *Mein Lebensabend*, Berlin 1919, 9.

41. Peter Altenberg, 'Lokale Chronik', *Liebelei*, 21 January 1896, 49–51.

42. Barker, *Telegrams from the Soul*, 25–27.

43. *Die Kaiserstadt an der Donau*, 202–203.

44. 'Wiener Stämmtische', *Österreichs Illustrierte Zeitung*, December 1912, 324–332.

45.ʹ Heike Herrberg and Heidi Wagner, *Wiener Melange: Frauen Zwischen Salon und Kaffeehaus*, Berlin 2002, 109.

46. Friedrich Torberg, *Tante Jolesch or the Decline of the West in Anecdotes*, trans. Maria Poglitsch Bauer, Riverside, California 2008, 98.

47. Joseph Roth, *The Radetzky March*, trans. Michael Hofmann, London 2002, 61–62.

Chapter 2

TIME AND SPACE IN THE CAFÉ GRIENSTEIDL AND THE CAFÉ CENTRAL

Gilbert Carr

The German exile writer Karl Otten's assessment that the coffeehouse was for modernist culture what the *agora* was for Socrates may resonate with other generalisations about the public sphere;[1] however, it also raises questions about the modern substitution of that open forum by the enclosed spaces of the coffeehouse, a place of intellectual encounters and literary production. As has been noted, Jürgen Habermas' theory of the public sphere has certainly influenced approaches to Vienna's rich coffeehouse culture.[2] Ursula Keller applied it in her 1984 monograph on Arthur Schnitzler, generalising about that 'very Austrian' hybrid, an *Ersatz* 'public sphere' with 'private functions', with contradictory features: on the one hand, a place of leisure and sociability, a literary market and information source, exempt from the pressure to consume; and on the other, compensating for the deficiencies of social life outside, a place of non-commitment, time-killing, gossip, a refuge for drop-outs and failures.[3] This is a theme that had been reiterated by essayists, among them Alfred Polgar in his 'Theorie des "Café Central"' (1926).[4] Friedrich Torberg claimed an 'indissoluble causal nexus' between 'types of coffeehouse and types of guest'.[5]

Generalisations about the coffeehouse, however, require careful qualification, as 'local' coffeehouses in the outskirts represented quite distinct milieus from central Vienna's literary cafés that continue to fascinate collective memory.[6] Reminiscences of the coffeehouse, like other retrospective narratives, are, of course, constructions of the past, but, in equating the Viennese café milieu metonymically with the creativity of those who frequented it, they are also problematic constructions. In the very perpetuation of a myth of the Viennese café as a centre of modernism, journalistic or autobiographical nostalgia often produces no more than a cliché and lacks the literary inventiveness to do justice to its subject. This, in turn, necessitates a further question: how far is narrative as such constrained by its linear, consecutive conventions when re-enacting that supposedly unique concurrence of intellectual interaction with the space and time structures of the coffeehouse? The contrast – well-established in literary studies – between the functions of narration (with its emphasis on the temporal) and of description (with its emphasis on simultaneity and suspension of 'the course of time')[7] does not preclude complementarity, such as the element of temporality in spatial description and the qualification of narrated dialogue (a temporally presented sequence) by its location.[8] The question of spatiality within the coffeehouse as a physical and narrated milieu, too, entails a temporal-spatial dimension, and it is this that would make the coffeehouse an exemplary topos not just for a cultural history of modernism but for the 'paradigm shift' in literary studies from temporality to spatiality, which has focused on 'topological rather than geometrical spatiality'.[9] A distinction has to be drawn between space and time in journalistic and autobiographical accounts, on the one hand (which are analysed in the first two sections of this chapter), and in the coffeehouse topos in literary fiction, on the other. The final section will examine the potential of some narrative devices to depict the socio-spatial dynamics of circles and yet encapsulate the time-specific cultural milieu of the coffeehouse as a productive ground of modernist discourse.[10]

Journalistic Accounts of the Coffeehouse in 1897

The received image of Vienna's turn-of-the-century coffeehouse culture is a construction of the collective memory of the inter-war (or, in some cases, early post-war) period, principally after the fall of the Dual Monarchy of Austria-Hungary and Vienna's loss of its imperial status. These recollections in turn borrowed from the nostalgic discourse of reminiscence at the *fin de siècle*, contrived collectively by journalists at the time of the closure for demolition of the Café Griensteidl (on 21 January 1897), which both then and since has been the milieu most often associated with Vienna's literary culture around 1890. As intellectual discourse was somewhat peripatetic, it would be too reductive simply to equate the Café Griensteidl with Jung Wien (Young Vienna, the literary group which formed around Hermann Bahr). Nevertheless, the Griensteidl – centrally situated as it was, at the corner of the Herrengasse and Schauflergasse, on the Michaelerplatz – certainly deserves attention, and the first section of this chapter will use contemporary sources to illustrate what kind of space this café was and what it was deemed to signify, before seeking corroboration from later sources.

Retrospective articles from 1897 give a sense of the variety of social groups frequenting the Café Griensteidl. The Socialists had been the constant element in the fluctuating modern cultural trends since the 1870s;[11] but this café's purely 'political' role had been superseded as this 'emporium' of public opinion became a magnet for 'politicians, non-politicians, jurists and philosophers, scholars reticent and loud, citizens from all districts', to play, read or to debate current affairs.[12] Alternatively, it was this café that was deemed the main meeting-place of 'literary and artistic professions and of numerous well-situated men, officialdom and academia';[13] since the Burgtheater had moved from the Michaelerplatz to the Ringstrasse in 1888, the actors' tables had become occupied by the Jung Wien circle.[14] The socio-spatial sub-division of the Griensteidl's interior, with its 'twenty-four walls',[15] i.e. six rooms, made cultural specialisation possible, although the proximity brought inevitable interactions: 'In the ... rooms looking out onto the Herrengasse ... journalists sit next to parliamentarians at all times'.[16] The space allowed for no privacy, except in the card-players' niches[17] (Figure 2.1).

One generalised account identifies writers and journalists as mediators who gave cohesion to the Café Griensteidl's otherwise 'many-faceted colony', liaising between the painters, sculptors and architects in the 'street-side' room, and the actors, singers and musicians on the other side.[18] That authenticates Edward Timms' schema – albeit not confined to coffeehouses – of the cross-fertilisation of 'circles' and groups with intersecting membership within Viennese modernism.[19] Given the fluctuating nature of such interactions even over a short space of time,

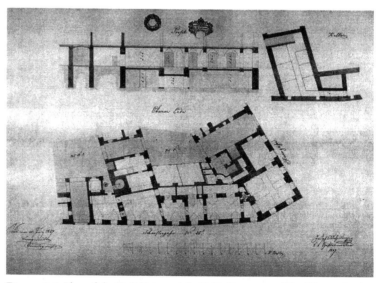

Figure 2.1 *Plan of the Café Griensteidl,* 1847. Courtesy of the Wiener Stadt- und Landesarchiv.

Timms' Venn diagram of the status quo 'around 1910' is, of course, somewhat idealised, as it of necessity freezes the constellations in time and has to assume regularity or continuity of affiliation. The visualisation of intersecting circles certainly invites questions about the real degree of interactions in and between those circles, in shared spaces.

Contemporaries in 1897 referred to the Griensteidl as a space divided by professions and class (with respected businessmen at the billiard and card tables, and, in a room at the back of the café on the Schauflergasse side, the intrigues of 'the jolly clan of Burgtheater artists');[20] or to a kind of solar system circling around revered centres, such as the great actors who met in the intimate *Sanktissimum* (inner sanctum),[21] attracting many aspirants, both literary and thespian, who gave the café its reputation as 'Café Größenwahn' (Café Megalomania).[22] Much of this is elaborated on in Stefan Grossmann's memoirs of 1931: the interior comprised outer rooms and 'sacrosanct rear rooms', separated by a 'small Biedermeier arch', and there was 'a so-called closed circle at a table in each window alcove in the outer rooms and at all the tables in the rear rooms'.[23]

Since a connection of discourse to the milieu is often claimed, it might be asked how essential the role assigned to spatial conditions in a description is, and what particular connotations they have. A problem for the thesis that equates the coffeehouse with modernity *per se* is that contemporary sources interpreted this intimate café with its niches as decidedly unmodern.[24] The characteristically Austrian tension around 1900 between tradition and modernity was ever-present in the flood of sentimental reminiscences about the Griensteidl as a 'familiar, beloved home',[25] where the 'art of salon conversation' was cultivated,[26] its modest, unmodern décor ('neither particularly elegant nor spacious') thus contrasting with its cultural importance.[27] Typical of the myth-making of 1897 is the journalist Ferry Bératon's personification of these 'smoky rooms with their nooks and crannies, narrow alcoves with their solid ceiling vaulting' as witnesses to cultural breakthroughs.[28] Others played off the 'homely, old-style Vienna establishment, simple and unpretentious like all that is inwardly noble and dispensing with screaming brash publicity', against the 'ostentation of modern luxury establishments'. Whereas the coffeehouse had once symbolised a symbiosis between 'old Vienna' and the emergent modernists housed in its interior, the widening gulf between the two was deplored.[29]

Autobiographical Nostalgia for the Coffeehouse

The Griensteidl's nearby rival, the Café Central, which came to dominate the scene before 1914, was an unequivocal symbol of modernism, despite its Neo-Renaissance architecture (Figure 2.2). Whereas there are some melancholic accounts of the circles there,[30] Berthold Viertel later recalled it as a 'house of life', and listed the 'many remarkable, smoke-filled rooms' of this multi-purpose space in vivid sequence: 'the large hall, in the background of which the billiard balls clicked neatly as they collided'; the quieter side rooms ('side valleys'); 'the special, smoky chess-room', with intimidating, dark groups of onlookers; 'the muted green card-rooms'; and the *Arkadenhof* (Atrium), 'an open, high courtyard

Figure 2.2 Marie Adler, *Café Central Interior,* undated, c.1910. Courtesy of the Wien Museum.

between houses, with its monumental fountain and its marble staircase with many arches and niches'. It is in this courtyard, 'this Viennese shaft', that Viertel – more critically – locates 'the most sophisticated intellectual life that is at all possible among completely idle sceptics', a select 'order, which seemed to have pledged itself to deriving reality only from reports and only as a reflection of the detailed features of a neighbour, who in turn did nothing but mirror'.[31] This concurs with the portrait of mentalities in 'Theorie des "Café Central"'. Whereas memoirs have little regard for the temporal and spatial conditions of intellectual productivity when paying tribute to specific personalities, Polgar's essay, with its witty *aperçus* and paradoxes, exemplifies the brilliance associated with this site of modernism, provocatively generalising social interactions and dissolving the concrete physical space of the café into the image of an aquarium full of personified contradictions, self-indulgent, self-negating attitudes and addictions. In a sardonic feat of metaphorical chemistry, he ventures that to grind up, 'put in a distillation chamber' and gasify 'all the anecdotes related about this coffeehouse' would produce 'a heavy, iridescent gas, faintly smelling of ammonia, … the so-called air of the Café Central', which 'defines the spiritual climate of this space', where 'unfitness for life' thrives.[32] Such a fate may well be merited by the nostalgic memoirs to be reviewed in the rest of this section, which complacently propagate the myth of the Viennese café.

In later, mainly autobiographical, testimonies, the atmosphere is invariably smoky, and frequently signifies intellectual excitement and claustrophobia, whether the Café Griensteidl is viewed nostalgically, as by Richard Specht,[33] or stigmatised, as by Gustav Gugitz's demotion of this 'fairy temple' to what was in reality a 'cavern', a site of modernity that had undermined its 'authentic' Viennese origins.[34] While contemporary journalistic accounts captured the demolished Griensteidl for posterity through physical descriptions and inventories of the location and a kind of historical roll-call of the socio-cultural networks, the second phase of collective memory coincided with the bitter ideological conflicts and political and economic upheavals of the 1920s, and, particularly after 1938, was cultivated as part of a broader nostalgia for the Habsburg 'world of yesterday', now lost forever. The self-reinforcing consensus in collections of anecdotes about the 'classic-modern' café seems to conform to Maurice Halbwachs' thesis that collective memory uses social frameworks 'to reconstruct an image of the past which is in accord, in each epoch, with the predominant thoughts of the society'.[35] In this case, the inter-war discourse, continued in exile, was to be re-invoked in the post-war period by mainstream Austrian society, coinciding with the 'forgetting' of the nation's complicity in the Nazi regime. Pierre Nora's thesis that an 'artificial hallucination of the past' is only conceivable in a 'regime of discontinuity', and that 'the *raison d'être* of a *lieu de mémoire* is to stop time, to block the act of forgetting, … to enclose the maximum meaning within a minimum of signification',[36] might account for the discrepancy in that post-Habsburg era between the emotional significance that the authors of memoirs invest in describing a 'unique' but bygone coffeehouse culture, on the one hand, and the repetitive or stereotypical narrative patterns which fall short of the originality that is being claimed. While such patterns may be inevitable in these text types, the effect, of reducing concrete presence or specific interactions to a function of a habitual collective identity (in the case of rootless exiles in need of reaffirmation), was readily absorbed in the post-war social vacuum too.

Reconstructions of real historical time fundamentally differ from narrative fiction, in which the preterite (the simple past tense) reconstitutes presence and is thus devoid of a temporal function relating to a historical past.[37] Yet the aim of many autobiographies, like Karl Rosner's *Damals* (*Those were the Days*, 1948), is to create a fixed past, a 'timeless' moment from a generalised series of repetitions. Whereas convention might dictate for coffeehouse narratives a temporal frame of regularity punctuated by unique moments, in the following examples of how temporal and spatial constellations are used, either an isolated scene is selected as typical or a homogenised version is composed out of what must have been repeated scenes – verbal tense and verbal aspect provide clues as to strategies of construction, which draw on devices common in fiction.[38] For example, there is some diachronic differentiation in Rosner's invocation of group members, but the repeated deictic adverbs ('there') affirm their presence as an emotionally significant memory, rather than specifying position: 'There was Rudolf Lothar – later to become the manufacturer of numerous operetta libretti and a journalistic Jack-of-all-trades – who in those days, in his literary beginnings, still had purely poetic ambitions. ... And there was Felix Dörmann, who made his début with his poetry volumes "Neurotica" and "Sensationen"'.[39]

Coffeehouse circles might invite description as internally configured groups, but in recalling the Café Griensteidl of the early 1890s, Richard Specht creates a certain synchronous concreteness in his passing reference to a demarcation of the café's space between 'two separate camps', the Jung Wien circle and the hostile adjacent table of 'Aryan' would-be poets.[40] A contrasting aim is to characterise the constant exchange in the coffeehouse as flux, as in Arthur Schnitzler's memory of the Café Central in his autobiography *Jugend in Wien* (Youth in Vienna, 1968).[41] To convey such fluidity, a journalistic account around 1897 replicates the informality of the Griensteidl syntactically, in the loose succession of 'giants of the Burgtheater' introduced as characters: 'Heinrich Laube liked to appear with his dog ... and let Meixner declaim to him about life being miserable, this "sly beast". Josef Wagner was there too'.[42] The phrase 'liked to appear' evokes frequency, which therefore frames the preterite ('was there too') – instead of (plausibly) being read as referring to a unique or chance appearance, it acquires a durative function, generalising Wagner's presence as a constant. A contrasting example can be found in Felix

Salten's memoir from 1932–1933: 'Hermann Bahr … joined our company. … Richard Beer-Hofmann joined us one day. … Otto Erich Hartleben turned up at our table in a peculiar costume. … Michael Georg Conrad, the old pioneer of Naturalism, had arrived from Munich. … An eccentric fellow showed up'.[43] Instead of a conventional diachronic perspective, as seen in Rosner's detachment from his own youthful admiration for Hermann Bahr in 'that long since bygone day',[44] here syntactical parallelism and the first-person plural perspective serves Salten's roll-call of a loose sequence of passing personalities; here it is only the point-of-view from a sedentary centre at the coffeehouse table that provides continuity amid the accumulation of verb phrases (characterised by their 'punctual', non-durative, aspect). Specht, too, vividly describes one of many 'curious presences' he witnessed in the Jung Wien circle, Friedrich M. Fels, in terms of a 'washed-up Kurt Aram', 'highfalutinly shabby', 'tyrannical' and yet not loud-mouthed, 'severely criticising all, carefully scrounging from all', 'until one day he was gone'.[45] The vividness here at first suggests a unique perception, but the Theophrastan generalisations of manner suggest recurrence, the sum of several occasions, which is confirmed contrastively by the perfective aspect of 'one day he was gone' – his disappearance is construed perfectively, i.e. as a singular action viewed as completed, to halt the series of 'habitual' appearances. It might have been more honest to have presented a 'spatial' sequence of discrete images of personalities and occasions, episodically linked by an 'Or', as Anton Kuh later did in structuring some of his memories of the Café Central.[46] In another example of Kuh's 'spatial' framing, in 'Zeitgeist im Literatur-Café', the impact of First World War casualties on intellectual life is recorded in a searching anti-revue set in a café, by deconstructing clichés about absent personalities: 'Here the black-haired theory of evolution should be sitting, still nervously looking up from his monthly ideological bible … Where are the painters and sculptors – all conscripted? … All that is missing there in the corner is one *avant-gardiste*'.[47]

Memoirs that crystallise a past scenically tend to blur chronology. For example, Richard Specht's value judgements on Felix Dörmann and *'soon afterwards'* Leo Ebermann,[48] when dated, appear to stretch the period of reference, as Ebermann's 'schoolboyish' play *Die Athenerin* (The Athenian Woman) was premièred in September 1896, at least five years after Dörmann's notorious début as a new Baudelaire. A similar question of dating arises with Stefan Zweig, who in *The World of Yesterday* (1943) describes visits to cafés as a schoolboy and locates his reminiscences of the old Café Griensteidl within his various precocious obsessions with culture and intellectual exchange at around the age of sixteen (Figure 2.3). His account of habitual practices, such as the reading and discussing of the Viennese and international press, is of necessity very generalised. Nevertheless, one could apply to Zweig's more specific recollections of this supposedly homogeneous 'world of yesterday' what Maurice Halbwachs observed about Chateaubriand's assembling 'in one single scene recollections of many evenings that were engraved in his memory', portraying 'the idea of a type of life', but resulting in a 'reconstructed picture'.[49] Briefly, while Zweig is quite insistent on dating his enthusiasm for the poetry of Stefan George and Rainer Maria Rilke to his school days,[50] and while it is impossible to determine a particular year for the group's reception of Kierkegaard,[51] his reception of 'a Wedekind production' and his attendance at the disrupted première of an atonal work by Schönberg have to have occurred after the demolition of the Café Griensteidl in 1897.[52] Confirmation that Zweig's memoirs are not confined to that café before its demolition – when he would have been fifteen – is contained in the memoir of Eugen Antoine, who, a year older than Zweig, admits to not knowing the old Griensteidl first-hand. He knew Zweig from frequenting the Café Glattauer,[53] the 'successor' café on that site built after the original's demolition.[54]

Of course, presentation of events from an extended chronological range as synchronous is itself a means of compressing the richness of years of exciting experience into a golden moment of recollection of a lost world. In his vivid account of Hermann Bahr's first meeting with the young Hofmannsthal,

Figure 2.3 C. v. Zamboni, *Café Griensteidl: Card Room*, 1897. Courtesy of the Wien Museum.

however, Zweig elaborates on how Hofmannsthal had 'suddenly' come up to Bahr's table.[55] Zweig does not claim to have witnessed this scene in the Café Griensteidl – he would have been nine at the time of that encounter – but he does claim to have witnessed Bahr's frequent recollections of it years later. This exemplifies how legends are made. A clue to the vividness of his account is that it is based closely on the well-known anecdote published by Bahr himself in his 'Loris' essay (1892),[56] which had ostentatiously presented his 'discovery' – an epiphany that had even made him drop his coffee-spoon in awe – of the precocious Hofmannsthal's review of his (Bahr's) play *Die Mutter*. This freeze-frame from Bahr's original version can evidently be repeated *ad nauseam* to Zweig, whose retelling of it in turn enhances his own link to Hofmannsthal.[57]

Zweig's own narrative seeks to prove the uniqueness of cultural activity and political controversy in the coffeehouse by name-dropping, inventorying cultural content and invoking group memory, rather than finding a literary form to exemplify the kind of 'spark' ('Zündung') that he attributes to Hofmannsthal's inspiration.[58] In some anecdotes about Vienna's coffeehouse personalities, nostalgia mutates into humorous or ironic commentaries on time patterns, on habit and predictability, as in Sigismund von Radecki's recollection of Karl Kraus's accurate predictive mimicry of a certain X.'s remarks on arrival.[59] Torberg's irony about time patterns is typical, when he contrasts continuity and discontinuity in his account of another habitué, whose exacting but unchanging demands had been fastidiously memorised by generations of obsequious waiters, only for this temporal chain of devotion to be broken by an unprecedented staff dispute, resulting in both trusted waiters resigning instantly and the client's being left dangling by an unaware novice.[60] However, to pursue further the question as to whether and by what formal means the discursive originality of Viennese coffeehouse culture could be portrayed, the focus will now switch to literary fiction. How inventively is the coffeehouse topos or setting used in literary genres? Kraus was no friend of the novel, but he is purported to have said that were he to write one, its plot would consist simply of a solitary coffeehouse guest moving from one room to an adjacent one over the course of twenty years.[61] While this mimics Viennese complacency, the elimination of characterisation and the long duration invoked also thematise the challenge that coffeehouse culture and its (dis-)continuities pose for linear narrative – whether narrative consecutiveness is 'spatially' modified by description or not. In the following literary examples, which include constructions of the pre-1897 Griensteidl as well as the Café Central in wartime, the question of how narrative can capture the social dynamic and do justice to the intellectual content and forms of discourse will be uppermost.

The Fictionalised Coffeehouse

In his novel *Neben der Liebe* (Besides Love, 1892), Hermann Bahr convention-ally uses the preterite to depict a fictive present, in a sequential depiction of a circle of regulars in the Café Scheidl (on the Kärntner Strasse), initially identi-fying each character in turn with a 'There was ...'. This novel's first coffeehouse scene is presented as a representative repetition of many other such scenes. Narratorial comments on the dialogues attribute certain habitual patterns to the group members' interventions, debating ploys and expected responses, and onlookers laugh respectfully (yet again) at the Wagnerite Hempel's joke from last winter.[62] Conversations range widely – from Ibsen to national identities and world domination, before shifting to Buddhism – but such allusions say little of the exceptional originality supposedly bred by the Viennese café. Narratorial pointers to characteristic stances and continuities in interaction prevail, under-lining the familiar and the repetitive structures that interested Naturalism, rather than the sparkling quality of discourse. Individuality is exemplified by the quick repartee of colourful characters interrupting or pre-empting a neigh-bour's diatribes. At two points, moreover, even while methodically developing character relationships, the Naturalistic narrative succeeds in incorporating the contiguous energies of the café's space. Firstly, the Doctor is distracted from his private thoughts on the speaker, Seeliger, by a voice behind him at the card table, and he goes over to greet a North German, von der Strass.[63] The arrival of another character, Lederer, provides a further distraction for the original circle, allowing the lofty conversation to switch to the topic of women. The second deployment of the space of the café occurs when Lederer himself turns away from another of Seeliger's diatribes, on the 'history of psychology from the Indians to Loris and Maurice Barrès', and begins listening to the casual remarks made by the adjacent card players, including von der Strass, about a female acquaintance (whose subsequent involvement with the German ends disastrously). The comments provoke Lederer to deliver an anti-German jibe, in a raised voice, loud enough for von der Strass to hear, but in fact Lederer is seeking affirmation from his own circle, as he turns back to them and instigates a change of topic.[64]

Contiguity thus functions well in Bahr's construction of the café, at the expense of inhibiting some intellectual exchange among the characters. Though often invoked as stimulating the vibrant interaction of intersecting circles, proximity is depicted to satirical effect in Alfred Polgar's early story 'Der Quell des Übels' ('The Source of Evil', 1908).[65] This minor experiment in the spatial patterning of coffeehouse relationships is played out between acquaintances at three tables, men whose contrasting professions provide a glimpse of modernity and in whose interactions dialogue is replaced by gestures and poses in a syntactically reductive sequence of minute-by-minute observations, such as contrasting the 'fabulous speed' with which the Medic's finger picks his ear, with the placidity of the Secretary of the Chamber of Commerce, smoking and watching the chess players.[66] The entrance of 'something white, feminine' is the frivolously designated 'root of trouble', triggering a series of strategic manoeuvres by these rivals for the woman's attention – to no avail, as she scarcely notices, and eventually leaves, whereupon dull order is restored in this egoistic world. The story closes with a hypothetical temporal extension of the 'evil', ironic speculation about 'what disgraceful things might have gone on' if the lady had read more than one journal.[67] (We are reminded that the mere reference to a vast supply of newspapers and journals in retrospectives like Zweig's or Rosner's implies a habitual aspect, expectations of continuity of custom, without an explicit verbal formulation of temporality.) Of more interest here are the metaphors that invest the supposedly neutral contiguity of the tables with nervous energy – not so much the attempt by the Writer figure to express an inner glow in his eyes, but his projection of them like opera-glass lenses and his 'casting invisible telegraph wires across to the ice-eating lady and cabling a large number of fan telegrams to her'.[68] This 'technological' fantasy, which completes the humorous sketch of a 'modern' repressed character attempting to bridge the alienating café space, is a modest example of the role of metaphorical invention in recreating (and mocking) the ambitious intellectualism of that era.

Metaphorical invention – even detached from the milieu that according to legend witnessed its production – was perfected by Karl Kraus and Robert Musil, whether in Kraus's pithy aphorisms, which are isolated from any narrative context, or, in Musil's *The Man without Qualities*, only integrated by virtue of his novel's 'essayistic' style. Kraus's early satire, *Die demolirte Literatur* (A Literature Demolished, 1897), is a self-consciously innovative variation on narrative conventions. Rarely does the 'verticality' of the quasi-feudal allegiance often noted in coffeehouse circles impinge on literary narratives, but in this, his literary demolition of the Jung Wien circle, Kraus reconfigures the open exchange of 'circles' within the enclosed space of the Griensteidl in a linear structure, by mimicking a pre-ordained hierarchical succession from the dominant central figure down. For example, the invisible narrator adopts a waiter's peripatetic vantage-point to effect a transition from one satirised figure to the next: 'And now from this man, to whom we have devoted unexpected attention here, away to other members of the table who are waiting for us and complaining of the favouritism of the service. The pale-faced poet of the Athenian theatrical hit, spoilt by success, is already becoming impatient'.[69] Kraus's pamphlet had a perfective title, yet was serialised in anticipation of the Griensteidl's actual demolition. The book version that followed concluded the linear review of its 'characters' by rounding up their literary pretensions in a metaphorical and metonymic 'last minute' inventory on the eve of the café's demolition. While a contemporary feuilleton summarily alluded to the 'inventory of marble tables, wooden chairs, billiard tables',[70] Kraus's rhetorical compilation of tropes and gimmicks breaks decisively with the nostalgic genre:

> In haste, all the literary gadgets are snatched up: lack of talent, premature mellowness, poses, megalomania, local girl, cravat, mannerisms, incorrect datives, monocle and mysterious nerves – they all have to go. Reluctant poets are gently escorted out. Fetched from their dim corners, they shy away from the day, the light of which dazzles them, and from life, the profusion of which will oppress them. Against this light the monocle offers only feeble protection; life will smash the crutch of affectation.[71]

A similar example is found in Polgar's ironic early story *Der Garten* (The Garden, 1908), about the temporary escape of a salesman from the coffeehouse smoke and brain-numbing chess-playing that would even infect the people at the next table. Here coffeehouse discourse is reduced to an inventory, of a circle that consists only of its own utterances, 'to be precise, of 127 conversational gambits, several frivolous quotations, an unclear, cynically soured world-view ... and numerous obscene jokes' – and once 'the world-view' leaves with its 'girl-friend', others decide to leave.[72] In these examples, the wit associated with coffeehouse discourse exploits (self-)critical metaphorical inventories of that sphere.

The third-person narrator of a novel can construct settings, follow interactions and review a character's (near-)simultaneous impressions in retrospective analysis. Indeed, Franz Werfel's novel *Barbara, oder die Frömmigkeit* (The Hidden Child, 1929) contains one of the most extensive characterisations of circles typifying the Café Central, set during and after the First World War. The fictional image of a decadent milieu is heralded when the protagonist, the newcomer Ferdinand, instantly detects the 'ammoniated reek of the urinal'[73] – familiar from Polgar's essay. The narrator vividly creates the impression of the unique space of the Café Central, but filters Ferdinand's 'unforgotten' first impressions through a more questioning retrospective point-of-view, that of the ship's doctor that he has since become. Ferdinand remembers first wondering about the 'immense, dimly guessed at', 'senseless' height of the 'cavern' of the café's 'Pillar Hall' and the indeterminate quality of the light, but he now suspects the dimensions of those 'towering cupolas' had become confused in his mental state at the time.[74] This self-critical insertion by the mature protagonist of later years can be read as a harsh authorial interpretation of the spatial distortion that Expressionist artists perfected in symbolically exteriorising inner existential turmoil. In the narrator's depiction, the café's 'towering darkness', unchallenged by the dim electric lighting during war-time, is only penetrated by a ray of sunshine from the adjacent chess-room on the street side. Although considerable interaction is depicted, as Ferdinand experiences the 'restless *va et vient*' between the six or seven occupied tables,[75] it hardly embodies cultural vitality.

Initially, Ferdinand loses track of time and place, as he 'unexpectedly' finds himself 'the centre of a group',[76] and he succumbs to the 'hidden spell' of the locale.[77] By means of indirect free style (a pluperfect tense) the reader becomes party to Ferdinand's emergence from this confusion, as he critically reflects that 'he *had* only had to face a barrage of words, a plethora of spectral faces'.[78] A proleptic insertion by the narrator intimates that Ferdinand '*spent* months' in these circles,[79] but the narrative continues with this first visit and Ferdinand's process of becoming habituated, as he guiltily tries 'from afar to catch the eye' of Gebhart, whom he felt he had been neglecting '*all the time* he sat at Basil's table' – the time phrase protracts the subjective impression of a 'long absence', only interrupted when Ronald Weiss moves to another table.[80] By contrast, time spent in coffeehouse circles can be concentrated into physical descriptions that are supposedly revealing of character, thereby reasserting temporal order, as in the sketch of Hedda, whose physiognomy bears the scars of 'consumption of thirty cigarettes a day, eternal intellectual discussion, and a habit of unselective promiscuity'.[81] Likewise, the perfective verbal adjectives in the sentence 'Burnt out cigar and cigarette stumps sagged from disgusted lips'[82] generalise an overwhelming sense of moribund reification. The scene, presided over by contemptuous waiters, is punctuated sporadically as individuals 'get up, shuffle a few steps, and sink down, without any attempt at ceremony, in the midst of a group of neighbouring guests'. Whereas coffeehouse anecdotes of necessity rely on the structural contrast of a continuous condition with unique moments, here the 'rare flashes of electrifying "temperament"'[83] that occasionally punctuate the prevailing lethargy are themselves all too ephemeral, tainted symptoms of decay. Even the 'genius' Gebhart only once dazzles the whole table, in a kind of intellectual reparation for his personal failings as a father.[84] Ferdinand later judges the staleness of Basil's discourse as 'a réchauffée [...] of things he *might have once felt*' and the ephemerality of Weiss's as 'some sudden, flashy notion, unsustained, *devoid of sequence, without either yesterday or tomorrow*'.[85] These temporal reductions to an end-effect thus reinforce the hyperbolical spatial match of the oppressive milieu to the decadence and dissoluteness of its clientele, as part of a larger-scale diagnosis of Habsburg decline, far removed from the world of redemptive modest piety embodied by the eponymous Barbara.

One final example, drawn from the essay genre, epitomises the temporal and spatial structures of café life in a unique intersection. In the inter-war period Anton Kuh reminds us, in his piece entitled 'Café de l'Europe', of quite a different café type. The Café de l'Europe was not a traditional coffeehouse, but a lively all-night café, and Kuh uses it as a topos to locate characteristically modern social paradoxes, in a finely observed suspension of segmentation – a structuring principle in spatial depictions of cafés – at a point along the temporal dimension of the daily round. In Kuh's sketch, at a certain time in the early morning the café is the place where the city's day and night shifts overlap in a moment of exchange ('from their remote worlds') that is pin-pointed both temporally and spatially as coincidence, with dissolute night-owls and bourgeois early risers sharing a table, 'contradicting each other like lacquered shoes on a dewy alpine pasture'. However, this moment is also a regularly occurring phenomenon. Whereas repetition is often a routine or unacknowledged aspect of coffeehouse nostalgia, Kuh's metaphor of this night café as being 'a metropolitan *perpetuum mobile*, a miracle of restlessness and incessancy and as such having a soothing effect on those anxious at night and afraid of death',[86] crystallises the temporally determined complexity of that space, as it briefly accommodates some existential fragility amid the city's abrasive social contrasts.

This 'Café de l'Europe', together with Polgar's 'Café Central' and Kraus's 'Café Griensteidl', may suggest literary resources that can reconfigure temporal-spatial intersections characteristic of the café's cultural diversity and social predictability, and thereby exemplify the performative aesthetic of modernism. The stereotypical structural devices of reminiscence, by contrast, may invite reflection less on the coffeehouse as a unique site of modernist creativity than on the memoir genre's own self-deconstructing myth-making. However, this conclusion has to be qualified by the concession that the intellectual stimulus of the coffeehouse had more diverse manifestations than are revealed in published narratives with coffeehouse settings – for example, inspiration that was consummated perhaps in a certain scarcely traceable intellectual energy or self-consciousness in artistic or philosophical work of very different forms. Nevertheless, it remains striking that only a few writers experimented successfully in depicting such a purportedly creative milieu – and it is characteristic of Austrian modernism that those, like Werfel, who incorporated the café milieu into a traditional novel form, suffused it with a discourse of cultural pessimism, as an atmospheric symptom of Habsburg decline, which overshadowed its significance as a hothouse of modernist germination.

Notes

1. Karl Otten, 'Eindrücke von Robert Musil', in Karl Dinklage (ed.), *Robert Musil. Leben – Werk – Wirkung*, for the State of Kärnten and the City of Klagenfurt, Zürich and Vienna 1960, 361.
2. Jürgen Habermas, *The Structural Transformation of the Public Sphere. An Inquiry into a Category of Bourgeois Society* (1962), trans. Thomas Burger et al., Cambridge, Mass 1989.
3. Ursula Keller, *Böser Dinge hübsche Formel. Das Wien Arthur Schnitzlers*, Berlin 1984, 47f. [All translations are my own unless otherwise stated. G.C.]
4. Alfred Polgar, 'Theorie des "Café Central"', in Alfred Polgar, *Kleine Schriften,* Marcel Reich-Ranicki et al. (eds), Reinbek 1984, vol. 4, 254–259. Translations quoted from Alfred Polgar, 'Theory of the Café Central', http://depts.washington.edu/vienna/literature/polgar/Polgar_Cafe.htm (accessed on 31 January 2011).
5. Friedrich Torberg, 'Traktat über das Wiener Kaffeehaus', in Kurt-Jürgen Heering (ed.), *Das Wiener Kaffeehaus. Mit zahlreichen Abbildungen und Hinweisen auf Wiener Kaffeehäuser*, Frankfurt 1993, 18–32, here 24.

6. On cafés with profession-specific clienteles, see Otto Friedländer, *Letzter Glanz der Märchenstadt*, 1947, quoted in Heering, *Das Wiener Kaffeehaus*, 91–97, here 94. On the history of specific Viennese cafés, see Felix Czeike, *Historisches Lexikon Wien*, 5 vols, Vienna 1992–1996.

7. Gérard Genette, 'Frontiers of Narrative', in Gérard Genette, *Figures of Literary Discourse*, trans. Alan Sheridan, Oxford 1982 (1969), 127–144, here 136.

8. Joseph Kestner, 'Secondary Illusion: The Novel and the Spatial Arts', in Jeffrey R. Smitten and Ann Daghistany (eds), *Spatial Form in Narrative*, Ithaca and London 1981, 100–128, here 100 and 107.

9. Reingard Nethersole, 'From Temporality to Spatiality: Changing Concepts in Literary Criticism', in Roger Bauer and Douwe Wessel Fokkema (eds), *Proceedings of the XIIth Congress of the International Comparative Literature Association (Munich 88)*, Munich 1990, vol. 5, 59–65, here 63.

10. On an exemplary café scene by the Moravian writer Petr Bezruč, see Gilbert J. Carr, 'Austrian Literature and the Coffee-House before 1890', in Judith Beniston and Debora Holmes (eds), *From Ausgleich to Jahrhundertwende: Literature and Culture 1867–1890: Austrian Studies*, 16, 2008, 154–171, here 168–170.

11. 'Das Ende des Café Griensteidl', *Arbeiter-Zeitung*, 9(20), 20 January 1897, 3.

12. 'Ein altes Wiener Kaffeehaus', *Fremden-Blatt*, 51(23), 23 January 1897, 13f.

13. 'Ein altes Wiener Kaffeehaus', *Neue Freie Presse*, 11641, 19 January 1897, 7.

14. 'Ein altes Wiener Kaffeehaus', *Fremden-Blatt*, 23 January 1897, 13f.

15. Ibid.

16. Ibid. See also Stefan Grossmann, *Ich war begeistert. Eine Lebensgeschichte*, Berlin 1931, 54, who distinguishes 'different camps and branches' within coffee-houses and between specific workers' cafés, businessmen's cafés, artists' cafés, politicians' cafés and medics' cafés.

17. 'Kehraus. (Die letzten Stunden des Café Griensteidl)', *Neues Wiener Journal*, 1166, 21 January 1897, 6.

18. 'Ein altes Wiener Kaffeehaus', *Neue Freie Presse*, 7 November 1896, in Ludwig Greve and Werner Volke (eds), *Jugend in Wien: Literatur um 1900*, Sonderausstellungen des Schiller-Nationalmuseums, Catalogue no. 24, Munich 1974, 265.

19. See Edward Timms, *Karl Kraus. Apocalyptic Satirist. Culture and Catastrophe in Habsburg Vienna*, New Haven and London 1986, 7–10.

20. T. Girhatz, 'Das "Café Griensteidl"', *Alt-Wien*, 5(10), October 1896, 203–207, here 204.

21. 'Ein altes Wiener Kaffeehaus', *Fremden-Blatt*, 23 January 1897, 13f.

22. 'Ein altes Wiener Kaffeehaus', *Neue Freie Presse*, 19 January 1897, 7.

23. Grossmann, *Ich war begeistert*, 55.

24. 'Kehraus', *Neues Wiener Journal*, 21 January 1897, 6.

25. 'Der Kehraus beim Griensteidl', *Neues Wiener Tagblatt*, 31(21), 21 January 1897, 7f.

26. Girhatz, 'Das "Café Griensteidl"', 204.

27. *Neue Freie Presse*, 7 November 1896, in Greve and Volke, *Jugend in Wien*, 265.

28. Ferry Bératon, 'Von der Woche. Plaudereien des Reporters', *Die vornehme Welt*, 1(4), 28 January 1897, 72f.

29. 'Das Ende des Café Griensteidl', *Arbeiter-Zeitung*, 20 January 1897, 3.

30. On contiguity as alienation in the Café Central after 1900, see Helga Malmberg, *Widerhall des Herzens. Ein Peter Altenberg-Buch*, Munich 1961, 133f. See also a letter of Berthold Viertel's from 1908 to Hermann Wlach about the Café Central, on the dehumanising and demoralising effect of claustrophobic proximity with phoneys and impotent idlers under the dominion of 'His Majesty Spleen'; in Greve and Volke, *Jugend in Wien*, 92f.

31. Berthold Viertel, 'Erinnerung an Peter Altenberg', in Berthold Viertel, *Dichtungen und Dokumente. Gedichte, Prosa, Autobiographische Fragmente*, Ernst Ginsberg (ed.), Munich 1956, 311–318, here 314f.

32. http://depts.washington.edu/vienna/literature/polgar/Polgar_Cafe.htm (accessed on 31 January 2011).

33. Richard Specht, *Arthur Schnitzler. Der Dichter und sein Werk. Eine Studie*, Berlin 1922.

34. Gustav Gugitz, *Das Wiener Kaffeehaus: Ein Stück Kultur- und Lokalgeschichte*, Vienna 1940, 189.

35. Maurice Halbwachs, *On Collective Memory* (1925), trans. Lewis A. Coser, Chicago and London 1992, 39.

36. Pierre Nora, 'Entre Mémoire et Histoire', in Pierre Nora (ed.), *Les Lieux de Mémoire*, Vol. 1. *La République*, Paris 1984, xvii–xlii, here xxiv and xxxv.

37. See Käte Hamburger, *The Logic of Literature* (1957), trans. Marilyn J. Rose, Bloomington and London 1973, 2nd edn, 97f.

38. See Bernard Comrie, *Aspect. An Introduction to the Study of Verbal Aspect and Related Problems*, London, New York and Melbourne 1976. For differentiations of temporal order in fictional narrative (diachronicity, duration, singularity and iterativity), see Gérard Genette, 'Discours du Récit. Essai de Méthode', in Gérard Genette, *Figures III*, Paris 1972, 65–282.

39. Karl Peter Rosner, '*Damals…*'. *Bilderbuch einer Jugend*, Düsseldorf 1948, 232.

40. Specht, *Arthur Schnitzler*, 33f. A similar hostile demarcation of coffeehouse space is recalled by Friedländer in Heering, *Das Wiener Kaffeehaus*, 94.

41. Arthur Schnitzler, *Jugend in Wien. Eine Autobiographie*, Therese Nickl and Heinrich Schnitzler (eds), Munich 1968, 102.

42. 'Ein altes Wiener Kaffeehaus', *Fremden-Blatt*, 23 January 1897, 13f.

43. Felix Salten, 'Aus den Anfängen. Erinnerungsskizzen', in *Jahrbuch für Bibliophilen und Literaturfreunde*, 18(19), 1932/33, 31–46, here 34–38.

44. Rosner, *Damals*, 233.

45. Specht, *Arthur Schnitzler*, 35.

46. Anton Kuh, '"Central" und "Herrenhof"', in Heering, *Das Wiener Kaffeehaus*, 157–166, here 161.

47. Anton Kuh, 'Zeitgeist im Literatur-Café', in Heering, *Das Wiener Kaffeehaus*, 169–172, here 170.

48. Specht, *Arthur Schnitzler*, 34f. [My italics. G.C.]

49. See Halbwachs, *On Collective Memory*, 60.

50. Stefan Zweig, *Die Welt von gestern. Erinnerungen eines Europäers*, Stockholm 1947, 60; Stefan Zweig, *The World of Yesterday. An Autobiography*, London 1943, 42.

51. Zweig, *The World of Yesterday*, 41f.

52. Ibid., 45. Wedekind was not performed anywhere before the première of *Erdgeist* in Leipzig in February 1898; see Günter Seehaus, *Frank Wedekind und das Theater*, Munich 1964, 15. The first disruption of a strictly atonal work by Schönberg was at the première of the Second String Quartet on 21 December 1908. I am grateful to Michael Taylor for this information.

53. Eugen Antoine, 'Erinnerungen an das Cafe Griensteidl', in *Agathon: Almanach auf das Jahr 1948*, Vienna 1947/48, 41–55, here 43.

54. On the expected opening of Rudolf Glattauer's café on the site of the Griensteidl in the autumn of 1898, see 'Ein neuer Besitzer des Café Griensteidl', *Illustriertes Wiener Extrablatt*, 91, 2 April 1898, 3.

55. Zweig, *The World of Yesterday*, 46f.

56. Hermann Bahr, 'Loris', in *Das Hermann-Bahr-Buch*, Berlin 1913, 253–260, here 254.

57. Zweig, *The World of Yesterday*, 46f.

58. Ibid., 49.

59. Sigismund von Radecki, 'Erinnerungen an Karl Kraus', in Friedrich Pfäfflin (ed.), *Aus großer Nähe. Karl Kraus in Berichten von Weggefährten und Widersachern*, Bibliothek Janowitz, 16, Göttingen 2008, 136.
60. Friedrich Torberg, 'Café De l'Europe. Café Imperial', in Heering, *Das Wiener Kaffeehaus*, 103–110, here 109f.
61. Radecki, 'Erinnerungen an Karl Kraus', 169f.
62. Hermann Bahr, 'Neben der Liebe. Wiener Sitten', in *Freie Bühne für den Entwicklungskampf der Zeit*, 3, 1892, 1009–1048, 1121–1154, 1233–1258, here 1015.
63. Ibid., 1017.
64. Ibid., 1020f.
65. Alfred Polgar, *Der Quell des Übels und andere Geschichten*, Munich 1908, 9–16.
66. Ibid., 10.
67. Ibid., 16.
68. Ibid., 10–11.
69. Karl Kraus, 'Die demolirte Literatur', in Karl Kraus, *Frühe Schriften*, Johannes J. Braakenburg (ed.), vol. 2, Munich 1979, 277–297, here 291.
70. 'Das Ende des Café Griensteidl', *Arbeiter-Zeitung*, 20 January 1897, 3.
71. Kraus, 'Die demolirte Literatur', 297.
72. Polgar, 'Der Garten', in Polgar, *Der Quell des Übels*, 71–80, here 71–72.
73. Franz Werfel, *Barbara, oder die Frömmigkeit*, Berlin, Vienna and Leipzig 1929, 424; Franz Werfel, *The Hidden Child*, trans. Geoffrey Dunlop, London 1931, 301.
74. Werfel, *The Hidden Child*, 302.
75. Ibid.
76. Ibid., 303.
77. Ibid., 316.
78. Ibid., 325. [My italics, G.C.].
79. Ibid., 320. [My italics, G.C.].
80. Ibid. [My italics, G.C.].
81. Ibid., 317.
82. Ibid., 302.
83. Ibid., 302f.
84. Ibid., 334.
85. Ibid., 327. [My italics, G.C.].
86. Anton Kuh, 'Café de l'Europe', in Heering, *Das Wiener Kaffeehaus*, 111–113, here 112.

Chapter 3

'THE JEW BELONGS IN THE COFFEEHOUSE'

Jews, Central Europe and Modernity

Steven Beller

In late 1895 Vienna was in the midst of a crisis of authority and power. In November of that year Emperor Franz Joseph had refused to confirm Karl Lueger as mayor of the city, but the Christian Socials had not accepted this setback. In early December they were still holding protest meetings against this attempt to subvert the popular will, that is to say to deny their victories in the municipal elections of that year. The 3 December issue of the *Neue Freie Presse* reported on one such meeting, a Christian Social 'Women's Meeting' in the Volksprater:

> In the Praterstrasse noisy and disgusting riots took place. Many women from the respectable middle classes, for whom such kinds of behaviour would not have been thought possible, took part.[1]

The newspaper reported that the meeting was dissolved by the police, and in the aftermath of this many women had headed through the local neighbourhood, the Leopoldstadt, invading shops, insulting Jews, and blaming them for engineering the dissolution of the meeting. (The newspaper printed this last detail in bold type.) The enraged female crowd then attacked coffeehouses. The report went on:

> At the Café Licht the crowd comes to a halt again: several Jewish guests are sitting at the windows, which enrages the mob, and several particularly fanaticized women tear open the doors of the locale and, shouting: 'Down with the Jews!', invade the Café. The coffeehouse owner and a number of guests rush to the door and just as quickly run the uninvited guests out as they had come in.[2]

The Café Licht was not one of the renowned literary and artistic coffeehouses we usually think of when we talk of 'Viennese coffeehouse culture', but there is a certain symbolism about this attack by Christian Socials on a 'Jewish' coffeehouse. Both this newspaper report, and the often used proverbial phrase that 'the Jew belongs in the coffeehouse', point to a long-held claim, by Viennese, Central Europeans and others, then and now, that there was a strong connection between the coffeehouse and Jews: not only that Jews 'belonged there', but that the coffeehouse as a centre of cultural innovation was a Jewish realm in the socio-cultural landscape of Vienna and Central Europe.

In one sense this was clearly not the case – the coffeehouse did not start as a Jewish institution and not all of the main players in the literary coffeehouses were Jewish – but, in another sense, there was a certain amount of truth in this claim. The character of the coffeehouse as a centre of the modern culture of Vienna 1900 did depend on its being in that part of the socio-cultural landscape of Vienna and Central Europe in which Jews, inclusively defined here as individuals of Jewish descent, predominated. And its symbolic power to this day lies in the fact that the coffeehouse was a vehicle for, and represented, a world – a world-view, a whole way of life – that was largely that of the region's 'assimilated' Jews.

Many have made this claim. Harold B. Segel, in *The Vienna Coffeehouse Wits, 1890–1938*, speaks of the literary coffeehouse's 'heavily Jewish character'.[3] The most famous advocate of the Jewish character of the literary coffeehouse was Friedrich Torberg, in his two nostalgia-tinged collections of anecdotes, *Die Tante Jolesch oder Der Untergang des Abendlandes in Anekdoten* (Tante Jolesch or the Decline of the West in Anecdotes, 1975), and *Die Erben der Tante Jolesch* (The Heirs of Tante Jolesch, 1977).[4] These did not, according to the author, start out as collections of coffeehouse anecdotes, but rather of the world of the emancipated, assimilated Jewish bourgeoisie. Torberg only 'realizes' (artfully) that the two worlds are virtually identical, and intimately linked, on page 136 of *Die Tante Jolesch*. It is here that he makes a double claim: not only is this 'Jewish' world unthinkable without the coffeehouse, but also the reverse:

> that the coffeehouse has taken on something from Tante (Aunt) Jolesch, that she is the missing link between the Talmudic tradition of the ghetto and emancipated coffeehouse culture, that she was, as it were, the female ancestor of all those people who found in the coffeehouse the catalyst and central focus of their existence, and she was their primal mother whether or not they realized it, whether or not they wanted it to be so.[5]

According to Torberg, it is precisely because Vienna's 'coffeehouse culture' was so Jewish, in this indirect, secularised sense, that it was so significant, and so much part of a world destroyed.

Torberg receives circumstantial, but strong, support from another prominent Viennese writer, Alfred Polgar. In a piece from 1906, an ironic Viennese feuilleton burying the Viennese feuilleton, Polgar situated the feuilleton within the socio-cultural landscape of Vienna:

> A quite special characteristic of the Viennese feuilleton is the jocose mixture of the ultra-Jewish and the ultra-Aryan. Of the melancholy of the synagogue and the tipsy humour of Grinzing. Is the sorrow over the thousand-year diaspora best drowned in Vienna's wine taverns? It seems so. Turning and twisting, that's my life – as sure as I live! The mixture manifests itself thoroughly in the construction and style of the Viennese feuilleton. It has a sensitive intellect and a remarkably intelligent emotional life. It practices logical mental games ornamented with feeling, and on the other hand always has a measure of emotion seated tenderly in the brain.[6]

The coffeehouse is not mentioned, but is present in its absence. In Polgar's deliberately stereotypical cityscape the one place that is not Jewish, but 'ultra-Aryan', is the Grinzinger wine tavern, with its 'ultra-Jewish' counterpart being the synagogue. Yet the feuilleton is supposedly a symbiosis of the spirit of these two spaces, and the reader knows that the feuilleton is, in actuality, written in neither, but rather in the spatial equivalent of the feuilleton itself, the coffeehouse, of which Polgar was one of the most frequent and famous habitués. By implication, therefore, the feuilleton and the coffeehouse are the terrain on which the Viennese-Jewish symbiosis – for good or ill – is taking place. As such, the feuilleton is part of the experience of Jewish integration and acculturation. By analogy, neither the *Grinzinger Heurigen* nor the synagogue is the site of this integration and symbiosis, but rather the coffeehouse, just as Torberg claimed.

The linkage between Jews and the coffeehouse in Vienna goes back to before 1848, and that linkage, as well as the Jewish predominance in the relationship, grew over time. It is of note that in Sigmund Mayer's history of Viennese Jewry the coffeehouse first appears in its role as a commercial site. Before 1848, it was as the space for informal commodity exchanges, of textiles, wheat, and spirits, often more significant than their official counterparts, that coffeehouses in the Leopoldstadt such as Cafés Friedrich, Café Mehringer, 'bei Stierböck' and Café Fetzer functioned.[7] This commercial side was actually a fairly common facet of café culture across Europe: Lloyds was also originally a coffeehouse before it became an insurance industry. Even before 1848, there was also a significant connection between Jewish writers and the coffeehouse. The most significant literary coffeehouse of the time, the 'Silver Coffeehouse', had few Jews among its literary lions, but, as Mayer points out, there was another coffeehouse, Café Geringer, in the Bauernmarkt, where Jewish writers and journalists did gather.[8]

In the era of Café Griensteidl, from 1848 until 1897, Jewish participation in literary life and the Jewish presence in the coffeehouse expanded, so that by the café's demise the most well-known literary group that met there, Jung Wien, was in a very large majority Jewish.[9] One should note, though, that there was also a *Stammtisch* in the café where another set of writers would gather, such as Hermann Hango and Fritz Lemmermayer, who thought of themselves as 'German', and who chose not to join the 'dilettantes' on the next table. This group, apparently with no Jewish members, was also part of the Griensteidl world, but they have largely been forgotten.[10]

Griensteidl's successor as the main literary coffeehouse was the Café Central, whose reign lasted until 1918, at which point its role was usurped by the new Café Herrenhof for the inter-war period. In the Café Central and the Café Herrenhof, the cast of characters, while not exclusively Jewish, was predominantly so: Franz Blei, Robert Musil and Otto Gross were not Jewish, but then there was Peter Altenberg, Karl Kraus, Hermann Broch, Anton Kuh, Alfred Polgar, Ernst Polak, Otto Soyka, Leo Perutz, Friedrich Torberg, Hilde Spiel, Elias Canetti, Joseph Roth, Franz Werfel, Egon Erwin Kisch, Gina Kaus and so forth. One of the non-Jewish writers who frequented the Herrenhof, Milan Dubrovic, once claimed (to me) that 80 per cent of the literary clientele of the café were Jewish. This might be a little 'generous', but I think Dubrovic's general attitude is interesting. In the 1840s Jewish writers had wanted to break in to the world of the non-Jewish literary lions of Viennese coffeehouse culture; by the 1920s, a young journalist wanting to enter the modern Viennese intellectual and literary world felt that he had to go to the 'Jewish' literary coffeehouses.[11]

But was there anything 'Jewish' about this? There were coffeehouses in Vienna before there were Jews, and there are still. Even during the heyday of Jewish participation in Viennese culture, there were many coffeehouses where Jews were not much of a factor at all. As has been noted in Charlotte Ashby's essay, different coffeehouses catered to many different walks of life in the city. So what was so special about the relationship of Jews to the coffeehouse? Even in the literary coffeehouse, did Jewish predominance make any difference to the cultural norms, style and atmosphere of the coffeehouse?

There were several reasons for Jews to feel an affinity with the coffeehouse as a space of social interaction. First, the coffeehouse and Jews shared the status of not being *bodenständig*, (literally 'of this ground'). The wine and beer taverns, including Polgar's *Grinzinger Heurigen*, had at their heart the purveyance of local products, for the local 'native' population – and Jews were never really included in the latter. The status of Jews was, I need hardly add, a matter of often dramatic and prejudiced debate, but they were never regarded as the 'host people' and were associated with difference, trade, and therefore somewhere else. Whether it was fair or not, Jews were identified as foreign, even exotic, hence their mystery – and danger – for many. But then so was that staple of Viennese life, the coffee served in coffeehouses: the coffeehouse was completely reliant on the sort of international trade in exotic, colonial goods that Jews were also associated with, and coffee's centrality to Viennese consumer culture thus reflected a globalisation, or exoticisation of European culture (even when domesticated) that paralleled the rise of tea in British consumer culture.

There was another quality of coffee that appealed to Jews in a way it did not necessarily to non-Jews: it was not alcoholic. This point should not be overstressed, as some prominent Jewish writers, such as Peter Altenberg, were notable for their alcohol consumption, but at the same time it does suggest a potential reason for the established patronage of the coffeehouse by the Jewish community. Aside from the traditional reservations about alcohol consumption, there were also economic considerations: coffee could be imbibed during business negotiations without jeopardising self-interest, so the coffeehouse could serve as an ideal place for trade. For the same reason – the lack of serious danger of inebriation – the coffeehouse could serve as a secular version of the synagogue: Jewish men could meet there either after, or increasingly instead of, going to the *Schul*, the traditional site of Jewish religious (intellectual) socialisation. The relative lack of emphasis within coffeehouse culture on food consumption similarly encouraged a concentration on the coffeehouse's twin functions: the ostensible one to consume coffee, and the real one to meet and talk with customers, business colleagues, friends and acquaintances. It was as a site for exchange, whether commercial, social or intellectual, that the coffeehouse truly flourished. Even coffee, I would argue, for all the fuss made about the various sorts of preparations of coffee available to the customer, was secondary to the coffeehouse's main function.[12]

Not only was it a site of exchange; what was particularly valuable to Jews was that it was a site of relatively open and inclusive exchange. One of the reasons that coffeehouses had served as sites for commercial exchanges before 1848 was that they filled a vacuum, or provided a bypass to obstacles: either there were no exchanges established, or those that were, were ones from which Jews were excluded. But Jews could meet in the coffeehouse. There is an interesting parallel here with the role of coffeehouses in British social history. If they did not develop into commercial and financial institutions, such as Lloyds, many coffeehouses went quite another, privatising way: they became gentlemen's clubs, which were characterised by the exclusion of the public for the sake of private socialisation. In Vienna the coffeehouse remained a relatively public space of civil society, where the purchase of a small cup of coffee was the equivalent of an entry ticket into a public version of a club.[13]

Many of the rest of Vienna's social institutions, especially regarding the court and aristocratic salons, and associations such as the student fraternities, were never open to Jews, were restrictive to most Jews, or became more restrictive and exclusive to Jews over time, with the rise of political (and social) antisemitism. But the coffeehouse remained open to them, and provided a social space, a site of social and cultural exchange, that was indoors but simultaneously quasi-public. As has already been noted in Ashby's chapter, even the forms of social exclusivity within the coffeehouse, such as the institution of the *Stammtisch*, where people were informally invited and disinvited from being 'members', were more informal and hence less exclusive than, for instance, club membership. A key figure in coffeehouse culture was the *Kibitzer*, the uninvited listener at the table. Social exclusions, personal rivalries and the like, clearly took place, but they took place within the larger, inclusive context of the coffeehouse.

Is it any surprise then that young Jewish writers and intellectuals, faced with the calamitous rise of antisemitism in Viennese politics and society in the 1880s and 1890s, should seek a form of refuge in the literary coffeehouse? And may they not also have brought their concerns, their fears, and their lack of security, their sense also of alienation and deracination, with them? That appears to have been what happened, in part, to the writers of the Jung Wien movement, if we are to trust Arthur Schnitzler as a guide. His most insightful novel, *Der Weg ins Freie* (The Road to the Open, 1908), is full of scenes inspired by Schnitzler's time in the Café Griensteidl, of Jewish writers pricking the balloons of other Jewish writers' vanities and illusions. Perhaps the most relevant scene for us is Heinrich Bermann's criticism of the young poet Winternitz for using the 'lyrical, subjective "Hei"' in a poem; such a word is denied to 'our sort', as Bermann puts it, for 'eternity'. That sort of easy 'inwardly free' approach is not the culture of the coffeehouse, for it is not available to young Viennese Jews in their existential crisis.[14]

It is not far from this depiction of the Viennese Jewish spiritual crisis, written in or before 1908, to perhaps the classic depiction of the most abstract form of coffeehouse culture, Polgar's 'Theorie des Café Central' (Theory of the Café Central, 1926). Polgar depicts the coffeehouse as a 'surrogate totality' for deracinated, alienated individuals, people 'who want to be alone but need companionship for it', a collective of individualists.[15] Is he not describing the coffeehouse as a refuge for Vienna's Jewish intellectuals, an escape from the crisis caused by the onset of antisemitism and the resulting denial of belonging and identity for these individuals? The same syndrome is expressed more bluntly by Albert Ehrenstein in his essay on Peter Altenberg, the ultimate coffeehouse man. Ehrenstein writes: 'Altenberg was ultra-Viennese and yet homeless when he died; the earth (*Boden*) beneath his feet did not welcome him. He was a Jew. Like Ahasverus he ran his whole life long from hotel room to hotel room, café to café'.[16]

In the spirit of the coffeehouse, however, we should take the gloom with a pinch of salt. Polgar and his coffeehouse colleagues were actually happily addicted to the Café Central, and later the Café Herrenhof (which was a far more modern and brighter place). This was partly because the coffeehouse did offer them a remarkable vehicle by which to exchange ideas, and partly because it was not, despite Polgar's half-playful suggestion, completely cut off from the world outside. Or if it was, it was only cut off from that Viennese reality that was threatening to the world of the coffeehouse *Literat*. The coffeehouse might have been cut off from the immediate, humdrum (and often antisemitic) political, social and economic world around it, but it was actually tied into, indeed a focal point of, a network of complexes and connections that extended deep into Vienna's cultural and intellectual life, and also far beyond the city.

Edward Timms' famous diagram of the circles of Viennese intellectual and cultural life can also be used to highlight the centrality of the coffeehouse in Viennese cultural life.[17] Many of those circles were actually centred around *Stammtische* in one coffeehouse or another. Café Griensteidl, Café Central and Café Herrenhof each account for a large proportion, and adding in Café Museum, Café Sperl, Café Landtmann, and Café Imperial would account for much of the rest. Individuals would move not only from table to table, but also from café to café, so much of Viennese cultural life was connected through the coffeehouses. These *Stammtische* in turn were connected through their members to several of the other more academic groupings, such as the Vienna Circle of logical positivism, which was linked to Café Herrenhof through Otto Neurath. In *Der Weg ins Freie* Schnitzler's characters move easily between the coffeehouse and the world of the literary salon (also largely Jewish) and this connection persisted: in the inter-war period Bertha Zuckerkandl, a leading *salonnière*, hosted her salon in an upper floor of the same building that housed Café Landtmann. Many journalists from the major papers were also coffeehouse regulars, and provided strong connections to the mass media of the day. Many of the librettists, and also the composers of the 'silver age' of operetta – Leo Fall was a regular at Café Central – were also coffeehouse habitués, linking in the Viennese version of show business. Coffeehouse intellectuals thus had their own community, through the connections between coffeehouses and other social nodes: this was the world that Torberg, Dubrovic and others describe, and this hinter-network, as it were, of the main literary and intellectual coffeehouses was a largely Jewish world.

It was also, for all the insularity and social insulation that Polgar discusses, a very outward looking world. The main coffeehouses were luxuriously equipped with a myriad of literary journals and newspapers from across Europe, and indeed, this access to such a panoply of information, in a pre-Internet age, was one of the prime attractions for many of the clientele. They were also part of a network of coffeehouses extending across Habsburg Central Europe and beyond, which offered the same context, or similar, for the coffeehouse literati. Café Arco in Prague, Café New York in Budapest, Café des Westens and then the Romanisches Café in Berlin, and less well-known satellites in outposts such as Czernowitz, Brünn or Lemberg, provided the nodal points of what was not so much a 'republic of letters' but rather a sort of 'consociational federation of coffeehouses'.[18] It was this complex of connections that provided the environment for a 'coffeehouse culture' that was also a Central European culture. One might say it was *the* Central European culture. It might not have been 'of the territory', of the *Boden*, of the earth, of central Europe, for the reasons given above, but it was what made 'Vienna' Viennese, what made 'central Europe' Central Europe, with a capital 'C'. What do I mean by this? To say that this coffeehouse culture was one of 'mercurial wit' might appear trivial cliché, but there is something deeper to this 'mercurial' characterisation. Yuri Slezkine has been criticised for the binary stereotyping that he used in his book *The Jewish Century*, between 'Mercurians' and 'Apollonians', but Slezkine's schema, for all its abstraction and rigidity, describes remarkably well the connection between coffeehouses, coffeehouse culture, and Central European Jewry that I have been discussing.[19] In this schema the Apollonians are the agrarian peoples, tied to the land, with a warrior ruling caste, a culture that prizes physical strength and beauty, and intellectual simplicity; the Mercurians are the minority trading peoples, that every society has in one form or another, who live next to or among the Apollonians but separately from them, yet who also provide the connections for that society. Hence the Mercurians are the traders, often the clerical administrators, and the money people, with a culture that prizes intellectual agility, hence 'mercurial wit', fears or looks down on physical strength and suspects physical beauty, and values above all intellectual complexity, what George Steiner would refer to, I suspect, as 'difficulty'.

If ever there was a Mercurian culture, it was that of the Central European literary coffeehouse. It was a culture that connected the region together, and connected the region with the rest of the world, but it was not heavily rooted in the 'soil', it was a culture and a community that consisted of its connections, not of its roots – it is almost as though it hovered slightly above the territorial reality of central Europe, not so much a Tower of Babel as rather a network of 'castles in the air'. It was this almost 'free-floating' network, of connected 'spaces of freedom' that provided the setting, the space of Central European culture, making that space inclusive of many points of view, a pluralistic space, open to the possibilities and varieties of human thought in a way that the narrow purviews of 'pure' national, conventional cultures were not.[20] The high level of Jewish predominance was key here. The way in which the possibilities of the coffeehouse were utilised to produce this Mercurian Central European culture had much to do with the needs and goals that Central European Jews brought with them when they entered 'this small, peculiar world, steeped in the soft, warm aroma of mocha'.[21] That is why I think Torberg was quite right when he claimed that the fall of 'Austria' – Austrian Central Europe – did not happen in 1918, but in 1938, March to be precise.[22]

What made the culture of the coffeehouse so significant, and in what way was it 'Jewish', in the central European context? Let me close by answering the question through the words of one of the coffeehouse's fictional literary characters, Ronnie Weiss. Weiss was a character in Franz Werfel's semi-autobiographical novel, *Barbara, oder die Frömmigkeit* (The Hidden Child, 1929). He was fairly transparently based on Werfel's close friend at the time when the novel was set (at the collapse of the Dual Monarchy of Austria-Hungary in 1918), the 'racing reporter' Egon Erwin Kisch. Turning to the non-Jewish hero of the novel, Ferdinand R., Weiss tries to explain why the regulars in the 'Colonnaded Hall' (the main room in the Café Central) could have tolerated having Spannweit, a left-wing publisher, among them, when they knew he was an informer. Weiss says: 'I suspect that you still do not understand the Colonnaded Hall, and never will … We *tolerate* everything. We live *sub specie aeternatis* like the swine'.[23]

Somewhere in that answer lies, I suspect, the answer to the cultural power of the coffeehouse, the creativity of Central European modern culture, and the huge debt we, today, owe to the cultural and intellectual contribution that Central European Jewry made to our, modern world.

Notes

1. *Neue Freie Presse*, morning edition, 3 December 1895, 6.
2. Ibid.
3. Harold B. Segel (ed.), *The Vienna Coffeehouse Wits, 1890–1938*, West Lafayette, Indiana 1993, 12.
4. Friedrich Torberg, *Die Tante Jolesch oder Der Untergang des Abendlandes in Anekdoten*, Munich 1977; Friedrich Torberg, *Die Erben der Tante Jolesch*, Munich 1981.
5. Torberg, *Die Tante Jolesch*, 136. The relation between the Talmudic tradition and the coffeehouse is also considered in Shachar Pinsker, 'Between "The House of Study" and the Coffeehouse: The Central European Café as a Site for Hebrew and Yiddish Modernism', in this volume.
6. Alfred Polgar, 'The Viennese Feuillton', in Segel, *Coffeehouse Wits*, 250.
7. Sigmund Mayer, *Die Wiener Juden: Kommerz, Kultur, Politik 1700–1900*, Vienna 1916, 224–230, 265–268.
8. Ibid., 275–277.
9. Karl Kraus, 'Die demolirte Literatur', in Johannes J. Braakenburg (ed.), *Frühe Schriften*, vol. 2, Munich 1979, 277–297.
10. Hans Weigel (ed.), *Das Wiener Kaffeehaus*, Vienna 1978, 58.
11. Milan Dubrovic, *Veruntreute Geschichte*, Berlin 2001.
12. Weigel, *Kaffeehaus*, 11.
13. For further discussion of the mores governing coffeehouse sociability, see Charlotte Ashby's chapter in this volume.
14. Arthur Schnitzler, *Der Weg ins Freie*, Frankfurt am Main 1978, 127.
15. Alfred Polgar, 'Theory of the Café Central', in Segel, *Coffeehouse Wits*, 267–270.
16. Albert Ehrenstein, 'Peter Altenberg', in *Menschen und Affen*, Berlin 1925, 68.
17. Edward Timms, *Karl Kraus, Apocalyptic Satirist: Culture and Catastrophe in Habsburg Vienna*, London 1986, 8.
18. See Shachar Pinsker in this volume for a further exploration of the pan-European dimensions of coffeehouse culture in relation to the Jewish community.
19. Yuri Slezkine, *The Jewish Century*, Princeton 2004.
20. 'space of freedom' from Weigel, *Kaffeehaus*, 10.
21. Ludwig Hirschfeld, *Das Buch von Wien: Was nicht im Baedeker Steht*, Munich 1927, 48.
22. Torberg, *Die Tante Jolesch*, 220.
23. Franz Werfel, *Barbara oder Die Frömmigkeit*, Frankfurt am Main 1988, 550.

Chapter 4

COFFEEHOUSE ORIENTALISM

Tag Gronberg

Of course, they have no coffeehouses here, but the few emigrants who live here meet on the main square every afternoon, on a street corner where a coffeehouse should be, and exchange news.

Friedrich Torberg, 'Epilogue', *Tante Jolesch or the Decline of the West in Anecdotes.*[1]

Tucked away in Khalidya in the Rawdah District is Crusty, the latest arrival on the café/bakery scene in Jeddah. A Viennese café would probably be a more appropriate way to describe Crusty – in German that's Wiener Kaffeehaus […].

Rashed Islam, *Arab News*, 2008.[2]

These two quotations might be read as indications of the persistence and ubiquity of the turn-of-the-century Viennese coffeehouse. They clearly pertain to very different historical periods and milieux. Torberg's poignant anecdote is one of many in his book *Tante Jolesch* chronicling the Jewish coffeehouse world of Austria, as it survived the First World War only to collapse in 1938. His book is a tribute to the rich culture fostered by the Viennese coffeehouse, but it is also a monument to a loss that occurred twice over. For Torberg, the coffeehouse more than any other place or social environment vividly embodied the 'afterglow' of the Dual Monarchy of Austria-Hungary, a golden age in which Jews might, to a certain extent at least, feel safe – at home – in the urban environment of Vienna. After 1938, emigration might facilitate faint glimmers of this vanished lifestyle (the anecdote quoted above is ostensibly taken from one emigré's letter to another, sent from Nairobi to Shanghai), but only 'thereby sealing its destruction'.[3]

Torberg's tract, alternately melancholy and witty, is a world away from the local reportage by the *Arab News* food critic, announcing the opening of a new snack venue in Jeddah. Crusty is evidently one more example of globalised consumption: not only Viennese coffee, but also French baguettes, American breakfasts and Caesar salad appear on the menu. (Similar international fare of course appears in many of today's coffeehouses in the Austrian capital.) Here too though we find that the café marks the juncture of different nationalities and histories. Readers of the *Arab News* are reminded that 'the first coffeehouse in Austria opened in Vienna in 1683 after the Battle of Vienna, by using supplies from the spoils obtained after defeating the Turks'. Sipping their drinks at Crusty, customers might well ponder this manifestation of the postmodern condition: the export of Viennese coffee (traditionally identified with the appropriation of a Middle Eastern beverage) to a Jeddah café whose name evokes that of a character in the Simpsons cartoon – Krusty the clown, son of a rabbi.

Crusty is obviously no more a 'real' Viennese café than a group of central Europeans gathering for the purpose of gossip and conversation on a street corner in Nairobi. Both scenarios however reveal the needs to which the idea of the coffeehouse might respond: companionship and mutual support in the case of the émigrés; refreshment for its customers, as well as a marketing and sales opportunity for the Austrian coffee company Meinl, in the case of Crusty. Along with the reference to the Turkish 'origin' of Austrian coffee drinking, these displacements of the coffeehouse to Africa and Saudi Arabia alert us to the fact that the experience of the coffeehouse has always involved a complex interplay of references to other cultures and historical moments. The title of this chapter signals my contention that the turn-of-the-century Viennese coffeehouse constituted a distinctive form of Orientalism.[4] I shall explore how the coffeehouse formed part of a mise-en-scène in which references (both implicit and explicit) to the 'Orient' played a crucial role in the articulation of identities, for individuals as well as for the city itself. My concern here is not primarily with the 'real' circumstances of cultural encounter and exchange nor with the décor and design of cafés at the time of their heyday in Vienna – although these issues are undoubtedly relevant. Rather, I am interested in the various dynamics sustained by this remarkably resilient Orientalist myth of origins.

It seems appropriate to begin a consideration of coffeehouse Orientalism on a street corner (a traditional site for inner-city Viennese cafés), and in particular with the 1885 monument to Georg Franz Kolschitzky, who had, according to legend, opened the first coffeehouse after the successful rout of the second Turkish siege of Vienna[5] (Figure 4.1). The metal monument was installed on 12 September, the anniversary of the 1683 Battle of Vienna, on the initiative of Karl Zwirina, proprietor of the Grand Café Zwirina, which occupied the corner site marking the juncture of the Favoritenstrasse and Kolschitzkygasse (Figure 4.2). Kolschitzky, born Jerzy Franciszek Kulczycki (1640–1694) near Sambor,

Galicia in what is now the Ukraine, spoke Ottoman Turkish and worked as a translator for the Wiener Orientalische Handelskompagnie. According to the widely held account of the 1683 liberation of Vienna, Kolschitzky, along with his servant Michailowitz, clad themselves in Turkish dress and managed to penetrate enemy lines, a feat that proved crucial in achieving victory over the Turks.[6] (According to a slightly different version of this story, Kolschitzky's role lay either in the intelligence he gleaned in wandering through the enemy encampments based to the northwest of Vienna or his communication with the leaders of Christian coalition forces rallying outside the city in support of the Habsburg Emperor Leopold I.)[7]

Figure 4.1 Monument to Kolschitzky, 1885, corner of Favoritenstrasse and Kolschitzkygasse, Vienna. Courtesy of David Brook.

In return for his heroic role, so the story goes, Kolschitzky was awarded several sacks of 'camel food' left behind by the fleeing Turkish army. These green beans proved to be coffee, a favourite drink of the Turks, and the rest is history. Kolschitzky was granted permission to open a coffeehouse in the Schlossergassl, near the Stefansplatz that became known as Zur blauen Flasche [To the Blue Bottle]. Over the years, historians have produced rather different, more historically accurate, versions of the history of Viennese coffee drinking and coffeehouses.[8] Due to the trajectories of trade and diplomacy between Vienna and the Ottoman Empire, coffee drinking was apparently already well known prior to the 1683 Turkish siege. Similarly, the city's first coffeehouses seem to have been run by Armenians. However, as with any myth of origins, historical accuracy is only part of the picture in assessing the significance of such stories. Torberg refers to Vienna as the 'city of functioning myth', asserting that 'it is reality that catches up with, almost emulates, the myth, and functioning legends to a large extent make Vienna what it is'.[9] Indeed, in a culture renowned for its inefficiency and laxity ('Schlamperei'),[10] for Torberg it was the case that 'what functions best in Vienna are supposed legends'.[11] (Note that the qualifier 'supposed' in no way undermines his claim for the efficacy of such myths.)

Torberg makes the point that while legends give sustenance to the present, they are not static but rather constantly regenerate themselves.[12] It is worth pausing therefore to consider in more detail the components of the Kolschitzky story,

CAFÉ ZUM KOLSCHITZKY

Wien, IV, Favoritenstraße 64

Mit dem Denkmal des ersten Wiener Kaffesieders Franz Georg Kolschitzky

Figure 4.2 *Café Zum Kolschitzky, Wien, IV, Favouritenstrasse 64*, illustrated in *250 Jahre Wiener Kaffeehaus. (1683–1933.) Festschrift*, published by the Gremium der Kaffeehausbesitzer in Wien, 1934. Courtesy of the British Library.

and in particular its Orientalising aspects. Visual depictions form an important part of this 'functioning legend'. The 1885 monument, for example, positioned right on the street corner, at first floor level shows Kolschitzky in 'oriental' dress: an outfit comprising fez-like cap, waistcoat, baggy breeches and finished off with pointed slippers. He holds a tray with two cups, into which he pours coffee. The figure's gaze is directed outwards to the street, a somewhat paradoxical scenario in which the guise of waiter (helpful but subservient) is combined with that of courageous national hero, as signalled by the emblems of military conquest at his feet (the Islamic crescent moon appears prominently on the display of spears and shields). In a sense, this figurative monument is the second commemoration to Kolschitzky here in Vienna's fourth district; the Kolschitzkygasse was thus named in the 1860s, another bicentenary reference to the Battle of Vienna. Karl Zwirina was thus in effect appropriating this mythic character on behalf of his own establishment (the sculpture stood directly over the rubric 'Café Zwirina').[13]

The iconographic parameters of the Kolschitzky figure were established early on; seventeenth-century prints show him as messenger and 'Kundschafter' (scout or spy), clad in much the same orientalising outfit as depicted in the later monument: fez, billowing trousers, pointed shoes and satchel (Figure 4.3). One of these prints includes a rubric drawing attention to the historical veracity of Kolschitzky's clothing. This, together with his language skills, was of course ostensibly the means of his being able to penetrate Turkish enemy lines: the disguise was both linguistic and vestimentary. A subsequent important development in the Kolschitzky iconography is revealed in an 1863 oil painting by Franz Schams, 'Das erste (Kulczyskische) Kaffeehaus in Wien' ('Kolschitzky's, The first coffeehouse in Vienna') (Figure 4.4). This shows a cosy seventeenth-century tavern-like environment, in which Kolschitzky himself serves coffee to his customers wearing Turkish costume. He holds a tray bearing a cup into which he pours coffee. It was a well-known part of the legend that Kolschitzky presided over his customers wearing Turkish clothing. Here, in Schams's picture, we have an earlier example of the conjunction of proprietor, waiter and war hero. Kolschitzky's exotic clothing functions both as entertainment and reassuring reminder of military conquest.

All too appropriately given the Viennese context, there is something almost theatrical not to say operatic about this story (some versions of the narrative recount Kolschitzky and his servant singing Turkish songs as they approached enemy lines). The performative aspects of the legend were highlighted by Franz Zwirina, as revealed by a 1905 photograph that shows Zwirina dressed as Kolschitzky with his son playing the part of the servant, Michailowitz.[14] At one level, this tongue-in-cheek re-enactment demonstrates Zwirina taking on the role of successful coffeehouse host, as 'originally' performed by Kolschitzky. It clearly responds to the Viennese taste for light-hearted theatrical masquerade, whether during Carnival season or with the numerous on-stage disguise narratives of

Figure 4.3 Martin Dichtl (attributed), *Georg Franz Kolschitzky as Scout in Turkish Dress, 13 August 1683,* published in J.C. Feigius, *Wunderbahrer Adlers-Schwung…Das ist: eine ausführliche historische Beschreibung des noch anhaltenden Türcken-Kriegs,* Vienna, 1694, vol. 2, p. 48.

Figure 4.4 Franz Schams, *Kolschitzky's, The First Coffeehouse in Vienna,* 1863. Courtesy of the Wien Museum.

opera and operetta.[15] Like the monument he installed outside his café, the photograph of Zwirina and son *en travesti* can be interpreted as a witty form of commercial marketing and self-promotion via reference to one of Vienna's best-known stories about itself. Nor were these the only such references in the case of the Café Zwirina. The café interior was decorated with murals (1899) depicting the 1683 Turkish siege of Vienna, executed by Reinhold Völkel.[16] For its guests in 1900 therefore, a visit to the Zwirina offered vivid reminders of the city's dramatic rescue from invasion by the forces of the Ottoman Empire.

We might argue that ceaseless reiteration of this rescue was the necessary means of assuaging the terror aroused by the spectre of cultural annihilation, a scenario in which the Christian Habsburg monarchy (and indeed Western Europe more generally) was saved from conquest by a powerful exotic, Ottoman 'other'. At the same time, the endless retelling – verbal, visual, and performative – of related stories, including those pertaining to Kolschitzky, firmly entrenched a dynamic of simultaneous anxiety and relief in the Viennese psyche. However, monuments and depictions of Kolschitzky were not the sole means of recalling Vienna's narrow escape. The Café Zwirina, with its explicit visual representations referring to the 1683 siege, was not unique; through its repertoire of coffees, every Viennese coffeehouse made tacit reference to this scenario of cultural encounter. There was surely no coffeehouse of the period that did not offer (among many other types) both 'türkischer Kaffee' (at least as evoked by the 'Mokka') and 'Melange'. The existence of these different ways of making coffee could be attributed to the trajectories of trade and diplomacy (as mentioned above) that had formed part of Vienna's history.

The Kolschitzky story, however, ensured that these drinks also functioned, however subliminally, as a reminder of Western conquest. Such reminders were couched in the reassuring form of assimilation: victory over the Turks had led to the adoption of their favourite beverage, either in a form closer to the original (Turkish coffee), or – more palatable to many Viennese – as a 'Melange', mixed with milk.[17] Even the ostensibly more authentic Turkish version could be rendered Viennese, as in the case of the 'Sperbertürk', the variation apparently ordered by one of Vienna's well-known lawyers.[18] Commemorations of conquest, demonstrated as assimilation of the defeated, could be found elsewhere in Vienna. The framing outer pavilions of the Upper Belvedere Palace, for example, built for Prince Eugene of Savoy, one of the military heroes of the 1683 siege, take the form of Turkish tents (recalling those pitched outside Vienna by the attacking Ottoman forces). More Turkish references can be found, not only in Prince Eugene's Baroque palace, but also in the wonderfully flamboyant bedstead designed for him, bristling with captive warriors (and yet again, a military tent).

Stories and reminders of the 1683 siege were not merely ways of assuaging anxieties; they also played on such anxieties in order to define what was most truly and quintessentially Viennese. It is of course precisely this constitutive dynamic – reference to a feared 'other' in order to produce articulations of self – that has been characterised as Orientalist. In this permutation, Orientalism functions as much to sustain fear as to offer reassurance. It might be argued that modern realms of relaxation and leisure, such as the coffeehouse, offered particularly effective spheres for Orientalising mise-en-scènes. Here recollections of danger could be contained by the sense of a reassuringly safe environment: battle and conflict are replaced by conviviality and enjoyment. If, arguably, the café performed this task exceptionally well (its very existence was, after all, ostensibly evidence of a threat surmounted), it was by no means the only Viennese manifestation of such Orientalism. In this respect it is important to stress that the dynamics of Orientalism are not necessarily always clearly signalled by the presence of exotic or 'eastern' motifs. If we recall for example the wall decorations in the Café Zwirina depicting the siege of Vienna, with Turks encamped on the hilly outskirts of the city, we will be alerted to the importance of spatial topographies for Orientalism.

The upper Belvedere Palace afforded inhabitants, and subsequently visitors, dramatic vistas of the city. Such exhilarating 'bird's eye views', with their implications of visual, spiritual and political omnipotence, were characteristic of the Austrian baroque, in art as well as in garden layout.[19] Facing towards the Wienerwald (Vienna Woods), the site of the final battle of the 1683 siege, it was as much the sightlines and the urban views as the palace itself that commemorated the victory over the Turks. Perhaps even more telling as a panoramic form of commemoration, however, are the twin peaks of the Leopoldsberg and the Kahlenberg, situated in the Wienerwald. The Leopoldsberg, a 425-metre hill, stands at the northern edge of Vienna and has long been one of the city's favourite outlooks. It was here in September 1683 that Austrian and Polish troops, under the leadership of the Polish King Jan III Sobieski, defeated the Turkish armies.[20] In 1693, building was completed on the Baroque chapel dedicated to Leopold (after the Babenberg Leopold IV, for whom the site had served as a fortification against the Magyars). It was with the consecration of this small church that the hill's original name, Kahlenberg, was transferred to the present-day Kahlenberg, located nearby in Döbling, the 19th District of Vienna. Both hills (the Kahlenberg is 484 metres) offer spectacular distant views of the city, and well beyond Vienna and the borders of modern-day Austria. If the Upper Belvedere Palace occupies a triumphalist position, glorying in conquest, the Leopoldsberg functions as a reminder that this elevated position was the vantage point of both the Muslim and Christian armies. Standing on the summit of the Leopoldsberg vividly recalls a defeat narrowly averted. Sobieski is quoted as saying: 'We came, we saw, God conquered'.[21] Both the baroque church and the views are tributes to Christianity's victory over Islam, that terrifying threat 'from the East'.

Painted depictions of the two hills became very popular. The Wien Museum displays a seventeenth-century canvas by Franz Geffels showing 'The relief troops at the battle – Turkish siege of Vienna 1683'. During the early nineteenth-century Biedermeier period, numerous paintings depicted both the view towards and from the Leopoldsberg and Kahlenberg.[22] These were not concerned in any overt way with siege and battle, but rather with rendering harmonious and idyllic scenes. Day trips to the hills formed a favourite excursion for the Viennese at this time and, as with other destinations in the Wienerwald, were catered to by *Heurigen* and taverns. Later in the nineteenth century, at the time of the 1873 Vienna World's Fair, a newly installed funicular railway (Drahtseilbahn) to the Leopoldsberg catered to international as well as indigenous visitors. This was followed shortly after in 1874 with the first Austrian cog railway (Zahnradbahn) to the Kahlenberg.[23] Showing off the host capital city through a panoramic view was of course often a feature of such large-scale exhibitions. The Eiffel Tower, erected at the time of the 1889 Paris exhibition, is perhaps the most famous example. As with the later Eiffel Tower, the railways to the Wienerwald hills would have presented visitors with the conjunction of new technology and long-established urban culture and tradition. The Leopoldsberg and Kahlenberg viewpoints were, however, distinctive in offering a bird's eye view not merely of Vienna, but also well beyond, into other countries of the Dual Monarchy of Austria-Hungary, revealing (and revelling in) the majestic sweep of Imperial Power. It was undoubtedly in the interests of the Habsburgs to keep alive the memory of the victory over the Turks.[24] It was certainly still alive in the 1920s, when the Austrian novelist Joseph Roth has one of his characters gaze out from the Wienerwald, over the panorama of Vienna, and pronounce: 'That Sobieski has been greatly overrated. The Viennese would have seen off the Turks anyway'.[25] Roth's irony produces a telling demonstration of how even this most mythic story of cultural rescue by coalition forces could ultimately be appropriated as 'Viennese'.

I have argued that notions of a quintessentially Viennese identity were produced by an Orientalist scenario in which the *gemütlich* (cosy) interiors of the coffeehouse and the wooded terrain of the Wienerwald played mutually reinforcing roles.[26] This dynamic relied on both the reiteration of a story (the 1683 Turkish siege) and a distinctive topographical layout. Vienna was (and perhaps remains) a city in which the urban Fernblick from its surrounding hills can easily prompt reflection on the shifting and unstable relationships of centre to periphery, and of self to 'other'. I mentioned earlier that this 'coffeehouse Orientalism' does not necessarily deploy Turkish or other 'exotic' forms of imagery. But as we have seen in the case of Zwirina and his son dressed à la Turque, such imagery did exist, and, indeed, specifically in connection with the coffeehouse. Nor was Zwirina an isolated example. One of the more frequently published photographs of the entertainer and writer Egon Friedell (1878–1938), for example, shows him dressed in Turkish dress, complete with turban, sabre and long pipe.[27] During the second half of the nineteenth century, the Habsburg Monarchy, in common with other European countries, saw a thriving Orientalist visual and literary culture. I shall return to this point shortly, but here I wish to consider in more detail how we might construe Orientalism in the context of the coffeehouse. I have referred to coffee drinking, as well as baroque design motifs, as examples of a cultural 'assimilation' that demonstrate the conquest of one culture by another. I would like to speculate briefly on something rather more allusive, which I tentatively refer to as the Orientalist 'tropes' of the café.

As in England and in France, the Habsburg Monarchy produced its own cohort of Orientalist painters. Rudolph Ernst (1854–1932), to take one example, trained at the Academy of Fine Arts in Vienna and went on to work in Rome and Paris.[28] In common with much English and French Orientalist painting, it is possible to discern a recurring cluster of popular subjects in Viennese Orientalist pictures: Muslim rituals of prayer, the hammam (baths), the slave market and the harem. There is a striking paucity of depictions of the 'oriental' coffeehouse. It hardly needs pointing out that cafés did exist in the Ottoman Empire, but as others have argued, Orientalist painting of this period was not necessarily (or even primarily) motivated by desires for realism or documentation. It is all too easy to explain the choice of such subjects as a means of titillating European viewers, either through the frisson of fear (as in the case of Islamic religious rituals), eroticism (the harem) or both – with the slave market, which played on widespread terrors about 'white slavers'.[29] The function of these representations in attributing despotism and cruelty to 'the east', while in fact catering to the erotic fantasies and sadistic tastes of Western audiences, has been amply demonstrated by recent scholars of Orientalism.

Returning to the domain of the coffeehouse, we might ponder whether such fantasies of the Orient had any purchase in a coffeehouse milieu, beyond the obvious references via Turkish coffee and fancy dress. Or, to pose the question somewhat differently, does the characterisation of the 'traditional' (one could say mythic) turn-of-the-century Viennese café in any way involve tropes that we might identify as somehow Orientalist? As we have seen, bicentennial commemorations of 1683 such as the Kolschitzky monument outside the Café Zwirina functioned as reminders of the Habsburg victory over the 'terrible Turk'.[30] By the later nineteenth century, however, such stereotypes of the Ottoman east no longer simply provoked terror and dread. As Paula Sutter Fichtner has argued, from the time of the decisive rout of the invading Turkish armies, Austrian attitudes towards the Ottoman Empire developed in various ways, academically, institutionally and in the arts.[31] This was partly a function of the need to procure information in order to maintain the political and trade interests of the Habsburg domains. 1754, for example, saw the foundation of the Imperial Royal Academy of Oriental languages. This institution, arguably a product of Enlightenment ideals as well as of imperial self-interest, trained scholars and translators who produced more informed, nuanced views of the Turks and of Islam.[32]

Such developments did not see the abolition of negative stereotypes, but as Fichtner convincingly demonstrates, they mark a shift in the range of attitudes towards the 'hereditary foe'. In the arts, in plays and in music, 'the Turk' could now appear as a comic figure (embodying a lack of discipline or debauchery), but also in a more noble guise, as with Pasha Selim, in Mozart's highly successful opera 'Die Entführung aus dem Serail' (The Abduction from the Seraglio, 1782). At the level of consumer culture and decorative arts, there was also a growing curiosity about the 'exoticism' of Ottoman culture. The fashion for Oriental exotica (widespread across Europe during the eighteenth century) reached its highest levels, as revealed by the Empress Maria Theresa choosing to have herself painted in Turkish dress.[33] These more relaxed attitudes existed in a historical context where the Habsburg monarchy aspired to present itself as the dominant power in central Europe. With the Treaty of Karlowitz, signed on 26 January 1699, the Ottomans returned many of the domains that they had conquered. Indeed this treaty is often considered a key moment in the 'decline of the Ottoman Empire'. Notions of 'decline' can further enhance a sense of allure. Constantinople, somewhat like Venice, emerged as emblematic of a once powerful force, the glittering remnant of a decaying culture.

Let us return now to the culture of coffee drinking and its significance. Fichtner cites a telling instance. Apparently shortly after the Treaty of Karlowitz, the Augustinian monk Abraham a Sancta Clara (1644–1709) installed a plaque in front of his cloister depicting two soldiers, one Christian, the other Muslim, drinking coffee together.[34] Sancta Clara, in Fichtner's words 'the man who had turned anti-Muslim invective into an art form', was the author of the rousing call to arms *Auf, auf, ihr Christen* (1683). It is noteworthy that a new phase of Christian-Muslim relations should be portrayed through the conviviality of coffee drinking. Such public assertions of good terms are of course frequently politically motivated. Over a century later, in the wake of the Napoleonic wars, when the Habsburg Empire found its sphere of influence severely reduced, the Chancellor Prince von Metternich was to pronounce: 'We look on the Ottoman Empire as the best of our neighbours … we regard contact with her as equivalent to contact with a natural frontier'.[35] Throughout the nineteenth century, diplomatic negotiations between the Habsburg and Ottoman empires formed part of a complex jockeying for position, as the balance of power in Europe, the Balkans and the Middle East was contested and fought over, especially in the face of mounting Russian military aggression. At a period in which imperial borders were (and remained) far from stable, Metternich's famous pronouncement that the East began at the Landstrasse was indicative of the Habsburg Empire's liminal position between occident and orient. As the century wore on, there was arguably a growing sense that such boundaries could be construed not only in terms of differentiating the 'otherness' of the East but also through an identification with it. By the late nineteenth century, it may not have been so difficult (at least subliminally) to recognise certain analogies between two great empires, both of which struggled to maintain unity in the face of diverse ethnic and religious groupings. Labyrinthine bureaucratic structures, as well as a court culture that insisted on maintaining tradition whilst simultaneously embracing aspects of modernity, were after all recognisable features of Austria-Hungary as well as of the 'mysterious' Orient. Not surprisingly then, given its legendary associations with the East, the fin-de-siècle Viennese coffeehouse offers a thought-provoking case in point.

Much has now been written about late nineteenth- and early twentieth-century literary cafés in Vienna. Their role as a site for intellectual exchange as well as in negotiating professional identities is discussed in a number of chapters in this volume. Already at the time however, contemporaries were quick to point out apparent contradictions inherent in this distinctive sphere of urban everyday life. Although many of the more famous coffeehouses – the Griensteidl, Central, Herrenhof – were located in the heart of the ancient inner city, it was the opportunities such cafés afforded for adopting a critical outsider's vantage point on society that was so often vaunted. Alfred Polgar famously referred to the Café Central in terms of a 'world view' and Felix Salten writing on Peter Altenberg (for his contemporaries perhaps the archetypal *Kaffeehausliterat*) pays tribute to the poet's determined existence 'on the periphery of the everyday'.[36] Such cafés functioned both as the site and the means for a productive intellectual life: places for social encounter, for reading and writing as well as a testing ground for the wits. But there was another aspect to this vibrant discursive, conversational life of the coffeehouse. Viennese coffeehouses also offered the opportunity for mindless habit and wordless regularity. In a witty anecdote, Torberg recounts the breakdown of normal routine at the Café Colosseum, when in the absence of his usual waiters, the arrival of a prominent habitué, District Court Judge Reiter, fails to provoke the appearance of his daily Melange and Kipferl.[37]

If, from an intellectual perspective, the principle raison d'être of literary coffeehouses was not primarily to provide or drink coffee (let alone food apart from light snacks), the cultural resonance of coffee was nevertheless highly significant. Coffee was both a stimulant, a tonic for sharpening up the mind, and the means of achieving a state of indolence. Polgar refers to the Café Central's 'tables of idleness', condemning it as a place to kill time.[38] As much as animated conversation, carefully cultivated boredom and lassitude formed a crucial component of the coffeehouse milieu. At one level this can be seen as an extension of the dynamics of the flâneur, that famous urban idler, as delineated by Baudelaire and subsequently by Walter Benjamin. When contemplating the flâneurial persona and mindset in the context of Vienna it is tempting to draw analogies between the coffeehouse and certain Orientalist scenarios, such as the baths and the seraglio. A heavy enveloping atmosphere characterises all these (cigarette smoke, steam, incense respectively), suggesting the separation of their inhabitants from the outside world. As with the flâneur, however, this state of waiting around and doing nothing is less a removal from the world than the necessary precondition for engaging with urban modernity, at least in imaginative terms. Elsewhere in Vienna at this time, the connection between what we might call productive reverie and Orientalism was made quite explicit. The psychoanalytic mise-en-scène of Freud's consulting rooms, with its couch, cushions and oriental rugs, cast patients in the reclining pose of an odalisque.[39]

Many of Freud's most famous patients (as they were written up in his publications) were women; the association of such feminising Orientalist tropes with the masculine domain of the literary coffeehouse, as I suggest here, may seem less expected or obvious. I have argued elsewhere that the gendering of Viennese coffeehouses and their inhabitants was always unstable.[40] It was common to disparage the literary *Kleinkunst* associated with cafés, as well as their habitués, as effeminate. In his artistic stance, Peter Altenberg was unusual in embracing (rather than rejecting) the effeminacy levied in such charges.[41] (Torberg points out that authors have always been quick to deny the identification of *Kaffeehausliterat*, apparently finding it trivialising and demeaning.)[42] Acknowledging the potential Orientalising effeminacy of the coffeehouse ambiance can prompt us to look anew at the plain, bright and airy spaces which Adolf Loos installed as part of his designs for the revamped interior of the Café Museum (1899). I have referred to Loos's designs for a prominent public space in the cultural heart of Vienna as a form of rhetorical engagement with contemporary debates on modernity and modern art.[43] Perhaps we can see this not solely as a rejection of ornament and historicism in design, but also as a move to present an updated and more emphatic Westernisation of the Viennese coffeehouse. As indicated by the title – 'Das Andere: ein Blatt zur Einführung Abendländischer Kultur in Österreich' – of his supplement to Altenberg's short-lived journal *Kunst: Halbmonatschrift* (later *Monatsschrift*) *für Kunst und alles andere* (1903), it was Loos's self-proclaimed mission to introduce modern, progressive 'Western' culture to a backward Austria.[44]

By the end of the nineteenth century, the conception of a threatening potentially invasive East may have somewhat abated, but in another sense it was further enhanced. This is rendered evident in the (what now seem rather shocking) 1869 original lyrics of 'The Blue Danube':

If you have not seen
Our beautiful city lately
You will not recognize it
The Ring is a Jewel inhabited by all of Israel.
In ten years time they will be able
To build a new Jerusalem here.[45]

The impact of extensive immigration into Vienna during the second half of the century from the eastern parts of Austria-Hungary has been well documented. Slavic and Jewish immigrants were perceived as a flood pouring in to the capital city from the East.[46] In his essay 'The Ethnic Immigrant in the Metropolis, or Containing the "Slavic Flood" in the Viennese Wurstelprater', Kristin Kopp explores the spaces of popular culture as a means of negotiating this 'threat', both for those who considered themselves indigenous to Vienna and for the immigrants themselves.[47] The much-vaunted symbiotic relationship between Jews and coffeehouse is complex, both historically and geographically contingent, with the turn-of-the-century representing simultaneously a golden age for assimilated Jews in Vienna and a period marked by rising antisemitic tension. I pause here briefly to ponder, albeit schematically, the ramifications of the Orientalising dynamics of the coffeehouse for a Jewish clientele.

The exploration of Orientalist tropes in relation to the coffeehouse suggests a further possible way of considering the association between the Jew and the coffeehouse. The question of why it should be the case that 'a Jew belongs in the coffeehouse' in Vienna at the turn of the century is one with many possible answers, some of them elaborated in the chapters of this book. Having access to the current intellectual debates of the period and making professional contacts were obviously key factors, as were for some at least, the varied aspirations for assimilation. Important too no doubt were the ways in which the coffeehouse kept in a state of flux the ostensibly opposed notions of belonging and alienation. Felix Salten wrote of Altenberg 'He is indigenous here and yet comes from elsewhere'.[48] Intellectually speaking (as we saw above), a self-determined position on the periphery of society, of not quite belonging, could be a desirable bohemian artistic stance, although in Vienna a potentially and increasingly dangerous one. The Viennese coffeehouse affords an interesting context through which to reconsider Georg Simmel's concept of 'the stranger' (as outlined in his essay 'Der Fremde' of 1908). Simmel writes of 'the person who comes today and stays tomorrow', the figure endowed with an objectivity based on 'a particular structure composed of distance and nearness, indifference and involvement'.

Simmel specifically cites the historic position of the Jews in society, and proposes 'the trader' as a recurring persona for the stranger, trade being 'the sphere indicated for the stranger'.[49] We might return at this point to the mythic Kolschitzky character, translator and spy turned (a kind of) tradesman in his role as proprietor of Zur blauen Flasche. Here was ostensibly a figure whose ability to transgress the boundaries of indigenous and 'foreign' enabled acts of heroism, his own and that of others. Widely credited as helping to save Vienna (and therefore also Western culture and Christianity), Kolschitzky clad in his exotic apparel could appear as a reassuring (rather than threateningly alien) figure. At the same time, he represented a kind of ongoing fluidity, an ability to shift back and forth between cultures as well as languages under cover of disguise, an embodiment of the mutability of modern identity, perhaps especially so for those who wished to feel themselves safely 'at home' in Vienna. An apt monument then, to grace the exterior of a coffeehouse, an institution which like Austria-Hungary itself occupied a liminal position between the symbolically charged spheres of East and West.

What of coffeehouse Orientalism today? Is the concept in any way still relevant, or operative, at a time when debates on modern-day Austria's role in negotiating relationships between East and West have become ever more conflicted and confrontational?[50] As the authors of 'The Ottoman Menace' Forum in *Austrian History Yearbook* point out, what is most striking about the 1683 'Turkish menace' trope is its malleability and multiplicity, as a metaphorical means of ahistorical application to more recent circumstances. Similarly, in his book *Uses of the Other: 'The East' in European Identity Formation* Iver Neumann stresses the importance of these dialogical relationships for modern-day Europe.[51]

I conclude by leaving this as an open question for a period where yet again we see moves to fuel and encourage anxieties about immigration from 'the East'. In the popular press, it has become commonplace to make reference to the country's historic position as bulwark against the Turkish foe when discussing Austria's position on Turkey's admission to full membership of the EU. This chapter began with a mention of the export of Meinl coffee to Jeddah, a small indication of the complex historic encounters (cultural, as well as economic and political) entailed by the dynamics of international trade. Indeed, when speculating on coffeehouse Orientalism in the context of a globalised economy, Julius Meinl (founded in 1862) forms an interesting case in point. The company unabashedly flaunts Orientalist associations: its website claims that in 1891 a modern roasting plant was built on the 'very site' where Pasha Kara Mustapha's army had abandoned its coffee bags in 1683.[52] Schams's painting depicting the first coffeehouse in Vienna is now owned by Meinl, whose extensive range of coffee roasts includes a Kolschitzky blend. Meinl has consistently (and prominently) used its distinctive logo – the silhouette of a 'moor', a young boy shown in profile wearing a fez – ever since it was originally formulated in the 1920s.[53]

The circulation of such imagery in the twenty-first century could be denigrated as being (at best) in poor taste, a form of historicist kitsch in the interests of commercial marketing. Worse yet, it might be taken as evidence of more widespread cultural prejudices and the desire to assert and sustain dominant positions of power. Fichtner holds what she calls an against-the-grain conviction that Orientalist stereotypes can function as 'a way-station on the road to greater understanding of, and accommodation to, the religion and culture of another'.[54] In its own small way, the existence of Crusty's in Jeddah should remind us that this reconception of stereotypes is always (at least potentially) a two-way process. Coffeehouse Orientalism, as I have tentatively sketched it, involves a multivalent dynamic, through which relationships can be reformulated and renegotiated. In this sense we may need to retain the figure of Kolschitzky, not as a national hero in defence against 'another', but rather as a means of destabilising entrenched positions and identities.

Acknowledgements

I thank the Meinl Archives in Vienna for allowing access to their rich collections. For his support and inspiration, I owe a great debt of gratitude to Paul Vivian Overy.

Notes

1. Friedrich Torberg, 'Epilogue', *Tante Jolesch or The Decline of the West in Anecdotes*, Riverside 2008, 170. This English translation also includes five essays written during the 1950s and 1960s.
2. Rashed Islam, *Arab News (The Middle East's Leading English Language Daily)*, 24 October 2008.
3. Torberg, 'Epilogue', *Tante Jolesch*, 170.
4. I derive the term from Edward W. Said's seminal 1978 text, *Orientalism*, drawing on his use of the word to indicate not only depictions of the 'East' by western commentators, writers and artists, but also the means whereby such representations produced notions of self through a contrast with the different, often negative, aspects of that 'other'. Said's book was primarily focused on Britain, France and the United States; he explicitly excluded German-speaking Orientalism. I refer to studies of Austria's distinctive position vis-à-vis Orientalism below. For examples of the extensive debate triggered by Said's work, see John M. MacKenzie, *Orientalism: History, Theory and the Arts*, Manchester 1995 and A.L. Macfie, *Orientalism: A Reader*, Edinburgh 2000. Said's book was republished as a Penguin Classic (under the title *Orientalism: Western Conceptions of the Orient*) in 2003.
5. See for example Karl Teply, 'Die Anfänge des Wiener Kaffeehauses – Legenden und Fakten', in *Das Wiener Kaffeehaus: Von den Anfängen bis zur Zwischenkriegzeit*, Vienna 1980, 19–26. In her essay '1883 in the Turkish Mirror', Maureen Healy outlines various celebratory events in 1883, which included an exhibition of Turkish artefacts in Vienna's town hall. See 'Forum: The Ottoman Menace', *Austrian History Yearbook*, Vol. XL 2009, 101–113.
6. On the 1683 Siege of Vienna, see *Die Türken vor Wien: Europa und die Entscheidung an der Donau 1683*, Historisches Museum der Stadt Wien, Vienna 1983, and Andrew Wheatcroft, *The Enemy at the Gate: Habsburgs, Ottomans and the Battle for Europe*, London 2008.
7. Bennett Alan Weinberg and Bonnie K. Bealer, *The World of Caffeine: The Science and Culture of the World's Most Popular Drug*, London 2000, 74–77.
8. See, for example, Helmut Kretschmer, *Kapuziner, Einspänner, Schalerl Gold.: Zur Geschichte der Wiener Kaffeehäuser*, Vienna 2006, and exhibitions such as the *250 Jahre Wiener Kaffeehaus*, Messepalast, Vienna 1933, and *300 Jahre Kaffeehaus: Von den Anfängen bis zur Zwischenkriegzeit*, Historisches Museum der Stadt Wien, Vienna 1980.
9. Torberg, 'Treatise on the Viennese Coffeehouse' (1959), *Tante Jolesch*, 206.
10. William M. Johnston, *The Austrian Mind: An Intellectual and Social History 1848–1938*, Berkeley 1983, 22.

11. Torberg, 'Urbis Conditer – The City's Confectioner' (1958), *Tante Jolesch*, 199.
12. Torberg, 'Urbis Conditer', *Tante Jolesch*, 194.
13. Indeed, it would seem that Café Zwirina was also known as the 'Kolschitzky'. See entry 152, 'Café Zwerina. Aussensicht', *Das Wiener Kaffeehaus: von den Anfängen bis zur Zwischenkriegszeit*, 89.
14. See Helfried Seemann and Christian Lunzer (eds), *Das Wiener Kaffeehaus 1870–1930: Das Wiener Kaffeehaus in Zeitgenössischen Photographien*, Vienna 1993, reprint 2000, 38.
15. For a discussion of the concept of *Gschnas*, the Austrian word for fancy dress, see Paul Overy, '"The Whole Bad Taste of Our Period": Josef Frank, Adolf Loos and "Gschnas"', *Home Cultures*, 3(3), 2006, 213–233.
16. See catalogue entry 153, *Das Wiener Kaffeehaus: von den Anfängen bis zur Zwischenkriegszeit*, 89.
17. Another of the chief developments characterised as 'Viennese' was the filtering out of the grounds.
18. This was 'an extra strong double Turkish coffee brewed with sugar cubes, which the Viennese attorney Hugo Sperber liked to consume in Café Herrenhof before strenuous trials'. Torberg, 'Treatise', *Tante Jolesch*, 208.
19. The bird's eye view of Vienna forms a major theme of my book *Vienna: City of Modernity 1890–1914*, Oxford 2007.
20. For details of the battle, see Wheatcroft, 'A Holy War', *The Enemy at the Gate*, 188–200.
21. A paraphrase of Julius Caesar. Wheatcroft, *The Enemy at the Gate*, 193.
22. Numerous examples of such paintings are illustrated in *Wiener Landschaften*, Historisches Museum der Stadt Wien, Vienna 1994. The exhibition catalogue also includes a short essay, 'Die Entsatzschlacht Wiens im Jahre 1683', 38–39.
23. Photographs of the Drahtseilbahn to the Leopoldsberg (Kat. 8/2/35, p.238) and the Zahnradbahn to the Kahlenberg (Kat. 8/2/37, p 238) appear in *Traum und Wirklichkeit: Wien 1870–1930*, Historisches Museum der Stadt Wien, Vienna 1985. There are further photographs of the amenities offered to visitors (including the 1873 Hotel Kahlenberg) in *Wiener Landschaften*, 136–139.
24. Fichtner refers to the 1683 rout as 'a struggle that would become the foundational epic of the Habsburg monarchy'. Paula Sutter Fichtner, *Terror and Toleration: The Habsburg Empire Confronts Islam, 1525–1850*, London 2008, 67.
25. 'We used to go into the Krapfenwaldl and stand in front of the Sobieski church, and your father would say: "That Sobieski has been greatly overrated. The Viennese would have seen off the Turks anyway." King Sobieski did not appeal to him. Basically, your father was a patriot'. Joseph Roth, 'Zipper and his Father', *The Spider's Web and Zipper and his Father*, Woodstock, New York 2003, 212–213. The novella is dated 1928.
26. Mention should also be made here of the Türkenschanz Park in the 18th district of Vienna, one of the city's largest parks. 'Schanz' refers to the 'sconce' (earthwork or fort) apparently used by the Turks in both 1529 and 1683. While not affording the dramatic views of the Leopoldsberg and Kahlenberg, the park does reinforce the sense of proximity of the attacking Turkish troops. It was a high profile project; the layout was designed by Heinrich von Ferstel and it was officially opened to the public by the Emperor Franz Joseph in 1888.
27. See for example, 'Egon Friedell', Harold B. Segel, *The Vienna Coffeehouse Wits 1890–1938*, West Lafayette, Indiana 1993, 193.
28. For an overview of Orientalist painting and interior design, see *Orientalische Reise: Malerei und Exotik im Späten 19. Jahrhundert*, Wien Museum and Residenzgalerie Salzburg, Vienna 2003.
29. For a study of the significance of Orientalist iconography (primarily in French painting), see Linda Nochlin's important essay 'The Imaginary Orient', *Art in America*, 71, no. 5 (May

1983), reprinted in Nochlin, *The Politics of Vision: Essays on 19th-Century Art and Society*, New York 1989, 33–59.

30. Until quite recently it was apparently the custom for Kaffeehäuser to display images of Kolschitzky to commemorate the 1683 anniversary.

31. This is the major theme of Fichtner's *Terror and Toleration*. Indeed, she argues that relationships between the two cultures were already considerably more complex prior to 1683.

32. See 'Servants to Government and Learning', *Terror and Toleration*, 117–161.

33. Fichtner, *Terror and Toleration*, 94. See also Eva B. Ottilinger, 'Kronprinz Rudolfs "Türkisches Zimmer" und die Orientmode in Wien', *Orientalische Reise*, 94–109.

34. Fichtner, *Terror and Toleration*, 71.

35. Wheatcroft, *The Enemy at the Gate*, 255. Referring to the work of Austrian social anthropologist Andre Gingrich on 'the east of Western Europe', Wheatcroft argues for a concept of 'frontier Orientalism' to characterise historical relations between the Habsburgs and the Ottoman Empire.

36. Segel, *The Vienna Coffeehouse Wits 1890–1938*, 267 and 171; although in Polgar's typically ironic characterisation of the Café Central (1926), 'It is indeed a worldview and one, to be sure, whose innermost essence is not to observe the world at all'. Salten opens his 1910 essay on Altenberg: 'Is it not curious how he wanders about on the periphery of the everyday, on the outer edges of the bourgeois life?'

37. Torberg, 'There's Coffeehouse in Everything', *Tante Jolesch*, 98. Torberg claims that this 'classical attitude' could 'serve as a definition of the term habitué'.

38. 'Only there, only at the tables of idleness, is the worktable laid for them, only there, enveloped by the air of indolence, will their inertia become fecundity'. Polgar, 'Theory of the Café Central', *The Vienna Coffeehouse Wits*, 269.

39. According to the London Freud Museum documentation, the rug covering the Freudian couch 'was woven by one of the tribes of the Qashqa'i Confederacy whose territories range through the west of Iran'. A table at the foot of the couch is covered with an asmalyk, woven by a Turkoman tribe, the Tekke nomads. Freud may have acquired some of his rugs from his brother-in-law Moritz Freud, an importer of carpets. 'Rugs', *20 Maresfield Gardens: A Guide to the Freud Museum*, London 1998, 88–89. In her preface to this publication Marina Warner refers to the rug on the couch as 'that flying carpet for unconscious voyaging' (viii). Mignon Nixon has written on the psychoanalytic scenario in 'On the Couch', *October* 113, Summer 2005, 39–76. For an interesting discussion of the role of 'the Orient' in Freud's thinking, see Steve Pile, 'Freud, Dreams and Imaginative Geographies', *Freud 2000*, ed. Anthony Elliott, New York 1999.

40. Tag Gronberg, 'Coffeehouse Encounters: Adolf Loos's Café Museum', *Vienna*, 69–96.

41. For a later pronouncement on his love-hate relationship with the Wiener Kaffeehaus, see Thomas Bernhard, *Wittgenstein's Nephew*, London 1986, 102: 'The more I hated the Viennese literary cafés, the more deeply I hated them, and the more often and the more intensively I visited them'.

42. Torberg, 'There's Coffeehouse in Everything', *Tante Jolesch*, 93: 'It was one of the unerring signs of a coffeehouse habitué to protest such a label (a claim that only drunks voice with equal insistence)'.

43. As note 40 above.

44. Loos's implication is that like the Ottoman East, Austria was not part of a more advanced Western culture. See Janet Stewart, 'Turkey and the Balkans: The Threat from the East', *Fashioning Vienna: Adolf Loos's Cultural Criticism*, London 2000, 66–67.

45. As quoted by Sonat Birnecker Hart, 'Afterword', *Tante Jolesch*, 227.

46. Studies include Marsha L. Rozenblit, *Jews of Vienna, 1867–1914: Assimilation and Identity*, New York 1984; Robert S. Wistrich, *The Jews of Vienna in the Age of Franz Joseph*, Oxford 1989; Steven Beller, *Vienna and the Jews, 1867–1938: A Cultural History*, Cambridge 1991.

47. Kristin Kopp, 'The Ethnic Immigrant in the Metropolis, or Containing the "Slavic Flood" in the Viennese Wurstelprater', *Felix Salten: Wurstelprater. Ein Schlüsseltext zur Wiener Moderne*, Vienna 2004, 181–195.

48. Felix Salten, 'Peter Altenberg', *Vienna Coffeehouse Wits*, 176.

49. Kurt Wolff (translator), 'The Stranger', *The Sociology of Georg Simmel*, New York 1950, 402–408.

50. In connection with this question, see Jamelie Hassan's provocative installation *Orientalism and Ephemera*, shown at the Centre A, Vancouver, March–April 2008.

51. 'Forum: The Ottoman Menace', *Austrian History Yearbook*, Vol XL 2009. Iver B. Neumann, *Uses of the Other: 'The East' in European Identity Formation*, University of Minnesota Press (Borderlines), 1999.

52. http://www.meinl.com/jmhistory.html (accessed on 3 February 2011).

53. For more on Meinl, see Margareta Lehrbaumer, *Womit kann ich dienen? Julius Meinl. Auf dem Spuren einer grossen Marke*, Vienna 2000. For a fascinating discussion of the artist Kara Walker's work as a response to such imagery, exploring how silhouettes might relate to stereotypes, see Therese Steffen, 'Between Transnationalism and Globalization: Kara Walker's Cultural Hybridities', in Frances Ilmberger and Alan Robinson (eds), *Globalisation*, Tübingen 2002, 96–102.

54. Fichtner, *Terror and Toleration*, 172.

Chapter 5

BETWEEN 'THE HOUSE OF STUDY' AND THE COFFEEHOUSE

The Central European Café as a Site for
Hebrew and Yiddish Modernism

Shachar Pinsker

Fin-de-siècle Vienna remains fixed in our imagination as an outstanding example of urban modernism and it is still common practice to regard the Vienna of this period as 'the focal point' of European modernism.[1] No account of fin-de-siècle Vienna can avoid discussing the Jewish aspect of this 'golden-age' of modernism. In his seminal study *Fin-de-Siècle Vienna*, Carl Schorske tends to both emphasise and downplay the role of Jews in Viennese modernist culture. He writes that 'the failure to acquire a monopoly of power left the bourgeois always something of an outsider, seeking integration with the aristocracy. The numerous and prosperous Jewish element in Vienna, with its strong assimilationist thrust, only strengthened this trend'.[2] Other scholars developed the insider/outsider paradigm articulated by Schorske in order to equate Viennese modernism with Jewish culture. Architectural historian Peter Hall writes: 'the Viennese golden age in its ultimate florescence was peculiarly a creation of that Jewish society: a society of outsiders, who, for all too brief a time, had become insiders'.[3] Steven Beller emphasises Vienna's highly acculturated Jewish population which had attained unprecedented cultural prominence by the turn of the century, and claims that this was especially apparent in literary circles of Viennese modernism.[4]

The role of the urban cafés in the creation of European modernism has been recognised (either in passing or in more detail) by many. In the introduction to their influential collection, Malcolm Bradbury and James McFarlane write: 'city living fostered the formation of literary centres and coteries; literary cafés, journals and publishing houses encouraged the development of new styles of writing to meet new realities and needs'.[5] 'Literary cafés' were indispensible for the creation of several modernist traditions in major urban European centres, and we are more or less well acquainted with the pivotal role of institutions like Café Griensteidl and Café Central in Viennese modernism, Café des Westens and the Romanisches Café in Berlin, the numerous cafés of the Left Bank and Montparnasse in Paris, as well as cafés in cities like Rome, Zurich, Lisbon, Prague, St Petersburg, Budapest, Odessa, Warsaw, and numerous others.[6]

Considering the pivotal role of the institution of the café in European modernism in general, and *Literarische Kaffeehäuser* of fin-de-siècle Vienna, it is hardly surprising to discover a certain conflation between literary modernism, Jewishness and Viennese café culture. This conflation is no doubt a product of well-known memoirs of the 'world of yesterday' by the likes of Stefan Zweig, Friedrich Torberg, Joseph Roth and Alfred Polgar, but it is also alive and well in many contemporary scholarly accounts.[7] Both Steven Beller and Harold Segal have stressed the predominant presence of Jewish writers and intellectuals in Vienna. Beller claims that 'the two institutions which provided the main milieu for liberal cultural life in Vienna at the turn of the century were the salon and the coffeehouse ... and both of them had very high Jewish presence. The coffeehouse was seen by the Viennese as "a Jewish space"'.[8] Harold Segal maintains that what distinguished the fin-de-siècle Viennese literary café from similar institutions in Europe is 'its heavily Jewish character'.[9]

There are social and economical dimensions to the historical link between Jews, coffee and cafés in Europe and beyond. In the eighteenth century, coffee (and other exotic imports like tea, cocoa, and sugar) was a new commodity that had not been explicitly prohibited for Jews to trade in, and they were quick to take up this commerce.[10] When coffeehouses were founded in Europe – some of them by Sephardic Jews who brought the commodity and the institution from the Middle East – Jews embraced them as well.[11] As has been noted in Beller's chapter, Jews were not always welcomed in more exclusive meeting places, in clubs and pubs where alcohol was at the centre; therefore, the new institute of the café emerged as an attractive alternative, first as a site for informal business and commodity exchange, and later as a site of political, cultural and literary exchange. In many European cities Jews were enthusiastic participants, and sometimes initiators of café culture.[12]

What was, then, the 'Jewish character' of the Viennese café of this period? Is it possible to define and identify its Jewishness? These are questions with which some of the Viennese writers themselves (Jews and non-Jews) wrestled. Since it is clear that the Viennese café was not a 'Jewish space' in any traditional or conventional way, these questions actually cut through some of the most profound dilemmas of Jewish cultural identity in modernity, especially in the period of 1880–1938, which Benjamin Harshav has called the time of 'modern Jewish revolution'.[13]

A key text in relation to the Jewishness of the Viennese café, already noted by Beller, is *Die Tante Jolesch oder Der Untergang des Abendlandes in Anekdoten* (Aunt Jolesch or the Decline of the West in Anecdotes, 1975). The work evokes the world of fin-de-siècle Viennese cafés and Friedrich Torberg makes clear that the 'Jewishness' of the café was very significant, and very much part of a world that was being destroyed:

> that the coffeehouse has taken on something from Tante Jolesch, that she is the missing link between the Talmudic tradition of the ghetto and emancipated café culture, that she was, as it were, the female ancestor of all those people who found in the coffeehouse the catalyst and central focus of their existence, and she was their primal mother whether or not they realized it, whether or not they wanted it to be so.[14]

The link which Torberg makes between the 'Talmudic tradition' of what he calls the traditional 'Jewish ghetto' and the secularised, bourgeois Viennese world of the café is oblique but fascinating. Torberg seems to suggest that there was a missing, hidden link – embodied, interestingly, in the female figure of the old aunt from the Jewish *shtetl* – between the traditional Jewish 'house of study' (*Beis Midrash* in Hebrew and Yiddish) where Jews studied Talmud for centuries and Vienna's café culture. Perhaps what Torberg had in mind is the intriguing idea that there is a strong link between the café and Talmudic culture of intellectual debate and (all-male) camaraderie that characterised the 'house of study'.[15] In this, Torberg is close to the Habermasian 'public sphere'.[16]

Interestingly, the 'Jewishness' of the Viennese cafés has also been seen as something very negative by emancipated liberal Jews. In Max Nordau's oft-quoted address to the Second Zionist Congress, *Muskeljudentum* (Muscular Judaism, 1898), he called for Jews to become 'men of muscle' instead of remaining 'slaves to their nerves'. Unlike the 'coffeehouse Jews' of the Diaspora, the 'New Jews', said Nordau, should 'rise early ... and not be weary before sunset ... have clear heads, solid stomachs and hard muscles'.[17] When Nordau's colleague, Theodor Herzl, the journalist of *Neue Freie Presse* who became the leader of the Zionist movement, wanted to portray what seemed to him to be the dire situation of Viennese Jews – and Jews in Western and Central Europe in general – he chose Dr Friedrich Loewenberg, a quintessential 'coffeehouse Jew' to be one of the main protagonists of his Zionist utopian novel *Altneuland* (1902). Indeed, the scene that opens this novel takes place in a fictional Viennese coffeehouse:

> Sunk in deep melancholy, Dr. Friedrich Loewenberg sat at a round marble table in his café on the Alsergrund. It was one of the most charming of Viennese cafés. Ever since his student days he had been coming there, appearing every afternoon at five o'clock

with bureaucratic punctuality. The sickly, pale waiter greeted him submissively, and he would bow with formality to the equally pale girl cashier to whom he never spoke. After that, he would seat himself at the round reading table, drink his coffee, and read the papers with which the waiter plied him. And when he had finished with the dailies and the weeklies, the comic sheets and the professional magazines ... there were chats with friends or solitary musings.[18]

Joseph Roth, the modernist Jewish-Austrian writer who immigrated to Vienna from Brody in Galicia, gives us a parallel yet totally different portrait of the 'coffeehouse Jew' during the inter-war period. In his novel *Zipper und Sein Vater* (Zipper and his Father, 1928), we find the following description:

After Arnold began working in the Finance Ministry, his visits to the cafés became a passion rather than habit ... he had found it difficult to spend an evening alone, he was now possessed by a real horror of solitude. Not that he wished to be part of a community. He just wanted to sit in a coffeehouse, nowhere else but his coffeehouse ... Arnold didn't play, but he was glad to look on. After a time he became for many of the players an indispensable spectator ... Only on entering this coffeehouse was Arnold free of his day. Here began his freedom, for although the revolving doors never ceased moving, Arnold could be certain that inside this coffeehouse he would never encounter anyone who reminded him of his work or indeed any work whatsoever.[19]

Acculturated Jews like Roth, Torberg and Stefan Zweig, who were *Stammgäste* (habitués, 'regulars') of Viennese cafés and have written about them, are well-known figures in Austrian and international modernism. However, the following pages focus on the less familiar and visible Hebrew and Yiddish modernist writers – those writers who grew up in the Talmudic 'houses of study' and experienced them first hand. In the first decades of the twentieth century, these writers immigrated from the Russian Pale of Settlement and Galicia and were equally attracted to the Viennese and Central European café for similar and different reasons. For them the café was, as it was for the fictional Arnold Zipper, a place to find a substitute of 'community' and a space in which they could meet, write and be what Roth has called 'effective spectators'.

My intention here is not to challenge the historical fact that the habitués in the coffeehouses were Jews or of Jewish decent, or even the more oblique link between café culture, modernism and Jewishness in fin-de-siècle Vienna. I would like to note, however, that these accounts produce a perception that Jewish modernist creativity in Vienna was idiosyncratic, and consisted of a relatively short period in which highly assimilated Jewish writers, artists and thinkers functioned as the primary promoters of modernism. Thus, these accounts tend to ignore the fact that Vienna – alongside other Central European cities like Lemberg and Berlin – has also been an important site of a different, and more marginal Jewish modernist creativity, namely Hebrew and Yiddish modernist literature produced between 1900 and 1930.[20] This literary and cultural production was another aspect of the 'modern Jewish revolution', part of a larger movement of Jewish immigration from Eastern to Central Europe in the period preceding and following the First World War. In what follows, I would like to discuss the crucial yet unexplored role of the coffeehouse in the emergence of Hebrew and Yiddish modernism in Vienna and in other cities and urban centres of Central Europe.

Lemberg: Uncertain Boundaries and Café Culture

At the beginning of *Tmol-Shilshom* (Only Yesterday, 1945), the celebrated novel by the Hebrew Nobel Laureate Shmuel Yosef Agnon, we are introduced to the main protagonist, Itzhak Kumer. Kumer is a young man who travels from his *shtetl* in Galicia to the cities and urban centres of Central Europe. He arrives in the train station of the city of Lemberg[21] – the capital of Habsburg Galicia – and immediately rushes to one of the local cafés about which he heard a great deal before embarking on the journey. Why is Kumer so attracted to the café, and why does Agnon devote such attention to the coffeehouses of Lemberg? The narrator of the novel supplies the readers with the following explanation:

> A big city is not like a small town. In a small town, a person goes out of his house and immediately finds his friend; in a big city days and weeks and months may go by until they see one another, and so they set a special place in the café where they drop in at appointed times. Yitzhak had pictured that café … as the most exquisite place, and he envied those students who could go there any time, any hour. Now that he had arrived in Lemberg, he himself went to see them.

Indeed, a few hours later Kumer finds himself,

> … standing in a splendid temple with gilded chandeliers suspended from the ceiling and lamps shining from every single wall, and electric lights turned on in the daytime, and marble tables gleaming, and people of stately mien wearing distinguished clothes sitting on plush chairs, reading newspapers. And above them, waiters dressed like dignitaries … holding silver pitchers and porcelain cups that smelled of coffee and all kinds of pastry.[22]

This explanation of the significance of the café in the big city is simple yet quite accurate. In contrast to the intimate and thoroughly familiar small town, the modern urban environment creates a sense of anonymity and alienation. At the same time, however, the city offers its inhabitants (locals, immigrants and even visitors) easy and immediate access to sites of mass consumption (where they can purchase coffee, pastries, etc.). These venues, such as the urban cafés, are also institutions of the public sphere where people can meet, converse and debate for the price of a cup of coffee, which even Kumer can afford. Kumer's experience as a slightly naïve, wide-eyed immigrant who sees the Viennese style café as a 'splendid temple', is more or less based on the biography of the young Agnon. He is also a good example of the path taken by many Hebrew and Yiddish modernist writers during the early years of the twentieth century.

Most of these writers were born and raised in *shtetls* and received traditional religious education in Talmudic 'houses of study', which gave them access to and knowledge of religious Jewish texts, necessary for their ability to create literature in Hebrew and Yiddish. But this was the period of the disintegration of the *shtetl*, and most Hebrew and Yiddish writers and intellectuals found themselves at very early age as restless (and usually penniless) immigrants in one of the metropolitan centres of Eastern and Central Europe.[23] To a large extent, modernist Hebrew and Yiddish literature was a result of immigration and an intense process of urbanisation. The encounter with the big city and with the disorienting pulse of metropolitan life was an overwhelming experience. The café fulfilled a decisive role in this encounter even in East European cities like Odessa, Warsaw and Kiev, but it was absolutely crucial in Central European cities like Lemberg, Berlin and Vienna.[24]

The example of Lemberg, the frontier city which Agnon described so vividly, and Joseph Roth aptly called 'a city of uncertain boundaries', is intriguing.[25] Until the First World War the city was Polish-Jewish-Ukrainian in terms of its ethnic make-up but considered 'Central-European' according to the mental cartography of its citizens.[26] Many young Hebrew and Yiddish intellectuals were attracted to the city. Some were native-born Galicians who came to study in the University of Lemberg; others immigrated to the city from the Russian Empire during the crisis years of 1904–1907 because it was the closest Austrian city to the Russian border.

There was a certain tension between 'Russian' and 'Galician' Jewish immigrants in Lemberg but it proved to be a creative one, and soon the city boasted an active Jewish press and publishing in German, Polish, Yiddish and Hebrew. As Agnon reminds us, the natural place for students, writers, intellectuals and political activists who came from very different backgrounds to Lemberg was the local coffeehouse. In memoirs and literary texts, Lemberg emerges as the place in which Jewish writers and intellectuals thrived in cafés, and various literary coteries were created in these establishments. Zvi Scharfstein describes the Lemberg of these years as 'the little Paris' of Galicia, with numerous cafés lining its streets.[27] Melekh Ravitch, a young Yiddish modernist poet from Galicia, wrote about Café Abatzya, an institution not far from the local Yiddish theatre, as the place where the entire Yiddish and Hebrew artistic and literary community was to be found: 'Like pigeons, who can only live in company, and who immediately begin pecking at one another as soon as they come across a grain of food – this is the conduct of the *Stammgäste* in Café Abatzya: the artists, the actors, and also we, the writers'.[28] The journalist and writer Moshe

Kleinman, who came to Lemberg from Russia, writes that when he was looking for the editor of *Tagenblat* (the local Yiddish paper) he was sent to Café Abatzya, 'where the writers and journalists would gather in a specific time'.[29]

Gershon Shofman, another Russian immigrant who was fleeing the Russian army during the war between Russia and Japan, testifies that the café culture in Lemberg was so robust that Jewish exiles and refugees from Russia also had their own cafés, restaurants and meeting places. In a short essay/feuilleton, Shofman evoked the cafés and restaurants of Lemberg with affection, but with the awareness of a certain critical distance and sense of alienation of the Russian émigrés from the local 'Austrian' bohemian life. He writes about Bacchus, a simple café and restaurant on Bozhnitza Lane:

> Were it not for 'Bacchus,' the owner of the restaurant in Bozhnitza Lane, who liked to joke and laugh, the Russian immigrants, who were traumatized by the riots of 1905, would not have been able to go on living at all … Famished, the young refugee eats for now, not knowing how things will work out in the end. To his delight, he suddenly feels someone tickling him with a piece of straw behind his ear, and he knows that it's Bacchus who's doing it.[30]

During the years in which he lived and worked in Lemberg, Shofman became one of the leaders of Hebrew modernism, publishing a number of short-lived but important journals and collections. He also became a *Stammgast* and developed a strong liking for cafés. He evoked the space of the café in a number of stories and essays. It was here that he began to experiment with what scholars of Austrian and German modernism call *Kurzprosa* or *Kleinkunst*, the miniature 'literary snapshots' ('sketches' as they are called in Hebrew and Yiddish) that capture different urban spaces, chief of them being the urban café.[31]

The story *Me-idach gisa* (On the Other Side, 1909) is a good example of the way in which Shofman gives a fictional representation to the cityscape and its cafés, and it contains some distinctively modernist accounts of the encounter of Russian Jewish immigrants with Lemberg.[32] The story focuses on a group of young Jewish socialist revolutionaries, most of them Russians and a few local Galicians. The group's story is interspersed with another plot focusing on the harsh life of Brunia, a young Jewish immigrant girl who falls in love with the non-Jewish Romanenko, a revolutionary messenger from Russia. The immigrants find some solace in 'the place to which their feet lead them'. This is Café Vladivostok, the 'Russian café':

> As if they had a will of their own, their legs take them to Vladivostok, the restaurant with the Russian sign outside – the only stronghold of the émigrés. Here the air is entirely theirs. It consists of two rooms at the end of the courtyard, windowless, where the gas is lit even during the day, so that it seems as if the night never ends here. The ground is damp and full of refuse and cigar butts. The conversation, which

is always both stupefying and soporific, like the rough faces with unshorn hair, can only be made out through a haze of blue smoke.[33]

The café is the place where there is a commune, where the female protagonist Brunia arrives, and where acrobats, revolutionary messengers from Russia and various characters appear. In the stories Shofman wrote in Lemberg these kinds of places and institutions become the spaces that fuse the private and public sphere, the real and the imaginary space, the individual artist and the mass, the masculine spectator and the feminine object of desire. In another story from the same year, *Glida* (Ice Cream, 1909), we find the following description:

> Exhausted from the heat, we sat, I and my compatriot, my young and pleasant acquaintance Sokolin, in one of the cafés that the great cities of Galicia are full of. We sat at a smooth, cold, round marble-topped table near a window, through which we could see the young women of this land walking by. Tanned, dark, in shiny, shimmering white dresses, they looked so beautiful to us through the clear glass, and their eyes, gray in the heat of the day, looked like glowing, rosy embers with rivers of fire flashing under them.[34]

Here, the café is the paradigmatic urban space, a place from which one can watch the urban spectacle of the crowd passing by, and it is primarily the women that catch the narrator's and the protagonist's attention. Shofman's narrator makes the liminal space of the café (both inside and outside, or 'through the looking glass') an occasion for impressionistic description of subjective reality. Thus he emphasises the contrasts between the heat and the coolness of the marble table, and between the women's white dresses and their gray, ember eyes.

Stammgäste and 'Strangers' in the Viennese Café

In 1912, Shofman moved from Lemberg to Vienna. He arrived at the Nordbahnhof, the train station that brought immigrants from Eastern Europe to the capital of the Austrian half of the Dual Monarchy, and settled in Vienna's second district, Leopoldstadt. This area, also known as *Mazzesinsel* (Matzo Island), had the highest proportion of Jews in Vienna, particularly newcomers from Eastern Europe.[35] With its many synagogues, Jewish shops, markets, and crowded apartment buildings, the area looked and felt like an East European Jewish enclave, but the presence of many cafés let no one forget that this was very much part of Vienna.

Shofman was not alone in Leopoldstadt or in Vienna. In the years before and during the First World War, an extraordinary group of Hebrew and Yiddish immigrant writers and thinkers congregated in the city. Beside Shofman, the list includes David Fogel, Avraham Ben-Yitzhak (Dr Sonne), Zvi Disendrook,

Ya'akov Horovitz, Ravitch, Melekh Chmelnicki, Meir Wiener and many others. The Viennese coffeehouse proved once again to be the place to bring these immigrant writers together and open new paths for them. They certainly spent much time in local cafés in Leopoldstadt, but they also ventured beyond. In the years before the First World War, the Arkaden Café, located opposite the Votivkirche near the University of Vienna, emerged as the chief gathering place.[36] The memoirs of Meir Henish, Michael Weichart, Daniel Charney and Ravich portray the Arkaden Café as the meeting place of 'students, writers, journalists, publishers, artists and bohemians from Austria and from all around the world', but especially the place in which Jewish immigrants from Galicia felt at home.[37] Henish wrote that Hebrew and Yiddish newspapers were available, and the Yiddish poet Chmelnitzky even wrote a sonnet about the Votivkirche as he looks at it from that café.[38]

The war years were challenging for the Jewish immigrant writers in Vienna. Some of them served in the Habsburg army and others found themselves 'behind enemy lines'. This was a time when the Hebrew and Yiddish centres in Eastern Europe (and the nascent centre in Palestine) were in effect defunct. Soon after the war, however, the Hebrew enclave in the city began to be very active in terms of publication. Shofman and Disendrook edited and published a short-lived but highly important journal aptly titled *Gevulot* (Borders, 1918–1920) and later *Peret* (1922–1924), which published innovative modernist works. This Hebrew activity coincided with the peak of Yiddish publishing activity in Vienna, with the journal *Kritik* and the publishing house *Kval*.[39] The importance of these publishing ventures transcended their small size and short life, because they appeared at a time of changing poetic modes and were edited and published by writers who absorbed and participated in Viennese modernist movements.

Vienna of this period proved to be a fertile ground for 'minor' Jewish modernism. The city fostered close collaboration between Hebrew and Yiddish writers at a time when these two literatures were gradually separating from each other.[40] Vienna also became a site of much contact between Hebrew and Yiddish writers and modernist figures working in German and other languages. Many of these encounters occurred in coffeehouses. Shofman, who met Peter Altenberg in Café Central during the war, came to know him quite well. He translated Alternberg's short stories into Hebrew, and this had a strong impact on Shofman's modernist style, which became more inclined to the Viennese *Kleinkunst*.[41] Elias Canetti, who met Ben-Yitzhak in the Café Museum, admired the modernist Hebrew poet. In his well-known memoir, *Das Augenspiel* (The Play of the Eyes, 1985) he writes:

> At the Café Museum, where I went every day after moving back to town, there was a man whom I noticed because he was always sitting alone and never spoke to anyone. That in itself was not so unusual, lots of people went to cafés to be alone among many … Only superficially did I bury myself in the paper. I peeked out constantly in the

direction of the door. He always came, a tall figure, thin, with a rigid, awkward way of walking, almost arrogant, as if he did not want to meet anyone, and so keep these garrulous creatures at a distance.[42]

Canetti recorded the connections between Ben-Yitzhak and figures like Musil, Hofmannsthal, Beer-Hofmann, Broch and Joyce.[43] The Hebrew and Yiddish writers Fogel and Wiener were acquainted with Viennese modernists of the post-war period, and these connections are clearly demonstrated in their poetry and prose fiction.

All this rich literary and cultural activity occurred both in spite of and because of the marginality of Hebrew and Yiddish in Vienna, a marginality that was not only linguistic but also spatial. Hebrew and Yiddish writers lived and worked on the visible and invisible borderlines between Vienna's cultural centres of modernism, and the geographically bounded sections of the city. Even in the 1920s and early 1930s, when Wiener, Fogel, Ben-Yitzhak and other Hebrew and Yiddish writers spent much time with intellectual friends who met regularly in central locations like the Café Herrenhof and the Café Museum, Leopoldstadt was still the tentative and provisional 'home' for them, and the base from which the writers and their fictional protagonists go to explore the cityscape, and the place to which they return.

The flowering of the enclave of Hebrew and Yiddish modernism in Vienna gave us many literary representations of the cityscape and its cafés. One of the most accomplished Viennese stories by Shofman, *Ba-matzor u'va-matzok* (In Siege and Distress, 1922),[44] is set in Vienna during and after the war, and follows the fate of a group of East European Jewish writers, artists and intellectuals.[45] This story builds on the familiar theme of the young Jewish male protagonist searching for cultural and intellectual self-fulfilment in the big city, as well as his disillusionment in the face of a disappointing reality. These two elements – aspiration and failure, hope and despair – are present from the group's very first encounter with the urban life of Vienna.

In *Ba-matzor u'va-matzok*, the Viennese coffeehouse, in which so much literary and cultural activity has occurred, and which serves so often as metonymy or metaphor for the city itself, is the space where these Jewish young men look for some sense of social belonging. It is of course also the place where they try to assimilate into the local and international bohemian and intellectual life. But the advent of the First World War shakes the relatively calm capital of the Dual Monarchy, and suddenly reveals the same café as a space that can also be dangerous, especially for émigrés and exiles from the East:

Never had there been as much smoke in the café as in these new, onerous days. People sucked on their cigarettes with all their might as if they intended to hide in their own smoke. But the police agents with the bristle moustaches peered through the windows with their sharp, crushing eyes, cutting through the clouds.[46]

Here, the public sphere of the café, which served as a replacement of sorts for home, community and the old 'house of study', reveals another, unfamiliar face. The same café, with its elusive promise of social engagement and sense of belonging, actually comes to prevent real human connection and communication. It is filled with thick cigarette smoke which masks people's faces. At the same time as it brings people together it also alienates them from one another. The café does not provide protection against the policemen searching for army defectors. Moreover, the young protagonists in the story quickly realise that the urban space of Vienna is comprised of many locations in which the public and private overlap, and that the desired 'outside' can actually become a series of closed and restricting spaces (the café can be similar to army prison, soup kitchen and sanatorium). On the other hand, the protagonists learn that the 'inside', the closed space in which they try to create a protective, homey environment, is itself permeated by the 'outside' world. Thus, two contradicting desires intersect in the city and its cafés: the desire for the outside, for the Viennese, Central European society, and the desire for an intimate protective place. This yearning is so strong in the story that the poet David Gol (who may be a fictional representation of Fogel) is indifferent to the prospects of sitting in an army prison, and the painter Mando gives himself to the police, and ends up in a sanatorium.[47]

The paradox of contradicting desires cannot be resolved. At the story's conclusion, the First World War ends and the borders are opened. 'The English, the Italians and the Serbs,' Shofman's narrator writes, are mixing with the Viennese. At the same time, the end of the war brings no real change, and the sense of 'siege and distress' is revealed as a kind of permanent existential condition. The end of the story casts into relief many social, historical and artistic questions about the life of the Jewish émigré writer in European cities like Vienna, questions that have been heightened by the violence of the war. The collapse of the Jewish 'old world', and the crisis of Jewish existence in unbearably shaky European cities, both parallel the collapse of the traditional experiences of time and space in the metropolis, and changing paradigms of how to represent time and space in modernist literature. The insane artist literally disturbs the legibility of our world; the promise of a portrait – its linguistic/ artistic transparency – is denied in the story's complex texture of ekphrasis, metonymy, metaphor, and abstraction.[48] Like Mando the insane painter, the modernist urban (Jewish) writer can offer only a fleeting portrait, a fragmentary sketch of urban Jewish characters and of the city itself.

In literary works written by Hebrew and Yiddish writers during the inter-war period in Vienna – a period in which Jewish modernism entered a new expressionist stage – cafés also play a central and important role. Perhaps the most fascinating are Wiener's unpublished Yiddish novel *Der Groyser Roman* (The Big Novel),[49] and Fogel's Hebrew novel *Chaye Nisu'im* (Married Life, 1929–1930).[50] *Married Life* was not received very well by the Hebrew readers of the time, but is recognised today as a masterpiece, the urban Hebrew modernist novel par excellence. Its protagonist, Rudolf Gurdweill, is the ultimate Jewish *flâneur*, a man who wanders around the streets and boulevards of Vienna.

Gurdweill and his friends spend much time in the Café Herrenhof during the period in which it was the favourite place of figures like Hermann Broch, Robert Musil, Alfred Polgar and Joseph Roth.[51] In Fogel's novel, however, Café Herrenhof is not described necessarily as a 'literary café'. Rather, it clearly becomes a metonymy of the city of Vienna itself: a substitute for a 'real' home, a space that fuses the public and the private, the inside and the outside, the culture of the bourgeoisie and the bohemian. The café brings the city inside, but also shields its regulars from the 'crowd' and the 'masses'. On one of the numerous occasions when Gurdweill and his friends meet at the Café Herrenhof, a female protagonist, Lotte Budenheim, asks the group: 'How long can you people go on sitting in cafés? Don't you ever get tired of it?' to which one of Gurdweill's friends, Ulrich, responds:

> Sitting in cafés is a barrier against the enforced activity which makes our lives miserable ... People like us always have the mistaken feeling that they are wasting time, missing something irretrievable ... As if a man had a set amount of things to get done in a set amount of time ... The harmful influence of our materialistic generation, a generation of physical labour and advanced technology ... But the minute you enter a café, you're in a holiday – the yoke is lifted from your shoulders, snapped in half.[52]

Ulrich's philosophy of the café, one which brings to mind Polgar's famous *Theorie des Café Central* (Theory of Café Central, 1926) and Roth's Arnold Zipper, is half ironic and half serious. It emphasised the contradictory features of the café: on the one hand, a place of leisure and sociability, a literary market and information source exempt from the pressure to consume; and on the other, a place of consumption and of non-commitment, time-killing, gossip, a refuge for drop-outs and failures who can only find their place in the café.[53] Thus, Fogel's narrator is far from idealising the café, and if camaraderie is presented as a key element of Viennese coffeehouses like the Café Herrenhof, the other side of the coin is the acrimony that is borne of the too-close, at times alienating, experience of the social space of the café. This ambivalent attitude towards the café captures much of the urban experience in *Married Life*.

In spite of the centrality of the Café Herrenhof in Fogel's novel, it must be noted that much narrative activity takes place in small and simple local cafés in Leopoldstadt and in Josefstadt. Here is how the narrator describes one of these small cafés:

> It was nine at night. One by one the Stammgäste of the little café near the university assembled: students and minor officials who sat in the same chairs night after night,

and ordered their 'Turkish' coffee as if they were finishing off their evening meal at home. These customers were as much a part of the café and its particular atmosphere as the ragged, threadbare velvet sofas around the walls and the dark, dirty, marble tables. It was rare for a 'stranger' to appear here.[54]

In this café, Gurdweill meets Thea Von-Tackow for the first time. Of course, it is exactly the fact that she is a 'stranger' who rarely appears in the café that first catches Gurdweill's attention and constitutes his uncontrollable desire for the 'other', who is in this case the gentile woman Gurdweill is unable to 'take his eyes off'. This charged encounter between Gurdweill and Thea sets in motion the entire sadomasochist plot of the novel. But much of the irony and the power of this scene, and the novel in general, stems from this position of Gurdweill as an immigrant East European Jew who lives in Leopoldstadt. Gurdweill is simultaneously an insider and an outsider, a *Stammgast* and a 'stranger' in the café and in Vienna. The same is true of Fogel and other Hebrew and Yiddish modernist writers who lived in Vienna during the most productive period of their lives.

Berlin: Between the Scheunenviertel and the Romanisches Café

Vienna, it should be noted, was not the only large Central European city to which Hebrew and Yiddish modernist writers migrated. In more or less the same period, Hebrew and Yiddish modernist literature was created in Berlin, and the urban cafés of the city played an equally important role in modernist activity. This can be attested in *Michtavim mi-nesi'a meduma* (Letters from an Imaginary Journey, 1937), the epistolary novel of the Hebrew poet and prose writer Leah Goldberg. Ruth, the thinly disguised autobiographical narrator of the novel, writes about wandering around various Berlin cafés:

> Because those who sit now at the Romanisches Café are Jews looking for sensational news in foreign press, and because Café Lunte doesn't exist anymore, and because the disciples of Jesus who worshipped Else Lasker-Schüler left the temple of Café des Westens a long time ago and found their Mt. of Olives in Le Dome and La Coupole cafés in Paris ... and because Mentzel who used to sit in café Josty had died before I was even born ... because of this and other reasons, I'm sitting in 'Quick,' a small café which our Jewish friends still frequent.[55]

Goldberg is clearly aware of the fact that the early 1930s, the time when she arrived in the city as a student and a young writer, was a time of 'twilight' in Berlin and that the 'golden age' of its cafés has passed: 'They say that the lions of the art and literature used to sit in the Romanisches café ... for anyone interested in Jewish literature there was a rare opportunity to encounter there some of their wild manes'.[56]

The period depicted by Goldberg, with its cafés and the 'lions' of art and Jewish literature, is the early decades of the twentieth century. Several cafés emerged during this period as important places for the creation and development of modernism in Berlin.[57] At Café Monopol near Freidrichstrasse in Berlin Mitte (not far from the Scheunenviertel) the Jung Wien writer Hermann Bahr and anarchist writers such as Gustav Landauer and Erich Mühsam mingled with young theatre artists, including Max Reinhardt and his circle. Several other Berlin cafés attracted writers who were critical to the formation and development of expressionist art and literature. Public recitals and cabarets of *Der Neue Club* appeared at Café Austria, Café Sezession and Café Josty, and the editorial activity of expressionist journals took place around their tables.

As is evident from Goldeberg's novel and from numerous accounts of café culture in Berlin, the most important institution in this period was Café des Westens on the Kurfürstendamm. By 1910 it had established itself not only as the chief gathering place for all of the expressionist circles centred in Berlin, but also as a magnetic pole attracting modernist writers and artists from all over Europe. It was famous for the extravagant dressing and eccentric behaviour of its habitués, such as the Jewish German poet Else Lasker-Schüler (who evoked it in her writings) as well as for its artistic and literary activity. Poets, painters, critics, philosophers, actors and directors packed the café in the evening. Periodicals such as *Der Sturm* and *Die Aktion* were founded and planned in the café, making it an indispensable ingredient of daily literary life for German modernists in Berlin before the end of the First World War.[58]

After the First World War and throughout the Weimar period, the huge and rather shabby Romanisches Café became the new headquarters for the expressionists, as well as the so-called *Neue Sachlichkeit* movement, and in fact of all writers, artists and many other intellectuals and bohemians. The Romanisches Café performed many of the roles of the Café des Westens in the 1910s, even inheriting the dubious name 'Café Megalomania'. Among many well-known figures who frequented the café were Lasker-Schüler, Franz Werfel, Kurt Tucholsky, Stefan Zweig, Alfred Döblin, Ludwig Meydner, Gottfried Benn, Joseph Roth, Berthold Brecht and Walter Benjamin, and many of them wrote in and about the café. They described it as a second home for writers during the daytime; a place where heated debates on various subjects lasted long into the night and where collective activities, such as the founding and editing of periodicals, were pursued.[59] What can be called the 'thirdspace' of the Romanisches Café reflected Weimar culture in many ways, including the fact that it was far from being the exclusive location of a small group of German expressionists, but rather a place in which 'insiders' and 'outsiders', locals and strangers, bohemians and bourgeoisie, politics and art, avant-garde and mass culture (both 'high' and 'low') coexisted in an elusive mixture.[60]

Although these well-known Berlin cafés have been described and their role in the various stages of Berlin modernism has been clearly demonstrated, these accounts rarely recognise the presence of Hebrew and Yiddish writers, intellectuals and artists who immigrated to Berlin from Eastern Europe. Like in Vienna, many of the East European Jewish writers and intellectuals settled in recognisably Jewish neighbourhoods like the Scheunenviertel, but they were attracted to places like the Café Monopol, the Café des Westens and the Romanisches Café.

In the first decade of the twentieth century, the Hebraists of Berlin had a *Stammtisch* at the Café Monopol. Aharon Hermoni and Itamar Ben-Avi (Eliezer Ben-Yehuda's son who came to Berlin from Palestine as a student) wrote in their memoirs that around 1908 even the waiter, Eduard, knew some Hebrew in order to accommodate the 'Hebrew' or 'Eretz-Israeli' table. This 'Hebrew Table' included Shay Ish Hurwitz, Reuven Breinin, Horodetzky, Itamar Ben-Avi, Aharon Hermoni and many other Zionist activists and Hebrew writers.[61] Y.D. Berkovitz wrote that plans for Hebrew publishing ventures were laid out on the black marble tops of this plush café, with its oriental-like appearance in the heart of Berlin.[62] Journals like *Ha-olam* and *He-atid* were edited in the café. The Hebraists in the Café Monopol were far from isolated. Next to their Hebrew table were many 'German tables' with which they interacted. There was also a 'Yiddish table' that enjoyed visits by luminaries such as Sholem Asch, whose play *El nekomes* (God of Revenge) was performed by Reinhardt's theatre, and Sholem Aleichem, who came to Berlin with a dream to have his plays translated into German and produced by Reinhardt's theatre as well.[63] There is less evidence of the presence of Hebrew and Yiddish writers in the famous Café des Westens during the 1910s, but it is known that Berdichevsky, Shay Ish Hurvitz and other Hebrew, Yiddish and German writers used to meet every Thursday evening first in the Café Monopol and then in the Café des Westens.[64]

However, the rather modest activity prior to the First World War was just a prelude to an expanded presence of Hebrew and Yiddish émigré writers in Berlin throughout the Weimar period, especially the first half of the 1920s when Berlin became, de facto, the most important enclave of Jewish modernism in Europe. Almost everybody who joined the Hebrew and Yiddish 'colony' in Weimar Berlin attested to the allure of the Romanisches Café. Uri Zvi Greenberg, Ya'acov Shteinberg, Yeshurun Keshet, Avrom Nochem Stencl, Dovid Bergelson, Nahum Goldman, Henrik Berlewi and numerous others mention the cafe. In fact, some accounts create the erroneous impression that the Romanisches Café was a kind of a pan-Jewish urban space. Thus, Nahum Goldman writes that 'each [Jewish] group had its own table; there were the "Yiddishist," "Zionists," "Bundists" and so on, all arguing among themselves from table to table'.[65] The Yiddish author Avrom Noach Stencl describes the scene at the Romanische Café from the angle of East-European Jewish intellectuals:

> From those fleeing the pogroms in the Ukrainian shtetls, from the famine in the Russian cities, and from the Revolution, a kind of Jewish colony formed itself in the west of Berlin, and the Romanische Cafe was its parliament. It was buzzing with famous Jewish intellectuals and activists, well-known Jewish lawyers from Moscow and Petersburg, Yiddish writers from Kiev and Odessa, with flying party-leaders from the extreme left to the extreme right wing – it buzzed like a beehive.[66]

In his characteristically fragmentary expressionist style, with expansive grammar and outrageous images, Greenberg writes in his essay on Lasker-Schüler that they 'drank together dark coffee in the Romanisches Café, and until midnight this bitter drink was dripping in our hearts, and sipping through even deeper to the "inner existence," around the heart and beyond it like dark blood'.[67]

The poet and critic Yeshurun Keshet described his encounters with the Hebrew and Yiddish writer Ya'acov Shteinberg who spent most of days in the Romanisches Café. In Keshet's memoir the café emerges both as a kind of 'Jewish urban space' but also as a place whose regulars are a 'cultural elite full of decadence, smoke and the syncopated rhythm of the metropolis'.[68] Shteinberg, who was attracted to this mixture of urban decadence and syncopated rhythms, and to the modernist literary activity in which he participated with a critical distance, devoted an entire cycle of sonnets to the Romanisches Café – *Sonnets from the Café* (1922) – which is surely one of the great achievements of modernist Hebrew poetry.[69]

While many Hebrew and Yiddish writers used to sit in the Romanisches Café and mention it in their writing, Shteinberg's cycle employs the urban space of the café in an unprecedented way. The cycle creates a tightly knit narrative that occurs solely in the café. The speaker-poet in the cycle is a lonely character who interacts with others only by the act of gazing at the regular and casual guests as well as at the habitual and uncommon incidents that occur in the space of the café. His participation in the world is one of an outsider, a witness and spectator whose only capacity is one of observation and introspection. In the beginning of the cycle the character of the speaker appears only by intimation and in the third person, as in 'then a man sits and watches in front of the lampshade'.[70] Towards the end of the cycle, he speaks to us directly, but only momentarily, before he disappears again, 'hiding in a screen of smoke'.[71] In the rest of the cycle the reader does not see him or hear about him at all. He exists only in the way in which he looks at the objects, events and characters that fill the café over a period of a few days and nights.

Hebrew and Yiddish writers' descriptions of the Romanisches Café, also known in Yiddish as *Café Rakhmonishes* (The Café of Pity), testify to the tensions between their 'bohemian' existence and a certain sense of marginality, both physical and spiritual, in the café and, by extension, in Weimar Berlin. A.N Stencl, U.Z. Greenberg and Shteinberg met Lasker-Schüler and other important figures of Berlin modernism in the Romanisches Café and the encounter strongly marked their literary and intellectual development. Their experience of the café, which became a metonymy for the urban space of Berlin in this period, emphasised both their participation in modernist Berlin culture and their marginality, the energy of the metropolis as well as its decadence, corruption, and sense of deep despair. East European Jewish Berlin was essentially no more than an ephemeral environment. Like the Romanisches Café, it was a kind of 'thirdspace' which turned into a hybrid urban culture, existing only on the margins where it intersected with majority society.

Conclusion

Hebrew and Yiddish modernist literature constitutes an important but overlooked aspect of the link between modernism, Jewishness and the urban café, especially in Central Europe. In this context, Vienna was certainly important but far from unique. The Viennese coffeehouse served perhaps as a paradigm, but it was also, like the East European Jewish migrants and like modernism, a transnational phenomenon that moved from one city to another. Moreover, what Viennese acculturated Jews like Torberg identified as an essential element of Jewishness of the café that belongs to the 'Jewish ghetto' was in fact not frozen in memory as a relic of a world that has passed, but alive and well in Jewish migrants who experienced the 'modern Jewish revolution'.

For the Hebrew and Yiddish modernist writers in Vienna, Berlin and Lemberg (and this was also true, but in a different way, in places like Odessa, Warsaw, New York City and Tel Aviv), cafés were often a substitute for a home and a community. During the first three decades of the twentieth century Hebrew and Yiddish modernist groups and movements were created in cafés, with journals, periodicals and other publishing activities taking place there. Cafés were often the spaces where Hebrew and Yiddish writers could interact with each other and with others working in German (or Polish and Russian). Last but not least, the café was the space where much of their literature was created, and was the very object of modernist literary representations of urban space. Some of the most distinctive representations of the cityscape focus on the café as a site of negotiation between inside and outside, public and private, real and imaginary, men and women, Jews and Gentiles, 'the local' and the immigrant.

Notes

1. Jürgen Nautz and Richard Vahrenkamp (eds), *Die Wiener Jahrhundertwende Einflüsse, Umwelt, Wirkungen*, Vienna 1993.
2. Carl E. Schorske, *Fin-de-Siècle Vienna: Politics and Culture*, New York 1981, 7.
3. Peter Hall, *Cities in Civilization: Culture, Innovation, and Urban Order*, London 1998, 5.
4. Steven Beller, *Vienna and the Jews, 1867–1938: A Cultural History*, Cambridge 1989, 22. See also Beller's contribution to this volume.
5. Malcolm Bradbury and James McFarlane (eds), *Modernism: A Guide to European Literature 1890–1930*, London and New York 1991, 96.
6. Apart from studies of the role of these cafés in the context of 'national' modernism, and a number of 'coffee-table books', the only comparative study of the 'literary cafés' that I am aware of is Michael Rössner (ed.), *Literarische Kaffeehäuser*, Vienna 1999. An important departure from this tendency is Edward Timms' mapping of several circles of Viennese modernism through various cafés in the city. See Edward Timms, *Karl Kraus, Apocalyptic Satirist*, New Haven 1986. Another recent study that makes an insightful use of cafés and teashops in English (but also in German and Czech) modernism is Scott McCracken, *Masculinities, Modernist Fiction and Urban Public Sphere*, Manchester 2007.
7. Many of these accounts can be found in the anthology, Kurt-Jürgen Heering, *Das Wiener Kaffeehaus: mit Zahlreichen Abbildungen und Hinweisen auf Wiener Kaffeehäuser*, Frankfurt 1991.
8. Beller, *Vienna and the Jews*, 40–41; See also Steven Beller, '"The Jew Belongs in the Coffeehouse"': Jews, Central Europe and Modernity' in this volume.
9. Harold B. Segal, *The Vienna Coffeehouse Wits 1890–1938*, West Lafayette 1993, 12.
10. Robert Liberles, 'Les Juifs, le Café et le Négoce du Café au XVIIIe Siècle', *Les Cahiers du Judaïsme*, 26, 2009, 4–14.
11. Brian Cowan, *The Social Life of Coffee*, New Haven and London 2005, 25.
12. See Sarah Wobick, 'Interdits de Café: L'influence de la Révolution de Juillet sur la Condition des Juifs de Hambourg', and Scott Ury, 'Juste un café? Le rôle des cafés juifs à Varsovie au tournant du XXe siècle', *Les Cahiers du Judaïsme*, 26, 2009, 14–23 and 26–30.
13. On the 'modern Jewish revolution', see Benjamin Harshav, *Language in Time of Revolution*, Berkeley 1991.
14. Friedrich Torberg, *Die Tante Jolesch oder Der Untergang des Abendlandes in Anekdoten*, Munich 1975, 136.
15. On these aspects of the Talmudic culture and the masculine ideal of the 'house of study', see Daniel Boyarin, *Unheroic Conduct: The Rise of Heterosexuality and the Invention of the Jewish Man*, Berkeley 1997.
16. Jürgen Habermas, *The Structural Transformation of the Public Sphere: An Inquiry into a Category of Bourgeois Society* (1962), trans. Thomas Burger et al. Cambridge 1989.
17. Max Nordau, 'Muskeljudentum', *Judische Turnzeitung*, June 1900, 10–11. For further comment on Nordau's characterisation of the café as degenerate, see Charlotte Ashby's contribution to this volume.
18. Theodor Herzl, *Altneuland*, Leipzig 1902; Theodor Herzl, *Old-New Land*, tr. Lotta Levensohn, New York 1960, 3.
19. Joseph Roth, 'Zipper und Sein Vater', in Hermann Kesten (ed.), *Werke*, Cologne 1956. While the novel does not state explicitly that Arnold Zipper and his family are Jewish, there is a clear sense that Roth depicted the largely Jewish milieu of the Viennese family and the coffeehouse. Moreover, *Zipper und Sein Vater* is a good example of the ways in which 'Roth's Jewishness is an influence on early texts not overtly concerned with religion …'. Jon Hughes,

Facing Modernity Fragmentation, Culture and Identity in Joseph Roth's Writing in the 1920s, Leeds 2006, 8–9. See also Kati Tonkin, *Joseph Roth's March into History: From the Early Novels to Radetzkymarsch and Die Kapuzinergruft,* New York 2008.

20. For a discussion of the 'marginality' of Hebrew and Yiddish see Chana Kronfled, *On the Margins of Modernism: Decentering Literary Dynamics,* Berkeley 1996.

21. We have taken the decision to use the German name for the city, in use by the administration of the Dual Monarchy of Austria-Hungary in the early 1900s. It was known as Lvov and Lwów to the large Russian and Polish populations that inhabited the city during that period and is now called Lviv and is a city in western Ukraine. The Hebrew and Yiddish writers who are the subject of this chapter referred to the city as both Lemberg and Lvov.

22. Shmuel Y. Agnon, *Tmol Shilshom,* Tel Aviv 1945, 13. See the English translation of the novel by Barbara Harshav, *Only Yesterday,* Princeton 2000, 9.

23. There was also mass immigration to America and in small numbers to Palestine. However, at least until the 1920s most Hebrew and Yiddish writers immigrated to large cities in Eastern or Central Europe.

24. See Shachar Pinsker, *Literary Passports: The Making of Modernist Hebrew Fiction in Europe,* Stanford, 2011.

25. Joseph Roth, 'Lemberg, die Stadt', in *Werke 2: Das journalistische Werk 1924–1928,* Cologne 1990, 289.

26. Delphine Bechtel, 'Lemberg/Lwów/Lvov/Lviv: Identities of a City of Uncertain Boundaries', *Diogenes,* 53(2), 2006, 62–71.

27. Quoted in Norman Tarnor, *The Many Worlds of Gershon Shofman,* New York 1989, 23.

28. Melekh Ravitch, *Dos mayse-bukh fun mayn lebn,* vol. 2, Buenos Aires 1962–1964, 115–116.

29. Moshe Kleinman, 'Galitzia lifney shloshim ve-chamesh shanim', *Moznayim,* 11, 1940, 227.

30. Gershon Shofman, 'Lvov', in *Kol-Kitvei G. Shofman* vol. 3, Tel Aviv 1948, 321–322.

31. On modernist *Kleinkunst,* see Andreas Huyssen, 'Modernist Miniatures: Literary Snapshots of Urban Spaces', *PMLA,* 122(1), 2007, 27–43.

32. Gershon Shofman, *Me-idach gisa,* Lvov 1909, 3–14. Reprinted in *Kol Kitvei,* vol. 1, 162–173.

33. Ibid., 160–161.

34. Gershon Shofman, *Glida* (1909). Reprinted in *Kol Kitvei,* vol. 1, 195.

35. See Ruth Beckermann and Teifer Hermann, *Die Mazzesinsel Juden in der Wiener Leopoldstadt 1918–1938,* Vienna 1984.

36. The Arkaden Café is not as well known today as Café Griensteidl or Café Central, but it was patronised by Wittgenstein and members of the philosophical Vienna Circle, as well as many students and musicians. See Allan Janik and Hans Veigl, *Wittgenstein in Vienna: A Biographical Excursion Through the City and Its History,* Vienna 1998, 188–189.

37. Ravitch, *Dos mayse-bukh fun mayn lebn,* 209–211; Daniel Charney, *Di Velt iz Kaylekhdik,* Tel Aviv 1963, 160–165; Michael Weichart, *Zikhroynes,* vol.1, Tel Aviv 1960, 229–248.

38. Meir Henish, *Mi-bayit u mi-chuts: pirke zikhronot,* Tel Aviv 1961, 145–147; Melekh Chmelnitzky, *Ruh un Imru,* New York 1948, 31.

39. Ravitch, *Dos mayse-bukh fun mayn lebn,* 363–369.

40. These ideological differences became strong after the 1908 Yiddish Language Conference, convened in Czernowitz. See Emanuel S. Goldsmith, *Modern Yiddish Culture: The Story of the Yiddish Language Movement,* New York 2000.

41. Peter Altenberg, *Ktavim nivcharim,* trans. Gershon Shofman, New York 1921.

42. Elias Canetti, *The Play of the Eye,* New York 1999, 112.

43. Ibid., 132–162; Hannan Hever, 'Acharit Davar', in Avraham Ben-Yitzhak, *Kol-hashirim,* Tel Aviv 1992, 107.

44. Shofman, 'Ba-matzor u'va-matzok', *Ha-tekufa,* vol. 16, 1922, 101–109. Reprinted in *Kol-Kitvei,* vol. 2, 125–137.

45. According to Nurit Govrin, the story is a kind of *roman à clef* and all the characters are based directly on the Hebrew colony – the group of Hebrew writers and artists in Vienna. Nurit Govrin, *Me-ofek el ofek*, vol. 2, Tel Aviv 1983, 345–349.

46 Shofman, *Kol-Kitvei*, vol. 1, 101.

47. Ibid., 125–126.

48. In this sense, what Shofman attempts in his short stories is the same project of modernist urban writing seen in Austrian writers such as Altenberg, Rilke, Hofmannsthal and Musil. See Huyssen, 'Modernist Miniatures', 30–32.

49. On Wiener's novel see Mikhail Krutikov, 'Yiddish Author as Cultural Mediator: Meir Wiener's Unpublished Novel', in Joseph Sherman and Ritchie Robertson, *The Yiddish Presence in European Literature: Inspiration and Interaction*, Oxford 2005, 73–86.

50. David Fogel, *Chaye Nisu'im*, Tel Aviv 1929–1930; David Fogel, *Married Life*, trans. Dalya Bilu, New York 1989.

51. Segal, *The Vienna Coffeehouse Wits*, 27.

52. Fogel, *Married Life*, 181–182.

53. See the fine analysis of Gilbert Carr, 'Time and Space in the Café Griensteidl and the Café Central', in this volume.

54. Fogel, *Married Life*, 21.

55. Leah Goldberg, *Michtavim me-nesi'a meduma*, Tel Aviv 1982, 15–16.

56. Ibid., 16.

57. For an overview of Berlin cafés and their role in modernist literature and culture, see Roy F. Allen, *Literary Life in German Expressionism and the Berlin Circles*, Ann Arbor 1983; Alfred Rath, 'Berliner Caféhäuser (1890–1933)', in Rössner (ed.), *Literarische Kaffehäuser*, 108–125.

58. Allen, *Literary Life in German Expressionism*, 67–73; Sigrid Bauschinger, 'The Berlin Moderns: Else Lasker-Schüler and Café Culture', in Emily Bilski (ed.), *Berlin Metropolis: Jews and the New Culture, 1890–1918*, Berkeley 1999, 58–101.

59. See Joseph Roth, *What I Saw*, 136–138; Walter Benjamin, *Berliner Chronik*, Frankfurt am Main 1972; Walter Benjamin, 'A Berlin Chronicle', in Michael W. Jennings, Howard Eiland and Gary Smith (eds), *Selected Writings Volume II*, Cambridge 1999, 595–637.

60. On the concept of the 'thirdspace', see Edward Soja, *Thirdspace: Journeys to Los Angeles and Other Real-and-Imagined Places*, Oxford 1996. For an analysis of the European urban café as thirdspace, see Shachar Pinsker, 'The Urban European Café and the Geography of Hebrew and Yiddish Modernism', in Mark Wollaeger (ed.), *The Oxford Handbook of Global Modernisms*, Oxford 2012, 443–.

61. Itamar Ben-Avi, '*Im shachar atzma'utenu*, Tel Aviv 1961, 146–156; Aharon Hermoni, *Be-ikvot ha-bilu'im*, Jerusalem 1951, 145–158.

62. Kitvei Y.D. Berkovitz, *Ha-rishonim ki-vnei adam*, Tel Aviv 1959, 209–210; Hermoni, *Be-ikvot Ha-bilu'im*, 151.

63. Berkovitz, *Ha-rishonim*, 210; Stanley Nash, *In Search of Hebraism: Shai Hurwitz and His Polemics in the Hebrew Press*, Leiden 1980, 172.

64. Immanuel Ben-Gurion, *Reshut ha-yachid*, Tel Aviv 1980, 64–72. See also Berdichevsky's German diary of these years, published in *Ginzey Micha Yosef*, 7, 1997, 90–113.

65. Nahum Goldmann, *The Jewish Paradox*, New York 1978, 21.

66. Avrom Nokhem Stencl, *Loshn un lebn*, 10–11, 1968, 25.

67. Uri Z. Greenberg, 'Dvorah be-shivya', in Uri Z. Greenberg, *Kol-Ktavav*, vol. 15, Jerusalem 2004, 127.

68. Yeshurun Keshet, *Maskiyot*, Tel Aviv 1953, 138.

69. Ya'acov Shteinberg, *Kol Kitvei Y'acov Shteinberg*, Tel Aviv 1957, 67–68.

70. Ibid., 67.

71. Ibid., 68.

Chapter 6

MICHALIK'S CAFÉ IN KRAKÓW
Café and Caricature as Media of Modernity

Katarzyna Murawska-Muthesius

Caricatures must have been produced at café tables all over the world. The significance of caricature for the aesthetics of modernity was declared by Baudelaire in mid-nineteenth-century Paris, while the uniqueness of the coffeehouse as a hub of the modernist literary movement has been discussed extensively in the context of turn-of-the-century Vienna.[1] What I am particularly interested in is the symbiotic interaction between these two – the medium of caricature and the socio-cultural institution of the café – and in their joint contribution to the process of fostering modern urban identities. This text examines the relationship between café-art and café-space in fin-de-siècle Kraków,[2] a self-declared suburb of Paris as much as Vienna.[3] It focuses on Jama Michalikowa (Michalik's Den), the most famous bohemian coffeehouse in Kraków, which opened in 1895 and was covered with caricatures from top to bottom[4] (Figure 6.1).

There are at least two ways to approach the interconnectedness of café and caricature. One, very tempting, is to look at this relationship in the context of liberal modernity, identified with experiment, synaesthetic impulse, performativity and subversion. Another way, more political, is to admit that, in spite of the concurrency with rebellion, both café and caricature also served as tools of the disciplining modernity, a modernity that controlled and proscribed as much as, if not more than it liberated.[5] Both made a parade of subversion while hiding their inimical adherence to rituals and formulas, and both were perfectly suited to ostracising the Other under the excuse of reforming urban society and behind the veil of anti-philistine laughter. There are two reasons why

KAROL FRYCZ, KRAKÓW. — CUKIERNIA LWOWSKA JANA MICHALIKA PRZY UL. FLORYAŃSKIEJ W KRAKOWIE.

Figure 6.1 Karol Frycz, *Interior of the Green Room of Michalik's Den,* c.1911, *Sztuka Stosowana,* 1911.

I feel I ought to place a stronger emphasis on this second aspect. The Viennese context and the Jewishness of the Viennese literary café, argued persuasively by Steven Beller,[6] provokes the question of the Jewish presence in Kraków cafés. At the same time, recent controversies about cartoons and freedom of speech give an urgency to the inquiry into the predisposition of the medium of caricature to serve both as an instrument of subversion and of discrimination.[7]

Café and Caricature

Caricature and the café have much in common as agents of modernity. Both were relative latecomers to European culture, emerging in the early modern period, roughly at the time of the first pronouncements of resistance against the pre-eminence of the classical paradigm. Both café and caricature, respectively, took part in the production of the model of an urban society, encouraging the distinction between Self and Other, and both were long associated with rebellions against the established order.[8] The partnership between caricature and café must have been facilitated to a large extent by their close relationship with the press. As is argued by David Kunzle in his discussion of the rise of cheap illustrated journals in Britain, broadsheet caricature – originally distributed by print shops and free from control – had by the 1830s become domesticated on the pages of illustrated magazines, losing much of its former independence and irreverence.[9] By that time, in many European countries, such journals had already been offered a home in coffeehouses, and networks of commercial alliances between the modern media had begun to form.

But clearly it was not just in the pages of magazines that caricature entered the space of the café. A much deeper kinship between café and caricature stems from their compliance with the new modes, conducts and themes of modernity, privileging distortion and irony, 'the ephemeral, the fugitive, the contingent', as Baudelaire famously put it in his much quoted text which, let us not forget, celebrated modern prints.[10] This camaraderie between the media of caricature and the café manifested itself in their mutual willingness to embrace each other within each other's space. Café walls were consistently used for the production and display of caricatures, while caricature, in turn, proved to be instrumental in developing the topic of the café interior into modern subject matter. By offering a space for display, café walls released caricature from enclosure within the pages of the press, as if restoring its lost freedoms and renewing its licence for the uncensored criticism of modern life, encouraging its spontaneous outflow and prompting the drive for formal experiments.[11] If, as is suggested by Werner Hofmann and further argued by Adam Gopnik, it was caricature's focus on exploring the limits of visual expression which paved the way for the modernist preoccupation with the medium, for the subversion of the canon of beauty and for the search for alternative ways of seeing,[12] then credit must also be given to the specificity of the space of the café and the sense of 'uninhibited freedom', or rupture associated with it. Indeed, the practice of drawing caricatures directly on café walls, or on large canvases attached to them, was widespread in Europe around 1900, from Montmartre to Vilnius.[13] Not infrequently executed to music or as part of cabaret shows, caricature transgressed the boundaries of the visual media, entering the category of those art forms which could be performed and improvised in front of the audience, encouraging chance and the participation of the viewer.[14]

But, apart from the walls, the café interior also provided a plethora of other surfaces to be drawn upon, such as café tables, as well as paper napkins – the most ephemeral kind of record of an idea, a poem, or a caricature. Evidence of the use of a café table marble top for caricature making, pointing to the ephemeral nature of the resulting work, is given in a drawing by Rudolf Bacher, one of the members of an independent artistic group, the *Hagengesellschaft*, whose activities originated in informal meetings in the Café Sperl in Vienna in the 1880s. The drawing, of 1888, represents a group of anthropomorphised creatures with hedgehog heads and pencils in their hands, busily covering a round marble table top with works of an unknown nature. Another drawing at the bottom of the page shows the same table, now empty, being washed clean with a sponge and water by an anonymous pair of hands. As is claimed by Marian Bisanz-Prakken, the early humorous drawings of the *Hagengesellschaft* were instrumental for future formal experiments of the Viennese Secession, thus turning the Café Sperl into the cradle of art nouveau.

Worth mentioning at this point is the pervasiveness of the mode of parody in café society of the fin-de-siècle, which is characteristic not only for caricature, but also for other forms of café-art, such as cabaret chanson and cabaret performance, as well as the feuilleton. In fact, one might argue that caricature, sketched briefly at the café table, exaggerating certain features and details, shares much with the technique of the genre of the feuilleton, which, even if not of Viennese origin, thrived in Vienna during the era of Kraus and Altenberg. According to the trope which often recurs in biographies of the bohemian artist, a sketch hastily produced at the cafe table was frequently used as the preferred currency by which its author was able to pay the café bill.

All those forms of coexistence between café and caricature – the walls covered with images, the significance of café tables and their marble tops, as well as caricature as currency of exchange – would reappear in the context of café life in Kraków around 1900. Before Michalik's Den, the centre of bohemian life was the Café Paon (Peacock). Established in 1897, Paon was the favourite place of the 'damned poet' Stanisław Przybyszewski and a wide circle of his admirers. Its walls were tightly covered by portraits and other images drawn by Stanisław Wyspiański. A good supply of paper and crayons was available to its guests in a dedicated room which also housed a huge canvas to be covered with caricatures and short poems by the café's habitués. The café and the canvas, preserved today in the collections of the National Museum in Kraków, was the topic of a feuilleton by Tadeusz Boy-Żeleński, 'Nonszalancki Paon' ('The Nonchalant Peacock', 1927).[15]

Apart from being activated and framed within the space of the café, caricature also activates the image of the café within its own frame. Since the end of the nineteenth century the topic of the café interior has established itself both in high art and popular culture, rising to become a potent metaphor of modernity. It served as an apt frame for the mapping of social, cultural, political and ethnic divisions, distinguishing between 'us' and 'them', hence recurring as one of the favourite visual tropes amongst the political cartoons in satirical journals. Above all, it kept reappearing as an emblem of modern forms of social relationships, displacing the salon as the testing ground of modern manners, a suitable microcosm for revealing the difference and the lack of polite etiquette on the part of various minority groups. In the same vein, the theme of the café served as a virtual battleground between the sexes, providing an opportunity to insist on the masculine nature of modernity and to mark women entering this modern space as prostitutes or, at best, actresses. And yet, at the same time, as is argued by Tag Gronberg in the context of the Viennese coffeehouse, the public space of the café helped to undermine the opposition between masculinity and femininity.[16] The café was, finally, an instrumental space for negotiating the ways of encountering the Other.

'Forges of Intellect' and the 'Painters' Table' at Michalik's Den

The peculiar geography and shifts in Kraków's cultural leanings form an important background to my argument, and it is helpful to devote a short paragraph to them.[17] Although it was part of the Austrian half of the Dual Monarchy, Kraków's relationship to Vienna was ambiguous from the start. Granted the privilege of a Free State soon after the partitions of Poland, the city was incorporated into the Habsburg Empire on a permanent basis only in 1846. With Galicia's capital in Lemberg,[18] Kraków found itself literally marginalised on the northern edge of this remote imperial province. Its rapid decline was marked symbolically by the transformation of the Royal Castle on Wawel Hill, the ancient seat of Polish kings, into the Austrian army barracks. As it happened, this was also the period which, following the influx of officers and civil servants from the centre of the empire, witnessed the proliferation of cafés in the Viennese style in Kraków, sure signifiers of imperial domination.[19] In turn, the relaxation of Austrian rule as part of the wider concessions secured in 1867 from the Austrian Imperial administration following its defeat in the

Austria-Prussia war of 1866 created the opportunity for restoring the damaged pride of the city. Under the benevolent eye of Franz Joseph, Kraków rose to become the spiritual capital of the dispersed Polish lands, focusing eagerly on the conservation of its noble past. Newly established institutions, such as the National Museum, collected large historical canvases to preserve the memory of national glory and martyrdom, building up the taste for monuments and solemn patriotic funerals. The same period saw a growing aversion towards Jews. The director of the School of Fine Arts, Jan Matejko, whose authority over Kraków's cultural life was confirmed by Franz Joseph's visit to his study in 1880, publicly accused Jewish students two years later of using art for material gain instead of serving the Polish national cause.[20] By the end of the 1890s, however, the intensity of the preoccupation with the patriarchal past faded and the city refashioned itself dramatically as the capital of Young Poland.[21] Not only did it expand rapidly beyond its medieval walls (an expansion which largely took place under mayors of Jewish origin), but it also granted female students access to the university and adopted all kinds of urban fashions and pleasures, including bohemian black coats, electric streetcars, cinemas, cafés and illustrated journals, the new theatre and the new exhibition pavilion which, like Olbrich's building in Vienna, was meant to signify the independence of new artist groups.[22]

The first years of the new century also marked the period of yet another cultural revolt in Kraków, this time conducted on a smaller scale by modernists themselves, and targeting not just the philistine – who remained the main object of laughter and was often identified with the Jew – but mocking with equal gusto modernist solipsism, the cult of decadence and the sanctity of art. Remarkably, this late stage in the accelerated shift of modern identities is strongly associated with Michalik's Den, the home of the legendary Green Balloon cabaret (1905–1912) and the site of many debates which, indirectly, dealt with the shape of modernity.

While examining the relationship between Kraków and Vienna's modernist trajectories,[23] the question of the presence of the Viennese café in Kraków's urban matrix offers one possible approach. Undoubtedly, the role of the coffeehouse as a cultural institution and discursive formation was much stronger in Lemberg which, having been made the capital of Galicia in 1772, was far more likely to treat the 'Viennese café' almost as a signifier of its new metropolitan status.[24] Kraków's sentiments were more ambiguous. As asserted by Irena Homola-Skąpska, the author of the first text on the cultural significance of coffeehouses in Kraków in the nineteenth century, the Viennese style adopted in the mid-nineteenth century was associated with elegance and modern comforts. Former taverns and numerous patisseries were turned into cafés, which became more profitable, and were often run by women. Wooden benches gave way to smaller tables, glasses were replaced with coffee cups, interiors enlarged and smartened up by mirrors and curtains; newspapers on the rack, billiard and card tables completed the transformation.[25]

Not all the cafés in Kraków turned Viennese, however, and there was no shortage of other venues selling coffee and cakes, in no particular style but cheaper, less salubrious, more tolerant of alcohol, open for longer hours and more crowded. Among them was Café Schmidt, remembered for its excessive grubbiness which, apparently, was conducive to heated discussions lasting until the early hours.[26] A remarkably modern cartoon, entitled 'The Youngest Poland after the closure of Café Schmid' (Figure 6.2), gives an insight into the perceived identity of its habitués, identified, ironically, as the 'youngest' members of the Young Poland artistic movement – a group of drowsy young men, walking against the striped background of the sky, somewhat menacingly, with their hands in their pockets, raised shoulders and skull-like heads buried between them. This remarkable Munch-like drawing proves that caricature served at that time as a medium uniquely suited to record those attitudes, body language and dress which were not representable in other media, and that it is precisely

Figure 6.2 A. Dobrowolski, 'The Youngest Poland after the closing of Café Szmid', *Liberum Veto*, 1903.

caricature which helped to made them visible, expanding the range of visual regimes and disseminating modern identities.

Another place which attracted students of the Academy of Fine Arts was Café Koziara. The lack of sophistication of the interior of the latter was recorded in a drawing by Witold Wojtkiewicz, entitled 'The youngest bohemians stimulate their talents with coffee at Café Koziara', published in *Liberum Veto*, 1904. The drawing not only gives a glimpse of the extreme simplicity of the café decor, furnished with plain rectangle tables and chairs, its interior filled with steam and puffs of smoke, coffee being served in huge ordinary mugs rather than elegant cups, but it also records the strikingly unassuming demeanour of the four young artists around the table. The caption labels them as 'young bohemians' ('najmłodsza malarnia') but, instead of an image of a distinctive company of young artists, conveying an aura of the fashionable *ennui* or extravagance, Wojtkiewicz shows a group of four unremarkable figures, entirely oblivious of the requirements of the bohemian self-fashioning. Hunched in their chairs, they are bending over and clinging to their mugs of coffee as if this was their only hot meal of the day. Their dwarfed bodies display, almost demonstratively, signs of weariness and imperfection. If, nominally, the image represents a *café des artistes*, Wojtkiewicz takes an ironic stance towards the myth of bohemianism and the exceptionality of the artist, challenging it with his down-to-earth record of the ordinary.

Obviously, Café Koziara, as represented by Wojtkiewicz, did not aspire to the Viennese rank; moreover, it seems that 'Vienneseness' at that time was not universally desired amongst the bohemian circles in Kraków. Tadeusz Boy-Żeleński, the eyewitness and most famous bard of Kraków's *bohème* and also a prolific translator of French literature, was inclined to dismiss the Viennese style for its 'cheap' elegance, background music and, most of all, for its attractiveness for 'families and ladies'. He recorded his memories of Kraków's cafés in an essay entitled 'Kuźnie intelektu' (Forges of Intellect, 1931). 'Amongst this buzz and airlessness, blind and deaf to the outer world, two young men orate passionately in a corner, wrenching words from each other's mouths, smashing each other with arguments, waiting impatiently for the moment when the interlocutor pauses for breath'.[27] For Boy-Żeleński, the essential feature of the cafés was neither their furnishing, nor the availability of newspapers, but above all the atmosphere encouraging passionate debates on 'the most important spiritual matters', including Kant, Ibsen, the *Übermensch*, ethics and truth, conducted until the early hours, and in exclusively male company. Boy-Żeleński was not oblivious to Vienna's fame for café disputes and of Peter Altenberg and Karl Kraus as the heroes of the Viennese café *bohème*, as it was the bohemian, the subversive that he was most keen on. Importantly, the essay's title, 'Forges of Intellect', remained associated with the concept of café life in Polish literary discourse throughout the inter-war period, as would his defence of both café and intellect as bastions of masculinity.

Many significant coffeehouses opened in Kraków at the turn of the century, but Michalik's Den, set up in 1895 as a type of *Café-Konditorei* by a confectioner from Lemberg, Jan Michalik, rose to become a landmark in Polish cultural history. Unlike Café Paon which lasted just for a few years, Michalik's Den has survived until today. Its notoriety as the hub of the modernist *bohème*, the epicentre of Young Poland, stems to a large extent from the fame of the Green Balloon cabaret (1905–1912) which, modelled on Montmartre, challenged the boundaries of social permissiveness, targeting clericalism, bourgeois prudishness, while not avoiding the dearest myths of Polish modernism, such as the massive cult of the artist-genius.[28] The cabaret was turned into a legend by its co-creator, the already mentioned Boy-Żeleński in a series of his much reproduced feuilletons on the Kraków of 1900. He presented the cabaret as the ultimate act of the city's modern transformation, capable of intoxicating its old walls with alcohol and of combating its morbid obsession with the past with 'a boisterous laugh whose echoes reverberated through all of Poland'.[29] It certainly initiated the fashion for cabarets in other Polish cities in the first decades of the twentieth century, dubbed by Boy-Żeleński 'cabaretiasis'. In spite of its elitism, political indifference, and its role as a safety valve preventing an active protest against power and authorities, the cabaret has been widely acknowledged as one of the most remarkable cultural products of Young Poland.[30]

While celebrating the cabaret, Boy-Żeleński admitted that it owes its existence to the extraordinary source of creativity which built up at the so called 'painters' table' at the café, the meeting place of professors and students of the Academy of Fine Arts. Comparing the Green Balloon team to a spiritual congregation which set the tone of Kraków life, he wrote:

> Rather naturally, it was the painters table, which became the nucleus of this assembly. Painters form the closest communities, a camaraderie of the school and crafts which are absent in other arts; joint parties, joint lampooning and revolts. Mimetic talent is frequent amongst painters, so is a literary one; and rarely is there a painter deprived of a sense of humour. The sharpened powers of sight and the habit of observation helps to register the automatism of gestures, to notice the work of muscles under drapery and the element of bestiality under the human mask. Almost every artist is to an extent a caricaturist, and that generation was particularly abundant in this kind of talent: suffice to mention Sichulski and Frycz.[31]

The agency of the painters' table was testified to in visual terms by contemporary 'portraits' which either represented the table on its own, or with a group of artists sitting around it, thus elevating the café to a 'natural' space and an active component of the artistic group identity, on a par with the artist's study or a dealer's gallery.[32] However, despite Boy-Żeleński's acknowledgement of the significance of the painters' table and of caricature in particular in the phenomenal success of Michalik's café and the Green Balloon cabaret, the huge monographic literature on the subject has paid little attention to the visual arts and caricatures which still decorate the café walls.[33] This relative lack of scholarly interest is all the more surprising given the high status at that time of caricature, which was often undistinguishable from fine art. Around 1900, as is argued by Irena Kossowska in her study of modern graphic arts in Poland, graphic arts surpassed painting in the search for new aesthetic conventions and caricature played an integral part in this process, also offering scope for the self-reflection of modernism.[34] It was practised by major Polish artists, including Stanisław Wyspiański, Jacek Malczewski, Jan Stanisławski, Leon Wyczółkowski, Wojciech Weiss, Witold Wojtkiewicz, Karol Frycz and Kazimierz Sichulski. The majority of those artists were the painter's table regulars at Michalik's Den, and their production turned the interior of the whole café into a unique exhibition space for the ongoing display of caricatures and cartoons produced in situ, which were framed and mounted, or painted directly onto walls, as well as sent off by post on invitations to cabaret performances (Figure 6.3). An example of this production was the *Teka Melpomeny* (The Melpomene Portfolio, 1904), a set of forty or so prints with caricatures of actresses and actors in their contemporary productions staged at the Municipal Theatre nearby, made in cooperation by Stanisław Rzecki, Frycz, Wojtkiewicz and others. It was again Boy-Żeleński who in a cabaret song praising the café owner Jan Michalik as a patron of art, gave a lively account of the process in which artists' works, mostly caricatures, came to dominate the space of the café. He drew from the existing trope of artists' sketches as the way of paying their café bills ('take this kitsch, you can stick it to the wall, your venue will be done-up'), while alluding also to the commercial sobriety of the owner, who, having realised the marketing potential of art to attract large crowds to his premises, was now prepared to commission the same artists to re-decorate the whole space of the café, and even to pay them 'gold for those doodles'.[35]

Unsurprisingly, the refurbishment of the café space was entrusted to one of the most versatile regulars, the young caricaturist and stage designer Frycz, who worked in co-operation with the architect Jan Mączyński. His design transformed all elements of the interior, including furniture, with strangely elongated chair-backs, and large benches with curved sides, huge doorways embellished with gigantic scrolls, colourful stained glass, as well as elaborate wood panelling with spaces destined for wall paintings (Figure 6.1). As is argued by David Crowley, Frycz's 'fantastic café-salon', owed more 'to the literary themes … of interiority, immorality and decadence', as promoted by the bard of Young Poland Stanisław Przybyszewski, than to the 'pragmatic world of the Arts and Crafts' which was steadily developing in Kraków at the same time.[36] Agreeing with Crowley's argument on the 'art for the art's sake' aesthetics underpinning Frycz's design, I would claim that the sheer eccentricity of his café decor could also be seen in reference to his adoption of caricature as the master idiom. Both works share the operational strategy of over-determination, exaggeration of detail, and the tendency towards the arbitrary distortion of scale and proportions, often achieved by either squeezing or elongating the shapes. In fact, for Frycz, caricature was an art form which dominated his early career. Unlike the majority of his fellow artists, who went to study in Munich or Paris, Frycz trained in Vienna, enrolling in 1902 as Alfred Roller's pupil in the *Kunstgewerbschule*, and he became one of the most innovative and sought-after stage-designers in Polish theatre.[37]

The agency of the painter's table at Michalik's Den might finally be measured in terms of the collaboration of many of the café regulars with the most ambitious Polish satirical magazine of the period, *Liberum Veto*, similar to Munich's *Simplicissimus*. Published between 1904 and 1905, first in Kraków and then in

Figure 6.3 Witold Wojtkiewicz, Invitation to the Green Balloon Cabaret Evening on 9 February 1907, with caricature of Tadeusz Boy-Żeleński, Muzeum Narodowe, Kraków. Courtesy of the Museum.

Lemberg, it opposed the conservative press, providing a radical commentary on social, political and cultural matters, and was amply illustrated with cartoons, drawn by Frycz, Sichulski, Wojtkiewicz, as well as Henryk Uziembło, Stanisław Kuczborski, Władysław Jarocki, Stanisław Szreniawa-Rzecki, Frydeyk Pautsch and Antoni Stanisław-Procjałowicz. Arguably, some of their drawings might have been conceived or even executed at the café table.[38]

Returning to Boy-Żeleński's assessment of the centrality of the painter's table and the claim that the caricaturist resides in every artist, I would like to argue that in Michalik's Den, the 'painters' table' was in fact the 'caricaturists' table'. It was indeed caricature which constituted the privileged medium and the dominant mode of expression, acting as a binding agent, or a common denominator, for all kinds of artistic creativity which were taking place there. Displayed on walls, present in the highly mannered shapes of furniture and other elements of the café decor, the spirit of caricature also motivated the aesthetics of the cabaret performances, which were bent on the strategy of de-familiarisation, parody, impertinence and improvisation as well as the active participation of the audience. If Michalik's Den's aesthetics could be seen as a particular kind of *Gesamtkunstwerk*, it was caricature which dominated its score.

'Forges of Antisemitism' and Bastions of Masculinity

The second part of this text moves on to the issue of café and caricature as mediums of the disciplining modernity, though which new frameworks controlling social interaction and regulating insiders and outsiders was established. Arguably, the most pronounced difference between cafés in Vienna and Kraków was the ethnic identity of their guests. As we know from the research of Steven Beller, the presence of Jewish intellectuals in Vienna coffeehouses was predominant, in parallel with their leading roles in Viennese literary, music and philosophical modernism.[39] In contrast, in the multi-ethnic Kraków around 1900, the Jewish presence in literary and artistic cafés in the city centre is very difficult to establish, having been rendered almost invisible by mainstream historiography. Until the very recent debates on antisemitism in Poland, even the books written by historians of Jewish origins have tended to bypass the issue of the Jewish identity of many prominent Polish intellectuals and artists, as if following the assimilationist approach and accepting the primacy of civil choices rather than ethnic roots. A study on the ethnic mix of the café society in Kraków of this time has yet to be written, and my remarks are therefore of a preliminary nature.

The Jews constituted twenty-eight per cent of Kraków's population at that time (ca 25,000), and the percentage of people of Jewish origin was even higher amongst certain professional groups such as doctors (forty-three per cent).[40] As was established by Jerzy Malinowski, the author of the first study on Jewish artists in Poland, at that time Jewish students constituted a small but perceptible faction at the Academy of Fine Arts in Kraków,[41] but were still underrepresented in comparison to other free professions, such as editors, journalists, or historians. Matejko's antisemitic diatribe, mentioned earlier, is indicative of the anti-Jewish sentiments prevailing amongst the artists serving the patriotic case. At the same time, however, one of the best known Jewish artists, Maurycy Gottlieb, was Matejko's pupil, while his much younger brother Leopold Gottlieb belonged to the well-established Kraków elite. So did the architect Jan Zawiejski who, having trained in Vienna, became the city architect and the author of the only new café building in Kraków, commissioned by a Jewish merchant Drobner. Zawiejski designed it in an extravagant style which displayed all the 'crimes' of *le gout juif*.[42] The café, called Drobnerion, was destroyed by fire in 1907 just after it had been built[43] but, luckily, it had been memorialised before that by Frycz in his series of six large caricatures which, made for one of the first cabaret nights in November 1905, became part of the permanent display as seen in photographs of the café interior. The caricatures, all accompanied by short verses, contributed to the current controversies on the reconstruction of the Wawel castle, and have been analysed in detail by David Crowley.[44] In 1905, the castle was finally vacated by the Austrian Army, and the style in which it should be rebuilt became a matter of the utmost importance in the debates on national identity. Frycz's cartoons suggested a bewildering range of styles in which the castle could be rebuilt, from Viennese Secession style to Socialist (Figure 6.4). In his nuanced interpretation Crowley argued that, unlike the high art of the time, these sketches proved capable of exposing the political agendas which underpinned the competing claims on Polishness at the beginning of the twentieth century. The effects of Viennese domination were seen as almost benign and reduced to the excess of ornament applied absurdly to the medieval structure of the castle, spoiling it in a most irrational way, with Café Drobnerion taking place of the Cathedral. If some anti-Jewish sentiments were already perceivable in this image, the disturbing scale of the anti-socialist hysteria in Kraków at the time of the 1905 Russian revolution was fully revealed in Frycz's representation of a 'Socialist Wawel'. It imagined the cradle of Polishness as having been taken over by socialists and turned into a nightmarish smoke-belching factory, totally industrialised by Jewish capitalists who replaced the cathedral with a kosher slaughter house ('rzeźnia koszerna'), a women's bath house ('mikva'), as well as offices of a socialist newspaper *Naprzód* (Forward) just above the printing house, owned at that time by the Jewish publisher Naftali Telz. These competing visions of Polishness, could equally be interpreted as the articulation of competing versions of modernity, perceived as threatening and as imposed by the outsider figure of the Jew/socialist.[45] In his conclusion Crowley takes a sympathetic stance towards the caricatures, arguing that those sketches should not be considered as a direct projection of the cartoonist's fears or desires and that, to the contrary, they sought to expose and ridicule the contrasting political claims and loyalties, putting them in inverted commas as it were.

This issue is central for my own inquiry into the specificity of the medium of caricature and cartoon, almost ontologically predisposed to sum up and sharpen claims and opinions, while maintaining an ironic distance on the part of the creator. This propensity to oscillate between the deceptive directness of the 'first person' claim and the detachedness of the 'third person' address, engenders constant travelling between meaning and counter-meaning, between familiar signifiers and their unfamiliar juxtapositions, both imposing and denying the authorial presence, and forcing the reader to complete the process of semiosis. The audience therefore plays a paramount role in fixing the meaning, and, as is to be suspected, the café frequented by the same guests, or, better, a cabaret performance by invitation, provided an occasion for a collective completion of meaning.

Figure 6.4 After Karol Frycz, 'Socialist Wawel' (1905), postcard 1946. Wawel Castle, Kraków. Courtesy of Wawel Castle.

This was precisely the case with cartoons in Michalik's Den. Although I fully sympathise with Crowley's argument on the possible parallel between the Wawel cartoons by Frycz and liberal pamphlets by the linguist Jan Baudouin de Courtenay opposing antisemitism, both using the parodic mode to bring attention to the blatant misrepresentation of the besieged minority, I am less certain about the prevalence of the same militant liberal attitudes amongst Michalik's Den's habitués. The rigid elitist profile of the Green Balloon cabaret, which imposed a very strict selection in terms of which guests were invited to its performances – even if that selection was based on the principle of revolt against the established norms rather than on ethnic or religious criteria – was not conducive to an inclusive ethos. While the architect Zawiejski was welcomed to this club, other prominent Jewish intellectuals, such as the art critic Stanisław Lack, or the historian Wilhelm Feldman have hardly or never been listed among the guests of the Green Balloon cabaret. The latter, a prolific writer, critic and the author of a controversial study of Polish contemporary literature, became instead one of the favourite targets of cabaret songs, which mocked not only his occasional blunders in literary criticism and his reputed lack of a sense of humour, but also one of the standard pointers of difference, his Jewish accent. This, in turn, provoked Feldman's series of articles sharply condemning the triviality of cabaret and its blunt indifference to the tragic events of the revolution of 1905, which he published in his own journal *Krytyka* (Critic), one of the most politically engaged and influential literary monthlies in Galicia (1901–1914).[46]

Nonetheless, it would be simplistic to accuse the Green Balloon cabaret of antisemitism, given the liberal outlook of many of its creators who, like Boy-Żeleński, would be soon vilified for his radicalism as an 'artificial Jew' by Polish nationalists.[47] And yet, the impossibility of confirming the Jewish presence at the café table might be linked, retrospectively, with the rise of modern antisemitism, and the associated intensification of anti-Jewish prejudices in fin-de-siècle Kraków. The emergent antisemitic press, such as *Kurier Polski* (The Polish Courier, 1889–1893) and *Głos Narodu* (The People's Voice, established in 1893), disseminated and naturalised opinions about Jewish criminality and conspiracy to take over Polish lands, Polish cities and free professions.[48] We may even assume that the derogatory jokes about Jews, which had long ago become commonplace and which were not strange even to the progressive *Liberum Veto*, might have actually been produced at Michalik's painters' table, frequented by the same caricaturists (Figure 6.5).[49]

Some of the opponents of antisemitism, such as the leading Polish feminist, the novelist and the playwright Gabriela Zapolska, made an explicit connection between the nationalistic press and the world of Krakovian cafés. In one of her novels entitled *Anty-semitnik* (Antisemite, 1897) she went as far as labelling one of them (leaving no clues as to which one) as a 'forge of antisemitism', thus forming a matrix associating the buzz and heat of the café interior with the process of intensified creativity. Zapolska's dark image of café life does not imply a comfortable space which is particularly suitable for disputes about spiritual matters, but to the contrary, invokes a repelling vision of a 'dark den', a breeding ground for the antisemitic slur, 'saturated with smoke and the murmur of gossip', with tables covered by linen stained with cheap alcohol and the remnants of food, the distasteful interior whose décor consists of unattractive mirrors which reflect the pile of empty hats on console tables in front of them and garish posters advertising a satirical event; amongst the guests pale, fatigued journalists who, having gambled their monthly wages overnight, now scribble hurriedly on the marble tops their pre-ordained reviews persecuting selected theatres, actors and directors, in the required antisemitic vein: 'He knew that he had to provide the *Kurier Narodowy* with a sensational piece about some Jewish villain, something about usury and its terrible effects – in short, something completely "new" and "piquant" on the subjects known and used by all those organs that supported themselves by rousing passions and fanning racial hatred'.[50]

Zapolska's novel was serialised in Kraków's most ambitious cultural weekly *Życie* (1897–1898) and her phrase identifying cafés as 'forges' of antisemitism may well have been noted by Boy-Żeleński and may indeed have inspired his use of the forge metaphor in his own famous account of café life in Kraków, ten years after his move to Warsaw.[51] While dwelling on the capacity of the café as the 'Forge of Intellect', he changed the meaning of the phrase entirely by displacing ethnic hatred as the final product with intellect. Although there was no shortage of other pronouncements commenting on the darker sides of café life as well as modernity in its complex entanglement with Jewishness, it was Boy-Żeleński's version of the metaphor of the forge, stressing the intellectual ferment while bypassing the issue of antisemitism, which remained hegemonic.

Z roku na rok zawsze w bród
Kuracyuszów polskich wód;
W oryentalny strojni brud
Starej rasy szerzą smród

Zanurzają się raz wraz
W mineralnej wody gaz
Zdrój wypiliby na raz
Gdyby tylko mieli czas.

Figure 6.5 Karol Frycz, 'The Jews at Polish Waters', *Liberum Veto*, 1903.

Equally problematic today is Boy-Żeleński's identification of Kraków's cafés with bastions of masculinity and his denial of the female presence. Indeed, his claim (made retrospectively in 1931) that many hours-long disputes about Kant are unsuitable for women who 'would not be capable of bearing them', ignores the fact that in 1897 women won access to study philosophy at the universities in Kraków and Lemberg.[52] Besides, as is confirmed by the memoirs of the Jagiellonian University's female students of this period, lunch-time breaks at Michalik's Den belonged to their almost daily ritual, and were considered to be as benign as walking along Kraków's green ring.[53] Other sources also testify to the increasing female presence in Kraków's cafés from the 1880s, and the photographs of the Carnival Ball at Michalik's Den record a good number of women taking part.[54]

A feminist approach to Boy-Żeleński's account of Kraków's cafés and to the texts of the Green Balloon cabaret extends beyond the framework of this paper, but a closer look would no doubt expose the blatantly sexist premises of his provocative anti-prudishness. The reduction of women to the type of the Hogarthian seduced maid, or to the puppet of a Suffragette, with her hair cut short and ready to be mocked, stood alongside the image of the iconic Jew Feldman during the Green Balloon cabaret's performances. And yet, even if the figure of the Suffragette was firmly placed within the staple range of comical Others, its appearance during the cabaret's nights did acknowledge the rise of the feminist movement in Kraków. It is also the case that Boy-Żeleński makes an uneasy target for a feminist attack because of his life-long campaign for the improvement of the status of women in Polish society, calling for civil marriage and divorce, as well as access to contraception and legal abortion.

Caricature and the Jew in a Café

Coming to my conclusions, I do not want to claim that Michalik's Den should be studied today primarily as a forge of antisemitism and misogyny rather than as the forge of intellect and anti-philistine outbursts of laughter. Inevitably, the Green Balloon cabaret, no matter how liberal and how subversive it was in terms of sexual mores, was at the same time the product of a world dominated by Gentile men, and therefore both the presence of Jews and women had to be mediated by the rules of the dominant discourse and the dominant representational codes, either moulding real people into the pre-existing roles of the Others, or rendering them invisible.

I do want to claim, however, that, remarkably, it is caricature which made up for the blind spots of other forms of discourse, capable of registering the presence of both Jews and women within the space of the masculinised bohemian café. If the specificity of the medium, as described earlier, lies in its effectiveness in both construing and exaggerating class, ethnic and gender differences in order to define the boundary between Self and Other, the same predisposition makes it also capable of recording those aspects of reality which cannot be represented in any other form, of making the invisible visible. If then the Jewish or female presence in the café could not have been recorded in the painting of this period in Poland for lack of a suitable representational code, and if ethnic differences were not visible on a snapshot photograph of the carnival ball, then it was the caricature which stepped in as precisely that medium which was capable of noticing and marking the Others, and thus introducing them into the image of the café and legitimising their participation in modern life.

I wish to conclude this text with a caricature of a bohemian café, drawn by Witold Wojtkiewicz, which provides a striking counter-point to Boy-Żeleński's mythography (Figure 6.6). Wojtkiewicz, a regular of Michalik's Den, was one of the most unfathomable artists of the Polish fin-de-siècle, who began his short-lived career as an author of satirical illustrations for periodicals and postcards.[55] Like Baudelaire's Monsieur G., he was a passionate lover of crowds and the passing moments of modern life, captivated by the new angles of vision which would rarely be noted or considered at the time by high art. He would represent people dancing the cake-walk, pensioners in public parks, moving increasingly towards the topic of human misery, continuously obsessed with ugliness elevated to an aesthetic category, with pathological bodies, embarrassed sexuality,

Figure 6.6 Witold Wojtkiewicz, *Bohemians,* 1903. Muzeum Narodowe, Warsaw. Courtesy of the Museum.

infantilised adults, eroticised children, marionettes, clowns and mental asylums. This image of a café comes from an early period of his activity, and was first published in June 1903, just before his move to Kraków to begin his studies at the Academy of Fine Arts.[56]

The drawing provides a complex ironic comment on the modernist myth of bohemianism, and its primary venue – an overcrowded café, registering both the presence of women and Jews. In contrast to the usual assembly of the solitary newspapers readers, the dominant code within the larger theme of the café, Wojtkiewicz's interior presents a conversation piece, fragmented into disjointed narratives that unfold at small tables, with coffee cups to sustain creative thought, and trails of tobacco smoke to mark their meandering routes. Satirical magazines on the racks and glitter on the floor complete the perception of urban pleasures. Two men by the table on the left appear to be discussing a text or drawing lying on the table: one of them examines it with great intensity; the other one, standing by the table, looks the most bohemian: he is wearing a short Parisian coat, a scarf, and a soft hat. His large nose alludes to his Jewishness. Although he might have been standing there for a while, perhaps waiting for a decision from the other man, there are no signs of his diminished confidence. On the contrary, he appears self-assured, his body well balanced; while smoking a cigar he points to something on the piece of paper. There is no shortage of women either. Two of them, plain and deprived of any signifiers of sexual allure, are chattering over a coffee. In contrast, a lonely woman on the right, with a heavily made-up face, might conform to the image of a *demi-monde*: she looks as if she is waiting for her companion who must have left an issue of the contemporary satirical journal *Bocian* (Stork) on the empty chair opposite. The woman in the middle, equally seductive but entirely relaxed, is engaged in a conversation with a man who is evidently overpowered by her charms.

Is this a caricature which warns against the subversion of dominant social norms by the bohemians, and thus upholds the social codes which apply to women and Jews in the 'normal' world? This might be suggested by the subtitle, 'Actresses' stock exchange', given to this drawing when it was published in Warsaw's most respectable illustrated journal *Tygodnik Ilustrowany* (Illustrated Weekly), which would not question the standard regimes of representing women and Jews in a café. The title indeed trims off the excess of meaning, marginalises the Jewish figures, and reduces the richness of the world presented in this café to a comment on actresses in search of jobs. Or, is it instead a socially committed drawing which makes the invisible visible, approves of and legitimises modern liberties? Looking at this caricature in the context of Wojtkiewicz's art, his close friendship with contemporary Jewish artists, and his feelings for the underprivileged, disempowered, condemned and rejected, I believe that the latter is the case. Both café as the topic and caricature as the medium played primary roles in Wojtkiewicz's own artistic development, confirming their significance as factors of modernist rupture, and their primary roles in the hunt for new themes and metaphors, for modern identities and modern bodies, and for the new regimes of seeing, as much aesthetic as social.

Notes

1. Charles Baudelaire, 'On the Essence of Laughter and, in General, on the Comic in the Plastic Arts', in Jonathan Mayne (ed.), *The Painter of Modern Life and Other Essays*, trans. Jonathan Mayne, London 1995 (1st edn 1964), 147–165, and Charles Baudelaire, 'Some French Caricaturists: Carle Vernet – Pigal – Charlet – Daumier – Monnier – Grandville – Gavarni – Trimolet – Traviès – Jacque', in Baudelaire, *The Painter of Modern Life*, 166–186. The importance of the essays on laughter and on caricature in Baudelaire's aesthetics of modernity is argued persuasively in Michele Hannoosh, *Baudelaire and Caricature: From the Comic to an Art of Modernity*, Pennsylvania 1992.

2. The decision has been taken to refer to the city of Kraków by its Polish name, reflecting the Polish-centric subject matter of this essay. In around 1900 the city fell within the Austrian half of the Dual Monarchy and was known in German as Krakau. English speakers may also know the city as Cracow.

3. Jan Paweł Gawlik, *Powrót do Jamy*, Kraków 1961, 54. For more reflections on Kraków around 1900 and its cultural relationship with Paris (seen as desirable) and Vienna (often perceived as oppressive and destructive), see essays by Tadeusz Boy-Żeleński, and especially 'Prawy Brzeg Wisły' (*Rive Gauche* on the Vistula River), in Tadeusz Boy-Żeleński, *Znaszli ten Kraj? … Cyganeria Krakowska* (1931), Tomasz Weiss (ed.), Warsaw 2004, 3–11. For the significance of the Viennese culture in Kraków, see Larry Wolff, 'Dynastic Conservatism and Poetic Violence in Fin-de-Siècle Cracow: The Habsburg Matrix of Polish Modernism', *The American Historical Review*, 106(3), 2001, 735–764.

4. For a detailed description of Jama Michalikowa, see Zenon Pruszyński, *Jama Michalika, Lokal 'Zielonego Balonika'*, Kraków 1930. An inestimable source for studies on Kraków's cafés and on Jama Michalikowa are essays by Tadeusz Boy-Żeleński, 'Kuźnie Intelektu' (1931), 'Jan Apolinary' (1931), 'Legenda Zielonego Balonika z perspektywy ćwierćwiecza' (1930), reprinted in Boy-Żeleński, *Znaszli ten Kraj*, 111–119; 119–127, 241–256. Amongst post-1945 studies, see Jan Paweł Gawlik, *Powrót do Jamy*, Kraków 1961; Tomasz Weiss, *Legenda i Prawda Zielonego Balonika*, Kraków 1987; Bolesław Faron, *Jama Michalika: Przewodnik Literacki*, Kraków 1997; Jakub A. Malik, 'Bal w cukierni. Zielony Balonik – fenomen młodopolskiej kultury śmiechu', in S. Fita and J.A. Malik (eds), *Wśród tułaczy i wędrowców. Studia młodopolskie*, Lublin 2001, 205–235. For a pioneering study in English on Michalik's café and its decor, see David Crowley, *National Style and Nation-State: Design in Poland from the Vernacular Revival to the International Style*, Manchester and New York 1992, 35–36, and David Crowley, 'Castles, Cabarets and Cartoons: Claims on Polishness in Kraków Around 1905', in Anna Kwilecka and Francis Ames-Lewis (eds), *Art and National Identity in Poland and England*, London 1996, 103–118, the latter text republished in Malcolm Gee, Tim Kirk and Jill Steward (eds), *The City in Central Europe: Culture and Society from 1800 to the Present*, Aldershot 1999, 101–122.

5. For the term 'disciplining modernity', informed by Foucault's analysis of the disciplinary society, see, for example, Gearóid Ó Tutathail, '(Dis)placing Geopolitics: Writing on the Maps of Global Politics', *Society and Space* 12(1), 1994, 537; Pamela Caughie (ed.), *Disciplining Modernism*, New York 2010.

6. Steven Beller, *Vienna and the Jews 1867–1938: A Cultural History*, Cambridge 1989, 40–41, 214–217 and ff; also Steven Beller's contribution to this volume.
7. There is a huge literature on the Muhammad cartoons controversy: see Tariq Modood et al., *The Danish Cartoon Affair: Free Speech, Racism, Islamism and Integration*, a special issue of *International Migration*, 44(5), 2006; David Keane, 'Cartoon Violence and Freedom of Expression', *Human Rights Quarterly*, 30(4), 2008, 845–875; also Katarzyna Murawska-Muthesius, 'The *Yyllands-Posten* Muhammad Cartoons Controversy: Racism and "Cartoon-Work" in the Age of the World Wide Web', in Graham Huggan and Ian Law (eds), *Racism Postcolonialism Europe*, Liverpool 2009, 148–161.
8. Markman Ellis, *The Coffeehouse: A Cultural History*, London 2004; Martha Banta, *Barbaric Intercourse: Caricature and the Culture of Conduct, 1841–1936*, Chicago and London 2003, 1–17. On caricature and modern art, see Adam Gopnik, 'Caricature', in Kirk Varnedoe, Adam Gopnik, *High & Low: Modern Art and Popular Culture*, New York 1991, 100–151.
9. David Kunzle, 'Between Broadsheet Caricature and "Punch": Cheap Newspaper Cuts for the Lower Classes in the 1830s', *Art Journal*, 43(4), 1983 (The Issue of Caricature), 339–346.
10. Charles Baudelaire, 'The Painter of Modern Life', in Baudelaire, *The Painter of Modern Life*, 12.
11. An earlier record of the covering of the walls of the artists' tavern with caricatures by members of the bohemian Dutch painters' society in Rome the Bentvueghels, see David A. Levine, 'Pieter van Laer's Artists' Tavern: An Ironic Commentary on Art', in H. Bock and T. Gaehtgens (eds), *Hollaendische Genremalerei im 17. Jahrhundert: Symposium Berlin I, Jahrbuch Preussischer Kulturbesitz*, 1987(4), 169–191.
12. Adam Gopnik, 'High and Low: Caricature, Primitivism, and the Cubist Portrait', *Art Journal*, 43(4), 1983 (The Issue of Caricature), 371–376; Gopnik, 'Caricature', in Marie-Noelle Delorme et al. (eds), *Picasso: From Caricature to Metamorphosis of Style*, Barcelona 2003. For the Viennese context, see Marian Bisanz-Prakken, 'Die Hagengesellschaft: Eine Unbenkannte Vorgeschichte der Secession', in *Heiliger Frühling: Gustav Klimt und die Anfänge der Wiener Secession 1895–1905*, Vienna 1999, 35–39.
13. Many instances pointing to the dynamic interdependency between caricature, café, music, cabaret and other media, and on the performative aspects of caricature making, can be found in Philip Denis Cate and Mary Show (eds), *The Spirit of Montmartre: Cabarets, Humor, and the Avant-Garde, 1875–1905*, New York 1996, and Harold B. Segel, *Turn-of-the-Century Cabaret: Paris, Barcelona, Berlin, Munich, Vienna, Cracow, Moscow, St. Petersburg, Zurich*, New York and Oxford 1987. A caricature by Stanisław Bohusz-Siestrzeńcewicz of 1911, showing a performance in a Vilnius cabaret *Ach* with a female artist drawing a row of galloping horses to the strains of a guitar played by a musician dressed as Pierrot, is reproduced by Laima Lauckaite, 'La Belle Epoque in Vilnius', *Lituanus: Lithuanian Quarterly Journal of Arts and Sciences*, 53(4), 2006, online at http://www.lituanus.org/2006/06_4_03_Lauckaite.html, accessed on 20 August 2008.
14. Caricature performed in front of the audience was capable of transgressing the limitations of the visual arts, as defined by Lessing, who distinguished the arts of space from the arts of time. Unsurprisingly, the classicist Lessing expressed his profound distaste towards the medium of caricature which obtains 'likeness by exaggerating the deformities of the model'; see Gotthold Ephraim Lessing, *Laocoön* (1766), in Lorenz Eitner (ed.), *Neoclassicism and Romanticism: 1750–1850: Sources and Documents, Vol. 1*, London 1971, 22. On performativity and visual arts, see Evelyn Welch, 'Painting as Performance in the Italian Renaissance Court', in Stephen Campbell (ed.), *Artists at Court: Image-Making and Identity, 1300–1550*, Boston 2004, 9–18. On the 'synaesthetic impulse' of modern art, see Simon Shaw-Miller, *Visible Deeds of Music: Art and Music from Wagner to Cage*, New Haven 2002.

15. Tadeusz Boy-Żeleński, 'Nonszalancki Paon' (1927), in *Znaszli ten Kraj*, 158–162; see also Barbara Małkiewicz, '"Paon" – Pierwsza Kawiarnia Artystyczna Młodej Polski', *Rozprawy Muzeum Narodowego w Krakowie*, Seria Nowa, 2, 2004, 107–122 (I want to thank Ula Kozakowska for drawing my attention to this article).

16. Tag Gronberg, *Vienna, City of Modernity, 1890–1914*, Oxford 2007, 89.

17. On Kraków's history and its shifting political allegiances, see Jacek Purchla, *Cracow in the European Core*, trans. Tersea Bałuk-Ulewiczowa, Kraków 2008.

18. Lwów in Polish, and Lviv in Ukranian.

19. Irena Homola-Skąpska, 'Krakowskie Cukiernie i Kawiarnie w XIX Wieku', *Annales Universitatie Mariae Curie-Sklodowska, Lublin- Polonia*, 51(5), 1996, 53–54.

20. Matejko's anti-Jewish speech was published by his pupil and adviser, the militant antisemite Marian Gorzkowski, in the conservative paper *Czas* in 1882 (Marian Gorzkowski, 'Ze Szkoły Sztuk Pięknych', *Czas*, 20 October 1882, 2–3); see Andrzej Żbikowski, *Dzieje Żydów w Polsce: Ideologia Antysemicka 1848–1914: Wybór Tekstów źródłowych*, Warsaw 1994, 119–121. See also Ezra Mendelsohn, *Painting a People: Maurycy Gottlieb and Jewish Art*, Hannover and London 2002, 205, and Dariusz Konstantynów, '"Matejko, Our Master" and Anti-Semites', *Kwartalnik Historii Żydów*, 2, 2007, 164–198.

21. On the art of Young Poland, see amongst others, Jan Cavanaugh, *Out Looking In: Early Modern Polish Art, 1890–1918*, Berkeley, Los Angeles, London 2000; Stefania Krzysztofowicz-Kozłowska, *Sztuka Młodej Polski*, Warsaw 2004; for an alternative interpretation, see Anna Brzyski, 'What's in a Name? Artist-Run Exhibition Groups and the Branding of Modern Art in Fin de Siècle Europe', *19th Century Art Worldwide* 6(2) (Fall 2007), http://www.19thc-artworldwide.org/index.php/autumn07/126–whats-in-a-name-artist-run-exhibition-societies-and-the-branding-of-modern-art-in-fin-de-siecle-europe (accessed on 20 August 2008).

22. The most engaging account of the modern transformation of Kraków is provided by the essays in Boy-Żeleński's *Znaszli ten kraj.*

23. Kraków's Austrian links were examined from various angles by Jacek Purchla, *Jak Powstał Nowoczesny Kraków*, Kraków 1979; Roman Taborski, *Polacy we Wiedniu*, Wrocław 1992; Lawrence Orton, 'The Formation of Modern Cracow (1866–1914)', *Austrian History Yearbook*, 19/20(1), 1983–1984, 105–117; and Larry Wolff, 'Dynastic Conservatism', 2001.

24. Józef Mayen, 'Gawędy o Lwowskich Kawiarniach' (1934), *Rocznik Lwowski*, 2002, online at http://www.lwow.home.pl/rocznik/kawiarnie.html, accessed on 20 August 2008; Bogusław Bakuła, 'Świat Naukowo-Artystyczny Lwowskiej "Knajpy" lat 30', *Eurozine*, 17(08), 2004, online at http://www.eurozine.com/search.html, accessed on 20 August 2008. See also the chapter by Shaschar Pinsker in this volume.

25. Homola–Skąpska, 'Krakowskie Cukiernie', 54–55.

26. Boy-Żeleński, 'Kuźnie Intelektu', in *Znaszli ten Kraj*, 117. This essay gives a lively account of Kraków's cafés circa 1900.

27. Boy-Żeleński, 'Kuźnie Intelektu', in *Znaszli ten Kraj*, 115.

28. The Green Balloon cabaret critique of modernist myths could be compared to the merciless parody of the most exalted tropes of Viennese Secession performed by Berthold Löffler in the short-lived satirical journal *Quer Sacrum*, as analysed in Julie M. Johnson, 'Athena Goes to the Prater: Parodying Ancients and Moderns at the Vienna Secession', *Oxford Art Journal*, 26(2), 2003, 47–70.

29. Boy-Żeleński, 'Legenda Zielonego Balonika', in *Znaszli ten Kraj*, 252.

30. For a critique of the cabaret on socio-political grounds, see, among others, Wilhelm Feldman, 'Najmłodsi w Literaturze Polskiej: Piosenkarz "Zielonego Balonika"', *Krytyka*, 2, 1910, 329–330; Adam Łada-Cybulski, *Psyche Polska w Kabarecie*, Kraków 1911; Weiss, *Legenda i Prawda Zielonego Balonika*; Tomasz Stępień, *O Satyrze*, Katowice 1996, 136–149.

31. Boy-Żeleński, 'Szał', in *Znaszli ten Kraj*, 129–130.

32. Alfons Karpiński, 1905, The National Museum in Wrocław. Another 'portrait' of the table on its own was made by Karol Frycz, now in the collections of The National Museum in Kraków.

33. Zenon Pruszyński's description of the interior of Michalik's Den of 1930 lists 232 objects; Bolesław Faron's guide of 1995 includes 106. The absence of a monographic study devoted to the caricatures was noted by Weiss in his magisterial analysis of Jama Michalikowa and the cabaret on 1987 (Weiss, *Legenda i Prawda Zielonego Balonika*, 405), and, surprisingly, a major study on the topic has still not been produced. The most comprehensive information, with many good illustrations, is to be found in the catalogue of the exhibition of caricature of Young Poland in Wojciech Chmurzyński, Grażyna Godziejewska, Muzeum Karykatury w Warszawie, *Sztuka Karykatury Okresu Młodej Polski 1890–1918*, Warsaw 2003.

34. On the significance of graphic arts, including caricature, in Polish art worlds around 1900, see Irena Kossowska, 'A Smile of Modernism: Polish Caricature: 1900–1914', *Centropa*, 4(1), 2004, 39–47; also Irena Kossowska and Łukasz Kossowski, 'Uśmiech Końca Wieku', in *Sztuka Karykatury Okresu Młodej Polski*, 10–16; Irena Kossowska, *Narodziny Polskiej Grafiki Artystycznej*, Warsaw 2000, 40–42.

35. Tadeusz Boy-Żeleński, 'Nowa Pieśń o Rydzu, czyli Jak Jan Michalik Został Mecenasem Sztuki, czyli Niezbadane są Drogi Opatrzności' (1910), in *Słówka* (1931), Warsaw 2002, 123–125. On caricatures offered to Jan Michalik in lieu of payment, see also Pruszyński, *Jama Michalikowa*, 6.

36. Crowley, *National Style and Nation-State*, 35–36.

37. Lidia Kuchtówna, *Karol Frycz*, Warsaw 2004, 46–54.

38. On *Liberum Veto*, see Weiss, *Legenda i Prawda Zielonego Balonika*, 74–112.

39. See note 15.

40. Andrzej Żbikowski, *Żydzi Krakowscy i Ich Gmina w Latach 1869–1919*, Warsaw 1994; also Weiss, *Legenda i Prawda Zielonego Balonika*, 38–40.

41. Jerzy Malinowski, *Malarstwo i Rzeźba Żydów Polskich w XIX i XX Wieku*, Warsaw 2000, 76.

42. On Jan Zawiejski, born into a Jewish family as Jan Baptysta Feintuch, see the monographic study by Jacek Purchla, *Teatr i Jego Architekt/ Das Theater und Sein Architekt*, Kraków 1993. In the words of Jacek Purchla, Café Drobner was a blend of the features specific to the Viennese school of Otto Wagner and the style of Guimard's Metro pavilions in Paris. On the contemptuous attitude of Viennese modernism towards the excessive ornament associated with the 'Jewish taste', see Gronberg, *Vienna City of Modernity*, 89.

43. Purchla, *Teatr i jego architekt*, 97.

44. Crowley, 'Castles, cabarets and cartoons'. All Frycz's cartoons are reproduced there. See also Agnieszka Janczyk, 'Projekty Odnowienia z cyklu "Wawele"', in *Polski Korona: Motywy Wawelskie w Sztuce Polskiej 1800–1939*, Kraków 2005, 238–249.

45. Importantly, images preceded the texts of songs, which were later added to cartoons, and the primacy of the image over the word is also characteristic of certain types of café art.

46. Feldman, 'Najmłodsi w Literaturze Polskiej'; see also Weiss, *Legenda i Prawda Zielonego Balonika*, 388–396.

47. Antony Polonsky, 'Why did they Hate Tuwim and Boy so Much?', in Robert Blobaum (ed.), *Anti-Semitism and its Opponents in Modern Poland*, Ithaca and London 2005, 189–209, in particular 205–209. And yet, a close collaborator of the cabaret at the early stages of its existence, Alfred Neuwert Nowaczyński, famous for the sharpness of his pen (he coined the term *Gladiolus tavernalis* an equivalent for the German *Kaffeehauspflanze* which refers metaphorically to the habit of 'establishing roots' in a café by their guests), turned into one of the most aggressive antisemitic campaigner, see his *Mocarstwo Anonimowe: (Ankieta w Sprawie żydowskiej)*, Warsaw 1921. Also Weiss, *Legenda i Prawda Zielonego Balonika*, 112–

148; Jakub A. Malik, *Adolf Nowaczyński: Między Modernizmem a Pozytywizmem*, Lublin 2002.

48. Wolff, 'Dynastic Conservatism'; Irena Kamińska-Szmaj, *Judzi, Zohydza, ze Czci Odziera: Język Propagandy Politycznej w Prasie 1919–1923*, Wrocław 1994; also Blobaum (ed.), *Anti-Semitism and its Opponents in Modern Poland*.

49. Karol Frycz, [The Jews at Polish Waters], *Liberum Veto*, 190. An anonymous text below the drawing conveys a strongly antisemitic message: 'Plenty of them every year/ The visitors to Polish spa/Covered in oriental dirt/They evoke the smell of the old race// They immerse once and then/ In mineral water gas/ They would drink the whole source/ If they only have time'.

50. Gabriela Zapolska, *Anti-Semite* (1897/8), trans. Harold B. Segel in *Stranger in Our Midst: Images of the Jew in Polish Literature*, Ithaca and London 1996, 236–270; see also Harold B. Segel, 'The Jew in Polish and Russian Literatures', *The Sarmatian Review*, 22(1), 2002.

51. Boy-Żeleński, 'Kuźnie Intelektu'.

52. Dobrochna Kalwa's entry on Kazimiera Bujwidowa in Francisca de Haan, Krasimira Daskalova and Anna Loutfi, *Biographical Dictionary of Women's Movements and Feminisms in Central, Eastern and South Eastern Europe: 19th and 20th Centuries*, Budapest 2006, 85–88; Grażyna Kubica, *Siostry Malinowskiego, czyli Kobiety Nowoczesne na Początku XX Wieku*, Kraków 2006.

53. Urszula Perkowska, 'Czas Wolny w Kulturze Studenckiej na Przełomie XIX i XX w. (w świetle Pamiętników i Korespondencji Krakowskich Studentek', in Anna Żarnowska and Andrzej Szwarc (eds), *Kobieta i Kultura Czasu Wolnego*, Warsaw 2001, 286.

54. Photographs are reproduced by Gawlik, *Powrót do Jamy*.

55. Wiesław Juszczak, *Wojtkiewicz i Nowa Sztuka*, Warsaw 1965; Jerzy Ficowski, *Wiold Wojtkiewicz: W Sierocińcu świata*, Łowicz 1996; Irena Dżurkowa-Kossowska, 'Cykl "Rok 1905" Witolda Wojtkiewicza', *Rocznik Historii Sztuki*, 19, 1992, 303–353; Elżbieta Charazińska, *Ceremonie: Witold Wojtkiewicz (1879–1909)*, Warsaw 2004; Irena Kossowska, *Witold Wojtkiewicz (1876–1909)*, Warsaw 2006.

56. Although the drawing is often represented as a depiction of Michalik's Den – see, for example, the recent literary guide to Michalik's Den (Faron, *Jama Michalika*, 33) – there is no concrete basis for this attribution and it is likely that it simply represents an interior of one of the numerous cafés in Warsaw.

Chapter 7

The Coffeehouse in Zagreb at the Turn of the Nineteenth and Twentieth Centuries
Similarities and Differences with the Viennese Coffeehouse

Ines Sabotič

Introduction

'In Coffeehouses about Coffeehouses (Reflections around a Table)' is the title of a feuilleton by Nikola Polić, one of the famous young *Stammgäste* of Zagreb's coffeehouses. Published in 1921, it is a kind of résumé, balance sheet, or testimony to a lost world and way of life: 'Oh, how many nice institutions were destroyed by Mr War!'[1] The war woke up many a conscience, dispelled illusions, and changed the geography of Europe. Croatia no longer belonged to the Dual Monarchy of Austria-Hungary but to the Kingdom of Serbs, Croats and Slovenes. Polić reflected on the coffeehouse as an important element of Zagreb's pre-war culture. This study of the coffeehouse is comparable to the exploration of the coffeehouse as a focus of reminiscences, discussed by Gilbert Carr in chapter two of this volume, and to its metonymic function in relation to literary culture. By focusing on the associations the coffeehouse had for writers in Zagreb and on its role in urban life, we can discover a portrait of coffeehouse life, far removed from cosmopolitan Vienna. In addition, in the context of Croatian national issues, the coffeehouse emerges as a paradigm through which aspirations and anxieties about Croatian culture and society are played out in relation to dominant cultural models from Vienna and later from Paris.

In the above mentioned text, Polić observed that the Zagrebian coffeehouses followed the 'Western' model and not 'the eastern one, which fabricated uncultivated types and brandy drinkers with the accompaniment of the boring *sevdalinka*'.[2] This brief description of an eastern coffeehouse is, in some ways, a negative of the Western one, which could be characterised by its emphasis on a non-alcoholic drink – coffee – and of course Western culture, from music to manners. Even though coffee originated in the Orient, by the nineteenth century the Occidental world had adopted this beverage and given it a specific place, a home, which rapidly became a social and cultural institution. In his text, Polić enumerates the most famous patrons of the Western coffeehouse tradition, men of letters from different periods and countries: Molière, George Gordon Byron, Carlo Goldoni, Joseph Addison, Voltaire, Emilio Praga, Nikolai Gogol, Henri Murger, Paul Verlaine and Paolo Ferrari. He also mentioned the taverns of Villon and Pietro Aretino, the Poets' cook shop of Cyrano de Bergerac and politicians, such as Cardinal Mazarin, Camille Desmoulins and Napoleon. There are no Croatians and no women included in this illustrious register. With this list, Polić draws up a well-defined cultural sphere, a European and Western one, to which Croatian coffeehouses of the nineteenth century belonged.

In relation to the idea of the Western coffeehouse, two main models emerge: the Parisian café and the Viennese Kaffeehaus. Indeed, one could say that at the end of the seventeenth century, there are not one but two parallel 'stories of the coffeehouse': the French tradition, starting in 1681 with the Café Procope, and the Austrian tradition, inaugurated, in legend at least, in 1683 with the Zur Blauen Flasche. These dates do not coincide with the actual appearance of coffee or coffeehouses in European cities, but indicate the symbolic birth of coffeehouses as new sites of sociability for the bourgeoisie.

At the turn of the nineteenth and twentieth centuries, Parisian and Viennese coffeehouses shared similar functions in society and were significant sites of sociability. Each of these coffeehouse traditions has a name in their own language, café and Kaffeehaus, though the French word is also frequently used to denote Viennese establishments. Furthermore, it is far more common to come across explicit references to the 'Viennese Kaffeehaus' or the 'Parisian café', rather than to the 'Austrian' or 'French' café, indicating a strong specifically urban, as opposed to national identity. Indeed, coffeehouses are the product of the city and primarily used by the urban elite. The coffeehouse is identified with the city: the city as a place of modernity, a space of innovation and invention, culture and plurality. It is also the theatre within which many of the profound social and political transformations of culture over the course of the nineteenth century are played out. Vienna and Paris, around 1900, are prime examples of this phenomenon. The urban and the modern are consistently coupled, as are the city and the coffeehouse.

From its earliest emergence in the capital cities and university towns of Britain, France and the Netherlands, the culture of the coffeehouse spread all over Europe, including Zagreb. The story of the first coffeehouse in Vienna is a well-established legend; this is not the case in relation to Zagreb. It is not known who opened the first coffeehouse (or *kavana* in Croatian), where it was or what it was called. The earliest mention of a kavana dates back to 1749, though the first mention of coffee was in 1636 in a reference to merchants selling coffee at fairs.[3] It is apparent then, that cafés in Zagreb did not make a conspicuous entrance on the cultural scene. There is no legend, no oriental initiator and no mythical date of foundation. In Budapest also, the emergence of the first coffeehouses is undocumented. Indeed, South-eastern Europe, on the border of the Ottoman Empire, had been known for its coffee long before coffeehouses in Vienna became popular.

By the late nineteenth century Zagrebian kavana were commonly referred to in relation to Viennese cafés. As Zagreb was part of Austria-Hungary, these comparisons seem logical. In 1880, August Šenoa, a famous Croatian writer, remarked that 'kavana life in Zagreb has developed in a modern way, very much like the Viennese model'.[4] He said of the Velika kavana (Grand Café), which was situated in the city centre on Ban Jelačić Square, that 'even in Vienna one cannot find a bigger'. Antun Gustav Matoš, another famous Croatian writer, observed in 1912 that 'there are coffeehouses and hotels on Ilica Street and on the squares of the Lower city that have the comfort and service of the most modern ones in Vienna or Berlin'.[5]

At the turn of the nineteenth and twentieth centuries, Vienna was still in many ways the cultural capital of the region, though the Habsburg Empire became a Dual Monarchy in 1867 and political power was divided between Vienna and Budapest. In 1868 the Croatian Parliament and the Hungarian Parliament had signed the Croatian-Hungarian Agreement, which recognised the Kingdom of Croatia and Slavonia as an autonomous area within the Lands of the Crown of Saint Stephen, also known as the Kingdom of Hungary, the Hungarian portion of Austria Hungary.[6] Accordingly, the Croatian-Hungarian Agreement confirmed the *Ban* (traditional Croatian governor) and the *Sabor* (Parliament), with Croatian as the official language. It also gave Croatia some autonomy in matters of administration, religion and education, and also in justice (with the exception of Admiralty courts). Though this document mentions the existence of the Kingdom of Croatia, Slavonia and Dalmatia, Dalmatia remained under direct Austrian administration. It became a central aim of the Croatian national movement to 'restore' unity to these territories divided within the Austria-Hungary. Despite the Croatian-Hungarian Agreement, power was primarily in the hands of Budapest so the relationship between Zagreb and Budapest remained strained, occasionally exploding into open revolt. Although Vienna was no longer directly involved in the political life of Croatia, it still remained a dominant cultural paradigm. German continued to be extensively used in both halves of Austria-Hungary and still functioned as a kind of bourgeois *lingua franca*. However, as part of national movements across Europe, different national groups were clamouring for recognition.[7] The status of national languages played a particularly prominent role in the struggle. Thus Croatian identity and the use of the Croatian language were increasingly asserted across all public spheres and Zagreb was the centre of these efforts.

In 1900, Zagreb had 61,000 inhabitants and twenty-five kavana, while Vienna had 1,700,000 inhabitants and 600 cafés.[8] It may seem difficult, or even impossible, to compare a small regional city with a capital city like Vienna. There are, however, a number of interesting points of comparison between the Zagrebian and Viennese coffeehouses. The similarities and differences between these characteristic cultural institutions and their position in city life highlight the emergence of self-consciously Croatian urban culture. Additionally, this chapter raises questions of cultural transfer: the kinds of items (material and immaterial) which were transferred, the mediators and the obstacles, as well as the question of imitation or appropriation. More generally, this chapter considers relationships between the periphery and the centre, through a focus on Zagreb's relationship with Vienna.

What is a Kavana?

The first legal and complete definition of the kavana is given by the Statute for Trade related to hotels, inns, pubs, taverns, spirits shops, coffeehouses and coffee shops (1887).[9] This document was written according to the model given in the Trade Act of 1884 for the Kingdom of Hungary. Indeed, the Act compelled cities or districts to write their own statutes. It also had some important repercussions for alcoholic shops, catering and hotel businesses in the Kingdom of Hungary. The rules were stricter than in the earlier Trade Act of 1872. For instance, the concessionary licence was reintroduced and it was mandatory to apply for permission before opening a public hostelry of any kind.

The Statute included eleven categories of activities. Of particular interest to this study is the category of kavana and *kavotočje*, which share the common root *kava* (coffee) but are distinguished in the legislation. *Kavotočje* (literally 'to pour coffee') is defined as a place 'where one can be served coffee, tea, or chocolate along with rolls' (§40) while the kavana is defined as being a place 'where one can get coffee, tea, chocolate, spirits (twice distilled plum-brandy and liquors), all kinds of non-alcoholic beverages, ice cream, as well as rolls, which are consumed with the above-mentioned enjoyable products at any time' (§37). The main difference is that the kavana must have 'at least one billiard table for public use' while 'billiards, card games and every other games are forbidden' in a *kavotočje* (§41). The kavana is the only establishment which is legally defined not only by the drinks retailed but also by the mandatory availability of a particular game. Accordingly, a *kavotočje* is a kind of coffee shop, while a kavana is a coffeehouse where billiards brings an extra dimension to sociability.[10]

The kavana also has its own standards for premises, which were not required of a *kavotočje*. It was stated that there must be at least 60 m² of area and 4 m of ceiling height and it could only be located in a basement or the ground floor of a building (§38). It was to open from 4 a.m. during the summer, or 5 a.m. during the winter, until 1 a.m. *Kavotočje*, in contrast, were only permitted to stay open until 10 p.m. (§42). Music was prohibited (§39) but kavana were allowed to be located in any region of the city. The maximum authorised number of kavana was fifteen (§2), which was increased to twenty-five in 1897.[11] In 1887, the number of *kavotočje* permitted was fifty.

In order to explore the specific qualities of the kavana, it is also useful to compare it as an institution to the *krčma* (tavern). All kinds of beverages could be sold in the *krčma* apart from spirits (§27). The area of the premises had to be at least 30 m² and the height of the ceiling at least 3 m and it could only be located in the basement (§28). Taverns were not allowed next to public buildings (e.g., churches, schools, institutions, etc.) or in the city centre (§29), but music was authorised (§30). They were permitted to open from 4 a.m., or 5 a.m. in the winter, to 11 p.m. The maximum authorised number in the city was 150 (§2) and this was increased to 190 in 1903.[12]

These comparisons show how the legislators tried to enact a strict social hierarchy. The kavana was reserved for the elite, the bourgeoisie, thanks to the larger, and hence more expensive, space and the provision of billiards, while the *kavotočje* were limited to basic non-alcoholic beverages and rolls, and the retail focus of the *krčma* revolved around alcoholic drinks. The number of permitted premises reflected the comparative population sizes of their projected class of clientele. Even if later legal changes to the trading laws modified regulations on the sale of alcohol, this did not undermine the essentially distinct definitions and functions ascribed to these establishments. This strictly regimented hierarchy of establishments should be borne in mind when one considers statements that reflect on the café as a democratic space in the city.[13]

After 1867, the Austrian half of Austria-Hungary was subject to a completely different set of laws from the Kingdom of Hungary and therefore Viennese coffeehouses operated within a different legal framework to Zagrebian cafés. The Viennese coffeehouse was subject to the Trade Act of 1859, article 28, which defined six kinds of licences related to hotel businesses, catering and the sale of alcoholic beverages, as well as concessionary stalls.[14] The coffeehouse was defined as 'serving coffee, other warm drinks and refreshments'. Billiards, and more generally the hosting of 'authorised games', was permitted but not mandatory. In 1883 a law enlarging the range of drinks permitted mentions 'serving coffee, tea, chocolate, other warm drinks and refreshments'.[15] There are clear parallels between the definitions of premises contained in the Croatian (and Hungarian) legal texts and the Viennese ones, though it is obvious that the legal definition of a Zagrebian coffeehouse was more precise and restrictive than the Viennese. There is, for example, no formal differentiation between Viennese coffeehouses and coffee shops. So, the hundreds of Viennese coffeehouses presumably included within their number premises similar to the *kavotočje* as well as the kavana, which complicates direct comparison.

Another point of comparison is the location of coffeehouses within the city. The Viennese cafés most directly comparable to the kavana were located in similar positions in the city centre. The central location of the Zagrebian kavana, though not determined in the legislation, was a practical response to the legal requirements relating to their mandatory size and their bourgeois client base. They were primarily situated in the Lower city, the new and modern part of Zagreb, particularly on the Ban Jelačić Square, in the heart of the city, and along Ilica, the principal commercial street.[16] Even if Zagrebian kavana are more closely defined by the authorities than the Viennese café, they both occupied the same place in the urban space. The central position of these establishments determined the natural profile of the bourgeois clientele – and vice versa.

An examination of the legal parameters of coffeehouse life is useful in providing concrete information as to how they were run and how they were perceived by the authorities, but it is also necessary to look beyond this. The legal definitions, in their efforts to pinpoint and control reality, are unable to reflect the full complexity of these spaces. In particular, they exclude the needs and social practices of the patrons who were, without a doubt, key elements in the constitution of the café.

The Viennese Coffeehouse as a Model

If one compares photographs of coffeehouses in different cities across Austria-Hungary, it proves difficult to determine, without an accompanying caption, which was the Zagrebian kavana, the Hungarian *kávéház*, the Prague *kavarna*. Across Austria-Hungary, there was a common visual identity for the coffeehouse, considered by many as an extension of the bourgeois living room and marked by a familiar touch of luxury. These ideas and the interior design of the Viennese coffeehouse are explored in detail in Richard Kurdiovsky's chapter in this volume. The Zagrebian kavana echoed all the common elements of coffeehouse furnishing: ornate light fittings, billiard tables and game rooms, newspaper stands, the counter presided over by a female cashier and the familiar marble-topped tables and Thonet chairs. The niche, with upholstered seating, is another feature immediately recognisable from the Viennese coffeehouse tradition. Café Corso and Café Zagreb, for example, were furnished with all these attributes. Photographic records reveal the large windows with seating niches and tables that allow patrons to feel comfortably secluded but, at the same time, almost on the street, possibly the best observation post from which to monitor the life of the city. During fine weather, in both Vienna and in Zagreb, patrons took their place on the pavement, in *Schanigärten*. These occupy the pavement outside the café, marked out from the rest of the street by surrounding wooden fences and flower boxes. In 1903 seven of the twenty-five Zagrebian coffeehouses had such a terrace; all four coffeehouses on the main square had one. The biggest was 220 m². [17] The turn of the century also saw the increased involvement of professional architects in the design of coffeehouses. In Zagreb, the kavana Corso was refitted in an Art Nouveau style by the Croatian architect Otto Goldscheider in 1907. [18]

Waiters are frequently included in photographic records of the kavana. The staff wore the same formal clothing, black suits, white shirts and ties, and were denoted by the same job titles as in Viennese coffeehouses. In a publication edited by the Zagreb Association of Owners of Cafés, Restaurants and Hotels in 1892 are cited the names of all the members, their job titles and the establishments where they work. [19] The publication is in German as are the titles of professions related to the coffeehouse. The staff of the Zagrebian café is composed of the *Zahlmarqueur* (head waiter who bills the customer), *Marqueur* (waiter who serves), *Zuträger*, *Caféjunge* and *Cafékoch* (the youth and novices who bring and make the coffee) and *Kuchenbursche*. This elaborate hierarchy of service staff is typical of an Austro-Hungarian society, in which the rigidly stratified social hierarchy was mirrored in the organisation of many other institutions. In the same period, the French only used the titles *garçon* or *serveur de café*. [20] It is interesting to note that the association used the Austrian (originally French) terms *Marqueur* and *Zahlmarqueur* for the senior café staff and the German term *Zahlkellner* for the hotel or restaurant staff. The term *Kellner* is not used in the publication even though it was in common usage across the cafés of Austria-Hungary, including Zagreb. The nomenclature associated with the cafés was essentially as cosmopolitan as the institution itself, making it a site for a ready mixture of local and international vocabulary.

The use of German by the Zagreb Association of Owners of Cafés, Restaurants and Hotels can be seen as signalling their allegiance to the German-speaking bourgeoisie, at home in cities across Austria-Hungary and to the professional milieu of German-speaking coffeehouse proprietors who served them. However, the cosmopolitan character of the coffeehouse was greater than the dominance of any one cultural group. Among the eleven coffeehouse-owners who were members of the association, six were born outside of Croatia, one in Croatia and there is no information on the place of birth of the others. The situation among the hoteliers, a wealthy group, is even more pronounced: seven out of nine were not born in Croatia and the place of birth is not known for the last two.[21] The association did not reflect the ethnic make-up of Zagreb, which had a Croatian majority of around 70 per cent in 1890.[22] As the owners determined the appearance of the cafés and popularised the professional terminology in line with the Viennese model, coffeehouses in Zagreb and Vienna looked and functioned in an almost identical manner. The role of these owners as cosmopolitan mediators was crucial. Across Austria-Hungary, the familiar space of the café provided a venue for locals, visitors and newcomers.

The Coffeehouse Habitué: Jung Wien and Zagreb Moderna

The success of a coffeehouse is mainly shaped by its patrons. Social life within the café revolved around drinking coffee, smoking, reading newspapers, conversing, observing people and doing nothing. In Zagreb, as in Vienna, the coffeehouse was a kind of theatre with its particular scenery, an identifying name (the name of the coffeehouse), plots (anecdotes, stories) and actors-spectators (patrons). Indeed, the coffeehouse and the theatre characterised bourgeois sociability in both cities, frequented, as they were, by intellectuals, members of the liberal professions, pensioners, artists and bohemians. Even if the price of a cup of coffee was the only formally constituted requirement to stay in a coffeehouse for hours, in practice, membership of the bourgeoisie was an important factor. Indeed, the formality of the waiters and their rudimentary multilinguism were not a coincidence, but a necessity imposed by patrons. By the turn of the century, the languages spoken by patrons and staff were increasingly diverse and newspapers in a variety of languages were also a common feature. The bourgeoisie could be considered as a social group strongly marked by cosmopolitanism.

Of course, writers are just one subsection of the patrons of cafés. However, a specific symbiosis occurred between coffeehouses and writers in many cities. Coffeehouses gave them a place of freedom, while writers ensured the coffeehouses a kind of immortality through their writings. The Viennese version of the story is well-known and explored in depth through the chapters in this volume. The Viennese literati, Alfred Polgar, Hugo von Hofmannsthal, Karl Kraus and Peter Altenberg, are as famous as the coffeehouses they frequented – Café Griensteidl, Café Central and the Café Museum.[23] This is not the case for the Zagrebian coffeehouse writers.

Without delving too far into the complexity of literary movements around 1900, it should be noted that Croatia also had its generation of young men who championed new literary modes and sought to shrug off the stultification of the previous generation.[24] Their association with the coffeehouses of Zagreb provides an interesting picture of how the relationship between the coffeehouses and artistic modernity played out in a manner that both contrasts with and parallels the more famous coffeehouse culture of Vienna. This group, known as *Moderna*, emerged at the beginning of the 1890s. *The Power of Conscience* by Antun Gustav Matoš, published in 1892, is considered to be one of the first works of this new movement. Parallels between the Jung Wien and Zagreb *Moderna* are numerous. For instance, Milivoj Dežman, who has been described as the 'Croatian Hermann Bahr',[25] founded a literary journal, *Mladost* (Youth) in 1898, the Croatian version of *Ver sacrum*. In order to express their emotions and opinions, and to find a space for freedom and aesthetics, *Moderna* writers favoured the same short forms as their Viennese contemporaries: poems, short stories, feuilleton and literary criticism. Their enthusiasm led to an explosion of new periodicals, some of which lasted for only one issue.

Like their Viennese brethren, Croatian writers such as Vilko Gabarić, Zvonko Milković, Karlo Häusler, Fran Galović, Ljubo Wiesner, Nikola Polić and Antun Gustav Matoš passed their time in cafés in the centre of Zagreb. Among the most popular cafés frequented by this group were the Kavana Bauer, Hrvatska kavana (Croatian Kavana) and Kazališna kavana (Kavana of the Theater). The most famous among the *Moderna* was Matoš who dominated the literary scene in Zagreb from 1908, when he returned to Zagreb from an extended period abroad, until his death in 1914.[26] As a deserter from the Austro-Hungarian army, he had fled in 1894 to avoid prison. While living in Paris, Belgrade and Geneva, it had been his practice to submit articles to Croatian papers, providing an important channel for the transmission of new literary and cultural ideas, especially from Paris. On his return, when he could frequently be found in the kavanas of Zagreb, his mediatory role could be performed in person. Polić remarked that 'we felt Europe for the first time in him'.[27] Matoš was without a doubt the most popular and influential writer of the day.

In common with the dynamic noted by other authors in this volume in relation to coffeehouse society in Vienna, Kraków and Lemberg, the coffeehouse functioned as a space where writers could socialise and where newcomers could be initiated into the literary milieu.[28] For example, Polić met Matoš in 1909 in a coffeehouse. This first night among Zagrebian writers, he made a tour of coffeehouses and taverns. He started his 'literary career' soon after, with the publication of his first poem.[29] Ljubo Wiesner, another young writer, wrote of the importance of the café to the self-identity of these young writers: 'between the excess of youth and the violent will to serve artistic ideals, a paradox was born by which we despise healthy sports and cultivate unhealthy sitting about in coffeehouses or taverns'.[30]

It was not only a way of life for young writers; it was often where they worked and wrote, found inspiration, and discussed literature. Wiesner, chief editor of a collection of poems, *Hrvatska mlada lirika* (Young Croatian Lyricism), made the last corrections to his manuscript sitting in a kavana with his colleagues. Sometimes, coffeehouses were also the subject of their writings, in particular through the form of the feuilleton. This particular literary form was closely associated with the Viennese coffeehouse. The feuilleton was an important feature of Matoš' œuvre, which also featured coffeehouse themes, such as 'Kafanske varijacije' (Coffee Variations). Polić also produced similar works: 'U kavani o kavani' (In the Coffeehouse on the Coffeehouse).

The kavana was the home of anecdotes, wordplay, caricatures and jokes. As Polić put it: 'at that time, one did not debate in coffeehouses and entrance was forbidden to serious people'.[31] These light, casual conversations needed spirit and oratorical talent. Such wordplay migrated into both Viennese and Zagrebian feuilletons, which are full of aphorisms. Wiesner recalled 'the anecdotes, wordplay and jokes of Matoš, which took the form of critical observations, such as "the Habsburg dynasty is as old as syphilis", "Franz Joseph, the emperor with the ears of Midas"'.[32] Politics was readily included. Jokes could wield serious power, as Polić wrote:

> It is clear that a joke, even the simplest one, if said at the right place and time, can demolish the whole magnificent structure of the system and the ideas, which have been compiled with sweat and carefully passed down through decades, centuries and millenniums and written in a ponderous library. Such jokes, which are not funny, because good jokes never make us laugh, can only appear in coffeehouses, which have until today nurtured a certain mentality, identical by its importance in every nation.[33]

This quotation highlights Polić's understanding of coffeehouse life and coffeehouse consciousness as something common across national boundaries and as a place of freedom and free expression that sought to revitalise and revolutionise society and arts.

Through their work, both Austrian and Croatian writers depicted not only the spirit of the coffeehouse, but also more generally of their society. A coffeehouse was not just an ordinary place of recreation; it was a warm place where people could meet and exchange information. During the last years of the nineteenth century, society across Austria-Hungary was experiencing dramatic transformations, and significant tensions emerged between past and future, modernity and tradition. Such paradoxes appear frequently in new writing of the period, for example in the work of Polgar and Polić. The café as a site of such paradoxes – work and play, frivolity and seriousness, conviviality and loneliness – is a recurring theme. Alfred Polgar considered that the Café Central was 'at the meridian of loneliness'[34] and Polić noted that 'writers and intellectuals are often in truth pleasant company but always bad and cruel friends'.[35] The coffeehouse was also sometimes depicted as a disease and a drug. As Polgar put it, the 'Centralist' cannot be without his 'daily dose of Centraline',[36] while Polić said that 'if we miss just one day in a kavana, we are unhappy' and that 'we understand the poison of the kavana but we forgive it too'.[37] Polgar talks about the 'purposelessness', 'inertia' or 'nothingness' of café life and Polić about 'boredom'. Café patrons were waiting for something; in Vienna they were 'longingly awaiting their excavation yet hoping that it will not occur',[38] while in Zagreb they were 'always waiting for someone even if we are convinced that nobody will come'.[39] Polić explained that 'in this harassment of nerves, there is a fatal and perfidious magnetism to the kavana'. Their anxieties were not simply a reflection on café life, but on life in the modern city.

National Identity and the Zagrebian Kavana

While both Zagreb and Vienna went through a period of intellectual turmoil at the turn of the century, similarities between the two cities should not be over-emphasised. In Zagreb, nationalist tensions increased during the 1890s and 1900s. Croatians resented Hungarian domination and the magyarisation policies of *ban* Karoly Khuen-Hedervary, himself a Hungarian, who governed from 1883 to 1903. Writers were mobilised as part of wider efforts to advance Croatian culture and political life. In Vienna, in contrast, literary movements maintained a distance from politics and focused instead on the individual in his confrontation with the forces of tradition and modernity. The café life of both cities similarly reflected these different preoccupations.

Increasingly the Croatian national movement began to influence commercial activity. Language was a key area of concern and the language within which a business operated was viewed as a reflection of its stance on wider nationalist issues. The identity of the Zagreb Association of Hotel, Restaurant, Tavern and Coffee Owners started to shift from a German-language organisation to a Croatian one.[40] This change was led by the hotel owner Albert Breithut, the president of the association. Although born in Vienna, in 1894 he decided to greet the assembly of the association in Croatian, thereby showing his sympathies for Croatian nationalism. In 1903 he initiated the creation of a Croatian-language industry journal *Vjesnik hrvatskih konobara, gostioničara i kavanara* (News for Croatian Waiters, Restaurateurs and Coffeehouse Owners) which was part of a growing swell of activities aimed at affirming the Croatian language and identity, as the title suggests it. A few years later, the journal published by the association explained that Breithut was seeking to eradicate 'the German spirit' which until then 'reigned in the association, when every book and every file was exclusively written in German'.[41]

Further changes occurred in relation to coffeehouse management in 1904 when a new president, Mato Huzjak, a Croat and a tavern owner, was appointed as the head of the association. His appointment was a marked change in comparison to his predecessors, who had all been hoteliers or coffeehouse owners and non-Croats. Indeed, since the 1890s the structure of the association had been evolving. Membership was increasingly composed of Croatian tavern owners who belonged to the middle classes and who held nationalist sympathies.[42] Its purpose was to develop the hospitality sector in Croatia, with developments such as the foundation of the Croatian Federation of Associations of Hotel, Restaurant, Tavern and Coffee Owners (Savez gostioničarsko-krčmarskih zadruga – 1907), a nationwide organisation, and a specialist bank (Gostioničarska banka – 1907) which sought to provide members with greater financial freedom. It was also a way of affirming the Croatian language and identity through business and, ultimately, politics in the region. A number of members of the association sought to get involved in politics (alongside Croatian opposition parties) in order to serve both the interests of their profession and Croatian national interests more generally. Finally, efforts were made to find Croatian words for staff titles and some dishes in order to substitute German, and sometimes French, names. This again illustrates the engagement of the association with the national issue of the public usage of the Croatian language.

Though these small changes in nomenclature may seem minor, they were part of a wider political arena in which the Croatian identity, particularly the use of the Croatian language, was central. In 1883 and 1903, two revolts occurred in protest at the use of Hungarian inscriptions, alongside Croatian, on the flags hung on public buildings. Croatian was the sole official language in the Kingdom of Croatia and Slavonia, so the Hungarian inscriptions were seen as an act of provocation. Similarly, in 1895, when Franz Joseph came to Zagreb to open the new Croatian National Theatre, students staged a protest involving the burning of the Hungarian flag in protest against what they perceived as the Hungarian-dominated administration of Croatia under *ban* Khuen-Hedervary. Croatian students who were expelled from Zagreb University for nationalist agitation continued to study elsewhere, often in Vienna and Prague, providing another important conduit for new ideas to enter Croatian culture.[43]

The writers of the *Moderna* movement were involved in the Croatian national movement. In 1898 a group of young writers decided to secede from the Association of Writers (Društvo književnika) in order to found the Association of Croatian Writers (Društvo hrvatskih književnika). The addition of the adjective 'Croatian' is not insignificant and reflected their consciousness of Croatian identity. More generally, young writers were critical of the government and shared, more or less, the political opinions of the Croatian opposition, which despite the differences between the two dominant groups – the Yugoslav movement and the Party of Rights – demanded greater political autonomy for Croatia and the unification of Croatians lands. For example, Matoš was known to be quite close to the Croatian Party of Rights, and critical of the administrations in both Vienna and Budapest. When Milutin Cihlar Nehajev, a writer from the *Moderna* group, became the chief editor in 1912 of a journal *Jutarnji list* (Morning Paper), a pro-government organ, he was no longer accepted in the Zagrebian kavana and his books were boycotted by his peers.[44] After 1903, *Moderna* was no longer purely a literary movement but also a cultural movement oriented towards 'a Croatian cultural rebirth'.[45] While the Viennese were oriented inwards, concerned with self-reflection, the Zagrebians focused on national self-expression and looked outwards – towards Europe,[46] and towards modernity.

Matoš' writings frequently display a deep concern about the limitations of the life of the Zagreb and the underdeveloped nature of Croatian society. His concerns highlight the fact that the Zagrebian writers and coffeehouses we have been discussing here were part of a small, emerging, urban culture in Zagreb, without the backing of a substantial, nationwide literate middle class. Matoš wrote that the lack of a powerful Croatian intelligentsia would jeopardise the development of Croatian society.[47] He felt that the aristocracy was not Croatian – 'their spirit was Pesto-Viennese, so without spirit' – and he therefore believed that they could not be relied upon to lead the development of Croatia according to Croatian interests. Although the ecclesiastic circles set themselves up as the guardians of Croatian tradition, Matoš saw their contribution to the development of Croatian culture as flawed because 'there were no women'. The main opinion makers were the bourgeoisie and public administration. Again, Matoš expressed misgivings about these groups: the bourgeois were 'patriots often without intelligence' while the 'bureaucrats do not have enough money or patriotism when they are intelligent'.

According to Matoš, the main places of sociability for this bourgeois society were the kavana and tavern, where he saw sociability closely associated with alcohol and the absence of money, intelligence, patriotism, and women. He also commented on the absence of salon culture as place of sociability for high society, because there was no Croatian high society. According to Matoš, the implications were very serious. This lack of a true Croatian elite and the presence instead only of the petit bourgeoisie explained for him why Zagreb 'is the capital in name only' but 'not yet the political and even less commercial centre of the entire Croatian land'. The sociability of coffeehouses proved, according to him, the failings of Croatian society and more particularly of the bourgeoisie. These observations were based on a perception of the problems associated with imitation: it may look like a coffeehouse but does not have all the functions, particularly the function of creativity. Matoš, frustrated with the pace of cultural development in Zagreb, saw the city's coffeehouses there as hollow imitations of the creative and intellectual social café life of London and Paris. It is useful here to recall that he had been living for many years in Paris during his exile from Croatia. These opinions serve to illustrate that the parallels between the coffeehouse life of Vienna and Zagreb need to be understood against the background of the different cultural, social and political conditions that shaped both cities.

Conclusion

The culture of the Viennese coffeehouse, from the material to the immaterial aspects, such as decoration, furniture, literature, sociability, tastes, ideas, feelings, crossed national frontiers throughout Austria-Hungary. The Zagrebian and Viennese coffeehouses were both cultural institutions and places of sociability. They fulfilled similar social functions and had a similar profile of patrons – the bourgeoisie and in particular literary and intellectual circles. The coffeehouse owners were also a conduit for the transmission of the Viennese traditions of café service. This common café culture across Austria-Hungary reflected the existence of a German-speaking bourgeois society that linked urban centres across the region. Thanks to the permeability of the bourgeois strata of men of letters, to fellow members, regardless of nationality and to the facilitating medium of the German language, cultural transfer between members of the bourgeoisie was horizontal and transnational. The common identity of coffeehouses in different cities, from Vienna to Krakow, from Lemberg to Zagreb, is proof of that. One may talk about imitation as a characteristic of the response of the periphery to the centre. This imitation could be taken as a lack of originality and formative identity. However, it might also be seen as a way of proclaiming allegiance to a specific cultural sphere, of challenging the limitations of the periphery and, finally, of finding a way towards modernity and towards Europe.

However, despite all the similarities, the Zagrebian and Viennese coffeehouses reflected different cultural and political realities. The apolitical dimension of the Jung Wien group could not find fertile ground in Zagreb, where most of the Croatian young writers were deeply preoccupied with the fraught question of Croatian national identity. This divergence in motivation makes the Zagrebian café less an example of reproduction or imitation but one of transformation, invention and appropriation. Despite the criticism of Matoš, the Zagrebian coffeehouses became a place for the expression of Croatian identity because of the national orientation of the patrons and owners of the coffeehouses. The coffeehouse has long been the 'right' place to talk politics. There have been no revolutions without associations with coffeehouses. Even if around 1900 Zagreb had no 'revolutionary' coffeehouses as such, this shifted the focus of the coffeehouses of Zagreb towards an identity, no longer primarily urban, local or social, but national and political. The coffeehouse began to take on an identity that was no longer specifically Zagrebian but also Croatian, since the influence of the political and literary activities undertaken there had more than purely local significance and were seen as having implications for the entire country. But is it still a kavana, a coffeehouse, once it loses its ties, first and foremost, to the city? We can answer the question positively, because identities are never completely dissociated; urban and national identities, like social and political ones, are mixed and fluid. The city and the coffeehouse perform roles that are simultaneously local and national.

Notes

1. Nikola Polić, 'U kavani o kavani (razmatranje oko jednog stola)', in *Marginalia: feljtoni*, Zagreb 1921, 83.
2. For a discussion of the myth-making surrounding the origins of the Viennese coffeehouse, see Tag Gronberg, 'Coffeehouse Orientalism' in this volume. *Sevdalinka* is folk music, mostly love songs, from Bosnia and Herzegovina. Polić, 'U Kavani o Kavani', 85.
3. Rudolf Horvat, *Prošlost grada Zagreba*, Zagreb 1992, 330–331.
4. August Šenoa, 'Zagrebačke crtice', in *Narodne Novine*, 22 January 1880.
5. Antun Gustav Matoš, 'Zagreb i Zagrebi', in Dragutin Tadijanović (ed.), *Sabrana Djela* (Complete Works), vol. 5, 1973, 177.
6. Since the personal union between Kingdom of Croatia and Kingdom of Hungary in 1102, the Croatian State had had some degree of political sovereignty, at least on a symbolical level.
7. Sarah Kent, 'State Ritual and Ritual Parody: Croatian Student Protest and the Limits of Loyalty at the end of the Nineteenth Century', in Laurence Cole, Daniel L. Unowsky (eds), *The Limits of Loyalty: Imperial Symbolism, Popular Allegiances, and State Patriotism in the Late Habsburg Monarchy*, New York and Oxford 2007, 162–177; Bernard Michel, *Nations et nationalismes en Europe centrale. XIXe et XXe siècle*, Paris 1995; Jaroslav Šidak, Mirjana Gross, Ljubo Karaman, Dragova Šepić, *Povijest hrvatskog naroda 1860–1914* (History of Croatian People 1860–1914), Zagreb 1968; Josip Horvat, *Politička povijest Hrvatske* (Political History of Croatia), reprint, Zagreb 1989; Mirjana Gross, Agneza Szabo, *Prema hrvatskome gradanskom društvu. Društveni razvoj u civilnoj Hrvatskoj i Slavoniji šezdesetih i sedamdesetih godina 19. stoljeća* (Toward Croatian Bourgeois Society. Social Development in Civil Croatia and Slavonia in the Sixties and Seventies of the 19th Century), Zagreb 1992; William Brooks Tomljanovich, *Bishop Josip Juraj Strossmayer: Nationalism and Modern Catholicism in Croatia*, Ph.D. diss, Yale University, 1997.
8. See Ashby's chapter in this volume.
9. *Štatut za obrte, baveće se držanjem svratištah, gostionah, pivanah, krčmah, rakijašnicah, kavanah, kavotočjah*, Zagreb, 1887.
10. The importance of billiards in the Viennese café has been noted in Ashby's essay in this volume. Though almost ubiquitous in relation to the Viennese café, they were not integral to the legal definition of a café business there, as they were in Zagreb.
11. Hrvatski Državni arhiv, VI, 2545–2897.
12. *Zapisnik skupštine zastupstva slobodnog i kraljevskog glavnoga grada Zagreba* (Records of the City Council of the Free and Royal Capital Zagreb), 1903, §184.
13. See a similar discussion in relation to Wirtshäuser and cafés in Ashby's chapter in this volume.
14. Claudia Rossmeisel, *Das Gewerberecht im Wandel der zeit unter besonderer Berücksichtigung des 19. und 20. Jahrunderts dargestellt am Gasthaus-. Kaffeehaus- und Schankgewerbe*, Ph.D dissertation, Universität Wien, Vienna 1995, 22–27.
15. Rossmeisel, *Das Gewerberecht*, 39.
16. Ines Sabotič, *Les cafés de Zagreb de 1884 à 1914: sociabilités, normes et identités*, Ph.D Dissertation, Université Paris I Panthéon-Sorbonne, Paris 2002, 288–293.
17. Sabotič, *Les cafés de Zagreb*, 355–356.

18. *Vijesti hrvatskog društva inžinira i arhitekata u Zagrebu*, 1908, N. 4; Olga Maruševski, *Iz zagrebačke spomeničke baštine* (From Zagrebian Monumental Heritage), Zagreb 2006, 279.
19. *Rechnungs- und Standes-Ausweis des Agramer Bürgerlichen Wirths- und Cafétier-Vereins von 1892*, Zagreb 1892.
20. Henry-Melchior de Langle, *Le petit monde des cafés et débits parisiens*, Paris 1990, 98–99.
21. Sabotič, *Les cafés de Zagreb*, 159–161.
22. Ines Sabotič, *Etude d'histoire urbaine de Zagreb de 1880 à 1910 à partir des recensements*, Mémoire de maitrise, Université Paris I Panthéon-Sorbonne, Paris 1995, 77–80.
23. Harold B. Segel (ed.), *The Vienna Coffeehouse Wits, 1890–1938*, West Lafayette, Indiana 1993.
24. Slavko Ježić, *Hrvatska književnost od početka do danas 1100–1941* (Croatian Literature from the Beginning until today 1100–1941), Zagreb 1993, 296–305; Krešimir Nemec and Marijan Bobinac, 'Bečka i hrvatska moderna: poticaji i paralele' (Viennese and Zagrebian Modernism: Impulses and Parallels), in Damir Barbarić (ed.), *Zagreb-Beč fin-de-siècle* (Zagreb-Vienna Fin-de-siècle), Zagreb 1997, 84–105.
25. Nemec and Bobinac, 'Bečka i Hrvatska Moderna', 88.
26. Josip Kosor, 'Kratka Autobiografija' (Short Autobiography), in Vinko Brešić (ed.), *Autobiografije Hrvatskih Pisaca* (Autobiographies of Croatian Writers), Zagreb 1995, 579.
27. Nikola Polić, 'A.G.M. (Nacrt za Studiju)' (AGM, Plan for a Study), in *Marginalia: feljtoni*, 1921, 18–19.
28. The role of the coffeehouse as a meeting place facilitating connections between writers is discussed in the chapters by Charlotte Ashby, Gilbert Carr and Shachar Pinsker in this volume.
29. Nikola Polić, 'Susretaji sa A. G. Matoš' (Meetings with A.G. Matoš), in Milan Selaković (ed.), *Izabrana Djela. Ljubo Wiesner, Nikola Polić, Ulderiko Donadini* (Ljubo Wiesner, Nikola Polić, Ulderiko Donadini. Chosen Works), Zagreb 1970, 292.
30. Ljubo Wiesner, 'Nikola Polić', in *Izabrana djela. Ljubo Wiesner, Nikola Polić, Ulderiko Donadini*, 140.
31. Polić, 'U kavani o kavani', 87.
32. Wiesner, 'Nikola Polić', 139.
33. Polić, 'U kavani o kavani', 81.
34. Alfred Polgar, 'Theory of the Café Central', in Segel, *The Vienna Coffeehouse Wits 1890–1938*, 267.
35. Polić, 'Susretaji sa A. G. Matoš', 295.
36. Polgar, 'Theory of the Café Central', 269.
37. Polić, 'U kavani o kavani', 82.
38. Polgar, 'Theory of the Café Central', 269.
39. Polić, 'U kavani o kavani', 88.
40. Sabotič, *Les cafés de Zagreb*, 156–190.
41. *Gostioničarski list*, 1 May 1907.
42. Sabotič, *Les cafés de Zagreb*, 172.
43. Ines Sabotič, 'Stjepan Matković, Saborski izbori i zagrebačka izborna tijela na prijelazu iz 19. u 20. stoljeće' (Parliamentary Elections and Zagreb Electoral Body at the Turn of the 19th and 20th Centuries), *Društvena istraživanja*, 14(1–2) (75–76), April 2005, 157–183; Šidak et al., *Povijest hrvatskog naroda 1860–1914*; Horvat, *Politička povijest Hrvatske*; Kent, 'State Ritual and Ritual Parody', 162–177.
44. Krešimir Kovačić, *Priče iz staroga Zagreba* (Stories from the old Zagreb), Zagreb 1990, 242.
45. Nemec and Bobinac, 'Bečka i Hrvatska Moderna', 86.
46. Antun Barac, *Jugoslavenska književnost* (Yugoslavian literature), Zagreb 1954, 239.
47. Matoš, 'Društvenost', in Tadijanović, *Sabrana Djela*, 207.

Chapter 8

ADOLF LOOS'S KÄRNTNER BAR
Reception, Reinvention, Reproduction

Mary Costello

On a May evening in 2008, a large party was held on the Kärntnerdurchgang, a small side-street off the Kärntnerstrasse, in the heart of Vienna's Innere Stadt. The occasion was the centenary celebration of the street's most famous bar, the 'Kärntner Bar' or 'American Bar', designed by the architect Adolf Loos, and now known more commonly as the 'Loos Bar'. The celebration was part of a year-long campaign in honour of '*100 Jahre Loos Bar*', as posters placed across the city announced, but the actual date of the party did not correspond to the original opening date of the bar. Instead it was chosen because the tiny bar, its interior measuring just over 6 x 4 metres, was far too small to host the size of party its fame demanded. As the Viennese newspaper *Die Presse* reported, the manageress of the bar, acting like 'the English Queen', chose a warm month for the birthday celebrations, and transformed the small Kärntnerdurchgang into a canopied '*Loos-Gasse*', or 'Loos Lane', for a street party.[1] Invited guests came from all over the world to pay tribute to Loos and his famous creation, and by midnight the party area had to be extended to accommodate the burgeoning numbers.[2]

The Kärntner Bar, designed by Loos in 1907–1908, and opened to the public in the winter of 1908–1909, was one of the first so-called 'American bars' in Vienna.[3] These establishments, which began to appear in Europe from the 1890s, generally took the form of a standing bar, and served 'American' or 'mixed' drinks to an all-male clientele. The introduction of bars to Vienna provided an alternative space to the ubiquitous coffeehouse for intellectual and cultural exchange. Loos himself had designed a coffeehouse, the Café Museum, in 1899, which had quickly become a meeting place for Vienna's literati. The Kärntner Bar may have been a much smaller affair, but it was equally self-conscious in staking a claim to a share in the intellectual and cultural exchange of the city by displaying an over-sized portrait of the writer Peter Altenberg, perhaps the most famous Viennese coffeehouse habitué, as the eye-catcher for the bar. The connection has remained an important one, with the Loos-Altenberg history of the bar at the forefront of the 2008 centenary advertising campaign.

The centenary celebration reflected above all the currency of the name of Loos and the bar's status as an icon of his distinctly modernist architecture. More significantly, it demonstrates how the bar has come metonymically to stand for the architect and his architectural philosophy and practice. This status is no better evidenced than by a copy of the bar, which was installed in Trinity College, Dublin, in 1986, at the height of popular and academic interest in fin-de-siècle Vienna.[4] This little-known version has generally been regarded as a whim on the part of its Irish architects, Shane de Blacam and John Meagher. Its reception as an oddity situates it firmly within a tradition of eclectic Irish architectural practice and, as a result, its relationship to its famous Viennese model has been largely unexplored.[5] This chapter proposes to examine the relationship between the Dublin replica – which I will call the 'Trinity Bar' – and the Viennese original. Particular attention will be paid to the role of Loos's architecture – in both its original and reproduced forms – in the performance of intellectual and gender identities. The central premise is that the 1986 reincarnation of the bar resonates not so much with the original, but with the idea of that original as it is figured in the historiography of Viennese modernism. The Trinity Bar can thus be considered a key text in the reception history of the Kärntner Bar, demonstrating the hegemony of particular interpretations of the bar throughout the twentieth century.

A New Bar in Vienna: For Men Only

From its earliest reception, the Kärntner Bar has been written about as a masculine space, in terms of both its architecture and its social function. In February 1909, the first published review, written by Peter Altenberg, set the tone for what was to follow.[6] Altenberg wrote, 'only men are allowed entry to this bar'.[7] Altenberg's explicit statement is echoed implicitly by writers of later accounts, which imbue the architecture – and the social behaviour it conditioned – with a pervasive masculinity. An influential example of this type of account is that given by Ludwig Münz and Gustav Künstler in their 1964 monograph on Loos.[8] In their description of the interior architecture of the Kärntner Bar, Münz and Künstler focus on elements that have been culturally ascribed as masculine: hard, polished surfaces, dark colours, and materials such as leather and mahogany. They then go on to state that this interior 'demands a certain demeanour from the customer. He has his drink either at the bar, pleasantly supported by the 3 feet 6 inches high bar rail, or sitting comfortably in one of the alcoves … and gives himself up unconsciously and unreservedly to the experience of seeing'.[9]

The artist Oskar Kokoschka echoes these sentiments in his memoirs, first published in 1971, when he recollects his experience of the bar. He too discusses the ambience created by the architecture, and notes: 'You sipped your drink like a blasé man of the world … The discreet quiet of the bar afforded a change from the unrest that had begun to affect the coffeehouses'.[10] In Kokoschka's memoirs it is clear that he is referring to political unrest, but the comment has routinely been quoted detached from its context.[11] As such, the cumulative effect of the gendered discourse surrounding the establishment of the bar invites a reading of Kokoschka's comment in the context of an increasing presence of women in what was traditionally the male preserve of the coffeehouses.[12] Susan Henderson, in her essay 'Bachelor Culture in the Work of Adolf Loos', uses Kokoschka's comment to support her positioning of the Kärntner Bar as an alternative space to the coffeehouse – a male sanctum influenced by the model of American bars and British gentlemen's clubs, in which Loos uses a masculine architectural language to both articulate a stance in opposition to the ornamental, decorative, 'feminine' style of the Secessionists, and to provide a setting in which the social structure of coffeehouse culture is redefined to exclude women.[13] It is this view of the Kärntner Bar as exemplifying the perfect marriage between Loos's architectural practice and his ideological position on the gendered organisation of social space that has come to dominate the academic and popular imagination. The Trinity Bar in Dublin both attests to the influence of, and in turn reinforces, the prevailing orthodoxy.

Mirror Image? The Kärntner Bar Reproduced

In 1984, a disastrous fire gutted Trinity College's eighteenth-century Dining Hall on Front Square. The Dublin architectural firm of de Blacam and Meagher was given the commission for the restoration of the building. Part of their brief was the installation of a bar in the Senior Common Room, a suite of rooms within the Dining Hall. The architects' surprising solution to this part of the brief was to install a reproduction of the interior of the Kärntner Bar, mirrored and adapted to fit the available space, and complete with a reproduction of the portrait of Altenberg.[14] In purely architectural terms, de Blacam and Meagher's approach to the restoration project was informed by postmodernist architectural theory, and by contemporary debate on the conservation of old buildings, which stressed the need to be sensitive to a building's history.[15]

The original Dining Hall, designed by Richard Cassels in the 1740s, suffered separate incidents of storm and fire damage, before being completed in 1765 by Hugh Darley, who adapted Cassels's model. Its Palladian architecture demonstrates the influence of Inigo Jones and speaks of developments in country-house planning of this period, associated with the English landed gentry in Ireland. As John Olley has written, 'Trinity College has often been the point of arrival or perfection of many an imported influence, whether brought in by foreigners or tested by Irish architects'.[16] In light of this history, de Blacam and Meagher's use of Loos is less surprising than on first consideration. The architects made formal links between the bar and their architectural conception for the Dining Hall project as a whole. In particular, its truth-to-materials philosophy – local Irish materials and craftsmen were used throughout – was solemnly consistent with late twentieth-century debates about sympathetic restoration and with Loos's early twentieth-century architectural theory. The architects were also keen to stress the links between their version of 'modern classicism' and Loos's, particularly in their design of the atrium, a galleried space which makes impressive use of repeated simplified classical forms. The bar was thus conceived as a 'footnote' to the project, acknowledging their reference to Loos. More than this, it can be considered as an act of homage, demonstrating the high esteem that Loos commanded in architectural circles at this time.

The architects also acknowledged the bar's place in the social structure of Trinity College. According to de Blacam: 'We were interested in the college and its society. Our duty was to secure the social organisation of the institution'.[17] This structure had changed little since the sixteenth century. One of the seven ancient universities of the British Isles, and the only one not within the present-day United Kingdom, Trinity College was founded in 1592 by Queen Elizabeth I, during the period when the English were formally asserting their political control over Ireland.[18] It was founded as a corporation, consisting of the Provost, Fellows and Scholars.[19] Historically, this strictly hierarchical social structure has been symbolised by a number of traditions related to dining, and encoded in both the division of space within the Dining Hall and the architectural language employed. Dining for all took place in the imposing main dining room on the ground floor, with Fellows and Scholars enjoying the privilege of dining on Commons, a formal three-course meal served there each evening. Fellows were eligible to join a private social club called the Senior Common Room, which occupied an exclusive suite of rooms on the first floor (also called the Senior Common Room), accessed by means of a private staircase. As Olley has noted, 'the hierarchical repertoire ... in skirting, dado, cornice, architrave and balustrade, leave one in no doubt as to which is the way to the common room'.[20]

The hierarchical organisation of the college went hand in hand with a distinct gendering of the architectural space, both historically and in de Blacam and Meagher's restoration. Along with the eighteenth-century classical features already mentioned, the dark-oak panelling in the main dining room was painstakingly restored, as were the monumental full-length portraits of previous provosts and benefactors in the history of Trinity – all men – which hang above the panelling. The Senior Common Room and the adjoining Smoking Room retain the ambience of a British gentlemen's club. Tooled leather sofas, rich wooden furniture, an imposing marble fireplace, and more framed portraits of notable men from Trinity's history, all serve to reinforce the space as a masculine one.[21] Significantly, it is within this suite of rooms that the reproduction of the Kärntner Bar is located.

The architectural gendering of the Dining Hall reflects the historical exclusion of women from the social space of Trinity.[22] Female students did not gain entry to the University until 1904, ten years after the Board of Governors had ruled against their admittance, pronouncing: 'If a female had once passed the gate, it would be practically impossible to watch what building or what chambers she might enter, or how long she might remain there'.[23] Once women were admitted, a watchful attitude towards them prevailed and a number of limitations were placed upon them so that the male-centric social organisation of the college remained intact. The Dining Hall played a significant role. Separate dining for men and women was enforced until the 1960s. Female students were excluded from the less formal lunch buffet, and female Scholars – who had passed the same academic examination as their male counterparts – were denied attendance at the 'Scholar's Dinner', held each year in honour of the newly-elected Scholars and Fellows. Female Scholars were also prohibited from dining on Commons alongside the male Scholars. Membership of the Senior Common Room was forbidden to female academics until 1958, when they were admitted as associate members, with conditions of restricted access: they had to leave the rooms by 2 p.m. to give the men their 'peace and quiet'.[24] Despite the discriminatory limitations on access there were bitter responses in the university newspaper that 'the gates opened and let the enemy in' and 'another male sanctuary had fallen'.[25] It was not until 1968 that female academics were admitted to Fellowship and became eligible for full membership of the Senior Common Room with the same rights of access as their male counterparts.

Today, women have a stronger presence within Trinity. Recent figures indicate that women make up 36 per cent of all academic staff and 47 per cent of all research staff.[26] Women Fellows are now represented in the portraits that line the stairwell from the main dining room to the Senior Common Room, albeit by one double-portrait amongst the plethora of individual male portraits. However, at around the time of the restoration project and the installation of the bar, the masculine culture of Trinity was still strongly evident.[27] There was a perception that the college was dominated by the 'old boy network'.[28] The legacy of historical discrimination against women was not easily forgotten, and continued to exert an influence. Right up until her retirement in 1987, Professor

Ann Crookshank stalwartly refused to dine on Commons as a protest against her exclusion (as a woman) from the 'Scholar's Dinner' in 1947, the year she was elected a Scholar.[29] As recently as 2002, the results of a questionnaire sent to all full-time female academics, both currently employed and retired, revealed that the perception of the college as a male bastion remained strong.[30] According to one respondent, Trinity was 'still an institution which behaves as if the staff consists of bachelor dons who live on campus'.[31] Despite the official admittance of women to the hallowed gentlemen's club of the Senior Common Room in the 1960s, they continued to be alienated by its bachelor culture, and, I would argue, by its architecture, both before and after the restoration in the 1980s. In this context, the Trinity Bar, beyond acknowledging Loos at a formal level, resonates with the idea of strict male gendering of social space for intellectual and cultural exchange, which is central to the interpretation of the Kärntner Bar in the historiography of Viennese modernism.

The Kärntner Bar: An Edited History

As has been previously discussed, the idea of the Kärntner Bar as a masculine space pervades the literature. This is to a large extent due to the success of Loos's own rhetoric, which has provided a powerful frame of reference for his architecture, and been a crucial influence on the reception of the Kärntner Bar. In the highly competitive artistic and architectural culture of fin-de-siècle Vienna, Loos was negotiating a space for himself and his architecture through a canny use of public lectures and printed articles in which he expounded his theories for cultural reform.[32] His theoretical framework was essentially oppositional, and forthrightly argumentative, with the Secession and the Wiener Werkstätte as the principal foils for his own self-positioning. This stance meant that Loos relied heavily on binary oppositions for rhetorical effect: he denounced culture that was ornamental, feminine, primitive and degenerate (the Secession, as he proclaimed it), advocating instead a culture that was plain, masculine, civilised and progressive (that which he would introduce to Austria).[33] While Loos was rehearsing these ideas from as early as 1898, it was in piecemeal fashion, and it is his later essay 'Ornament and Crime' that has been taken as the paradigmatic example and aggregation of all his theories of cultural reform by architectural means.[34] The essay also constitutes one of Loos's most direct attacks on the Secession and the Wiener Werkstätte, referencing members by name (Josef Maria Olbrich and Josef Hoffmann) or through their works ('Miraculous Draft of Fishes' and 'The Enchanted Princess' by Koloman Moser).[35] Loos's compelling rhetoric has promoted a forceful editing of history in the case of the Kärntner Bar in two major ways. There has been an editing of time, through a persistent, anachronistic pairing of the Kärntner Bar and the key text 'Ornament and

Crime', and there has been an editing of both time and space in the photographic representation of the bar.

The compression of time in the historiography, which brings the Kärntner Bar and 'Ornament and Crime' into synchronicity, derives from the routine dating of the essay to 1908 – the same date given for the completion of the bar. However, there is no evidence to date 'Ornament and Crime' any earlier than 1910, as a lecture, or 1913, for a print version in French.[36] With the persuasive polemic of 'Ornament and Crime' moved back in time to break onto Vienna's cultural scene in the same year as the Kärntner Bar, the two are brought into a shared dialogue, which has powerfully shaped the bar's reception history. Two examples will serve to illustrate this point. The first is Otakar Máčel's account of the Kärntner Bar.[37] His description, which closely follows that of Münz and Künstler, concludes by noting that, 'The year of the bar's completion is memorable for another reason. It was in 1908 that Loos wrote what is probably his best-known and most controversial essay, "Ornament und Verbrechen" ("Ornament and Crime")'.[38] The second example is the aforementioned examination of bachelor culture in Loos's work by Susan Henderson. Henderson considers the Kärntner Bar in the framework of Loos's ideas in 'Ornament and Crime', and positions the bar as a key illustration of his reassertion of a masculine aesthetic. In support of her argument, Henderson quotes Claire Loos, Loos's third wife, recounting a story that Loos had told her about the exclusion of women from the bar:

> The revolt of the women was great. Daily the bar was over-flowing, full of loiterers, but the women were refused. Countesses and princesses demonstrated, entreated, threatened, but in vain. They were not allowed in. [...] Finally, after five weeks, the situation was no longer tenable. The women were forced into retreat.[39]

Claire Loos wrote in German, and the above quotation is Henderson's own translation. The last sentence, in the original reads: 'Die Frauen erzwangen sich den Zutritt',[40] which correctly translates as 'the women forced entry' – exactly the opposite of 'the women were forced into retreat'. Henderson's mistranslation tellingly illustrates the success of Loosian rhetoric in shaping the history of the Kärntner Bar: equating the bar with Loos's ideas in 'Ornament and Crime' is so seductive, that Henderson simply cannot see it as anything other than a masculine space. She writes: 'The bar remained a male sanctum'.[41]

In the historiography, the narrative representation of a masculine space is reinforced by a corresponding visual representation. This involves the editing of both time and space. Photographs of the bar are often presented uncritically, sometimes wrongly dated, and sometimes not dated at all. Two photographs are most commonly used to illustrate the interior of the bar, both of which present the view towards the back wall. One shows a landscape on the wall, and a row of stools alongside the bar; the other shows a portrait of Altenberg and no stools (Figure 8.1). The photograph with the landscape and stools has been captioned with various dates: 1907, 1908 and 1930. The correct date is 1930, and the image comes from a set of photographs of Loos's buildings by the Viennese photographer Martin Gerlach, who was a friend of Loos. The second photograph, the one with the Altenberg portrait and no stools, has been more consistently dated in the literature, to 1907 (the year of some of Loos's drawings), or 1908, or 1909 (consistent with the opening of the bar in the winter of 1908–1909). However, as with the dating of 'Ornament and Crime', this is also an instance of chronological compression. The second photograph is actually a photomontage, and the original that it doctors is Gerlach's 1930 photograph. In the montage, the portrait of Altenberg by Gustav Jagerspacher, which had hung in the bar at the time of its opening, has been reinserted in the place of the landscape, and the row of stools alongside the bar has been edited out. The image thus becomes one of a standing bar, which signifies a male-only clientele. When dated to 1908–1909, we read this photograph as a definitive representation of the bar at around the time of its opening. Significantly, of all the photographic representations of

Figure 8.1 Interior of the Kärntner Bar: view towards the back wall. Photomontage after 1930. Courtesy of the Albertina, Vienna.

the bar, it is this montaged version that the Trinity Bar (Figure 8.2) most closely resembles.

The photomontage has been ascribed to Loos, which would make it an example of a direct intervention on his part in his own reception history. Loos certainly expended considerable effort in controlling the photography of his buildings, and worked closely with Gerlach to achieve this end.[42] Retouching, combination printing, and photomontage techniques were frequently used.[43] Gerlach's 1930 photograph of the interior of the bar was certainly being doctored in Loos's lifetime, as a version with the stools edited out (but without the Altenberg portrait montaged in) appeared in Franz Glück's 1931 publication on Loos.[44] The timing is significant, as 1930 was the year of Loos's sixtieth birthday, and that of his architectural rival, Josef Hoffmann. Both architects marked the occasion with photographic exhibitions of their oeuvres.[45] Given Loos's lifelong animosity towards Hoffmann, and his characterisation of his work as overtly feminine, one can assume that in this exhibition 'face-off' it would have been important for Loos that the differences between the two architectural practices were strongly marked. The Kärntner Bar was represented in Loos's birthday exhibition at the Hagenbund, but as the catalogue is not illustrated, it is not possible to ascertain if the photomontage was used.[46] However, it was published in the aforementioned monograph by Münz and Künstler, alongside the customary textual narrative of a masculine space.[47] The material in this publication came from the Adolf

Figure 8.2 Trinity Bar, Trinity College Dublin. Architects de Blacam and Meagher. Photograph 2008, Declan Cusack.

Loos Archives established by Münz, a close friend of Loos, who began collecting the material during Loos's lifetime. As Münz had been authorised to look after the 'artistic questions relating to Loos',[48] it is reasonably safe to assume that the photomontage of the Kärntner Bar, constructed more than twenty years after its opening, but dated to the time of its opening, presents the vision of the bar that Loos wanted handed down for posterity.

Our conception of the Kärntner Bar, then, rests on a forcefully edited history, the two major components of which are a retrospectively edited 1930 photograph that purports to be a definitive visual representation of the bar in 1908, and a historiographical orthodoxy that has shifted Loos's key text 'Ornament and Crime' back in time to coincide with the opening of the bar. These significant edits, together with the persistently reiterated textual narratives, which present both the architecture and social function of the bar as strictly male gendered, allow only one story of the bar to be told. In this story the Kärntner Bar has to be the embodiment of the rhetoric of 'Ornament and Crime', and can only be positioned antithetically to the 'ornamental' and 'feminine' art and architecture of the Secessionists. However, the heavily edited nature of the received history of the Kärntner Bar suggests that there may be another story to be told about its design, opening and social function, and about where we position Loos and his architecture in Vienna 1900.

The Kärntner Bar Reconsidered

If the Trinity Bar is a mere simulacrum, an image of the image constructed in 1930, or later, by either Loos or those he trusted with his *Nachlass* (estate), and perpetuated by later writers and publishers, what was the real object, the original Kärntner Bar, that this representation has effaced? Was it the exemplar of a masculine space for intellectual and cultural exchange – a successful gendered organisation of social space through architectural means? Does it represent a point and place in time and space when Loos achieved a polarisation with the Secession?

In a recent exploration of Loos's Café Museum, Tag Gronberg has argued persuasively that the idea of the coffeehouse as a space for strictly masculine intellectual and cultural exchange was problematic: 'when articulated through reference to the Kaffeehaus, the binary oppositions so important to Loos's polemic are constantly threatened and undermined'.[49] Gronberg identifies three key elements that bring connotations of the feminine into the Café Museum. First, shared influences made the polarisation of Loos and the Secession impossible. Second, the rapid change, renewal, refurbishment and differentiation of product, that were key elements in the relentless struggle to make coffeehouses visible and attractive, meant that they were an important part of Viennese urban consumerism. Third, the association of the coffeehouses with literary *Kleinkunst* linked them intimately with the fashionable and the ephemeral. As Gronberg puts it, there were 'increasingly ambivalent cultural connotations of the Kaffeehaus around 1900, simultaneously connoting masculine intellect and feminine frivolity'.[50] The Kärntner Bar, although constructed as an unproblematic male space in the edited history, does not, however, transcend the gender tensions that Gronberg identifies in the Café Museum in 1899.

In addition to the much-published photomontage, there also exist two infrequently-published photographs of the interior of the Kärntner Bar, reliably dated to circa 1909, which provide a good starting point for a discussion of these tensions. One photograph shows the view towards the entrance, and the other the view towards the back wall (Figure 8.3). These photographs present a more lively image than the austere interior of the photomontage. Instead of dark leather on the seating there is floral jacquard upholstery, and ornamental jugs are symmetrically placed along the back wall. The portrait of Altenberg is both much bigger, and more square in format, than the rectangular one inserted into the montage. It is also integrated into the architectural scheme in what appears to be a gold-painted frame. The overall impression is more in keeping

Figure 8.3 Interior of the Kärntner Bar: view towards the back wall. Photograph 1909. Courtesy of Bundesdenkmalamt, Vienna.

with Secessionist decorative schemes than with the unremittingly plain, clean-lined and 'masculine' aesthetic presented in the montage. One could almost go so far as to say that the 1909 photograph depicts an interior design strategy of the very type that Loos castigates in his theoretical writings: a room designed around a painting.

In his 'parable' of 'The Poor Little Rich Man', published in the *Neues Wiener Tagblatt* in 1900, Loos tells the story of a happy man rendered unhappy by having his house 'made over' by an architect who designs everything down to the smallest detail.[51] The architect tells his patron: 'Don't you see that for every picture I have hung for you I have also designed a frame on the partition or on the wall? You can't even *move* a picture'.[52] The story is implicitly critical of Secessionist culture, and in particular of the collaboration between Josef Hoffmann and Gustav Klimt. Wealthy female patrons who had their portraits painted by Klimt would often employ the services of Hoffmann to design an interior suitable for the picture.[53] Yet Loos's integration of the portrait of Altenberg and its impressive frame into the back wall of the Kärntner Bar has some affinity with Hoffmann's design strategy.

While the 1909 photograph problematises the view that the Kärntner Bar represents an antithesis to Hoffmann's work, it also points to some of the differences between the two practices. As Eduard Sekler has shown, Loos and Hoffman both drew on an English tradition of architecture and applied arts, but differed in what they selected from that tradition and how they used it in their work.[54] Loos's use of fabric is significant in this respect. Although he may have originally considered green automobile leather for the Kärntner Bar seating,[55] in the actual installation Loos employed a floral jacquard of English design, stylistically dating to the early 1890s.[56] Loos sourced his upholstery fabrics from Victor Tepser, a Viennese interior decorator, upholsterer and antiquarian, who specialised in French and English textiles. Rolls of these textiles were also bought for the Museum of Art and Industry, by the then director and confirmed Anglophile, Arthur von Scala. Von Scala's decision to favour English over Viennese craftsmanship attracted much controversy in Vienna, with both Loos and Hoffmann taking active roles in the debate.[57] In one of Loos's many articles in favour of von Scala's approach, he wrote: 'The fundamental principle of the Scala vision emerges sharply in the Winter Exhibition: either imitate exactly, or create something new. There is no third way'.[58] Loos's use of existing English textiles in his interior designs contrasts with Hoffmann's practice of using textiles newly-designed by himself or fellow members of the Wiener Werkstätte, and executed by the Viennese firm Johann Backhausen and Sons. Loos's choice of fabric for the Kärntner Bar is therefore not insignificant; on the contrary, it firmly announces Loos's position in an existing artistic debate, and signals the point of divergence between him and Hoffmann in their shared appreciation of English design.

The Kärntner Bar is also linked with the Secession through Jagerspacher's portrait of Altenberg. The portrait references a drawing of Altenberg made in 1907 by the Secessionist Berthold Löffler.[59] In this drawing, Löffler had simplified certain elements and exaggerated others to create an image of Altenberg bordering on caricature. Jagerspacher's portrait replicates the key elements of Löffler's 1907 characterisation: the over-sized coat rendered in a grid design; the profile view emphasising the distinctive shape of Altenberg's balding pate, furrowed brow, and emblematic walrus moustache; and a wide-brimmed hat held in skeletal fingers. These shared characteristics implicate the Jagerspacher portrait, and thus the Kärntner Bar, in the creation of a distinctive identity for Altenberg, which was intimately bound up with Secessionist aesthetics and interior architecture due to Löffler's work for the Wiener Werkstätte and the Cabaret Fledermaus.[60]

Further evidence which problematises the positioning of the Kärntner Bar as anti-Secessionist can be found in one of the preliminary sketches for the bar that Loos made in 1907 (Figure 8.4). In this sketch, Loos drafts a number of possible names for the bar: 'Kärntner Bar' (twice), 'Marble Bar', and, perhaps somewhat surprisingly, 'Klimt Bar'. While it could be argued that Loos was simply being ironic in thinking of naming the bar after Klimt, the president

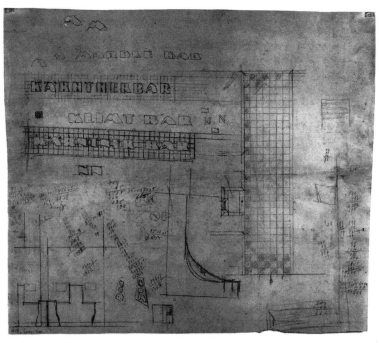

Figure 8.4 Adolf Loos, Sketch for Kärntner Bar, 1907. Courtesy of the Albertina, Vienna.

of the Secession, it must be noted that in a similar sketching of possible titles, this time for his journal *Das Andere*, Loos works very seriously through the possible alternatives, with no trace of playfulness or irony.[61] In addition, as I have shown, the antecedents of the Jagerspacher portrait, and the portrait's placement within the overall decorative scheme, make links between the Kärntner Bar and Secessionist aesthetics, which have been eliminated in the later edited history.

As well as the incursion of the feminine into the bar through certain intersections with the Secession, the subject of the portrait – Altenberg – together with the portrait's prominence, immediately implicate the bar in the promotion of the fashionable and the ephemeral.[62] Author of impressionistic sketches and poems, Altenberg was one of the key exponents of literary *Kleinkunst* in Vienna 1900. From 1905 to 1909 he also held a position reviewing variety and cabaret shows for the *Wiener Allgemeine Zeitung*, a role which also stresses an association with low, rather than high, culture, and which is explicitly referenced in the Jagerspacher portrait. Jagerspacher paints Altenberg against a backdrop of a starry night, and a wall of theatre posters, including one for the Apollo, a variety theatre on Gumpendorferstrasse, whose shows Altenberg reviewed. The portrait therefore celebrated a wide range of perceived 'lightweight' and therefore 'feminine' artistic productions. Moreover, the portrait not only referenced consumer culture in its subject matter, but had itself a practical function within the commercial arena.

Altenberg's public persona was intimately entwined with some of Vienna's most popular cafés and social establishments.[63] The installation of his portrait in the Kärntner Bar can therefore be seen as a commercial ploy on the part of Loos, or the bar's proprietor – in effect an advertisement suggesting Altenberg's approval of this particular bar. The timing of its installation is pertinent in this respect. Altenberg celebrated his fiftieth birthday in March 1909. Forever short of money and reliant on patronage, Altenberg, the consummate self-publicist, saw his birthday as an opportunity to launch a campaign which would bolster his public image and bring in some money. In the autumn of 1908 he wrote to Alfred Kerr suggesting that Kerr place a notice in all the German newspapers announcing a collection in honour of his birthday.[64] On 20 March 1909, an official birthday celebration was held at the Cabaret Fledermaus. A commemorative souvenir was produced, which consisted of a colour lithographic portrait of Altenberg by Löffler, a reworking of his 1907 drawing, discussed earlier.[65] Each copy was hand-signed and dated by Altenberg and sold for the price of two kronen. The graphic qualities that the Jagerspacher portrait shares with Löffler's meant that it too could be easily reproduced – two known copies in watercolour exist[66] – further implicating the bar in both the creation of, and cashing in on, a highly marketable image of Altenberg. The Kärntner Bar was not the only establishment which exploited Altenberg's birthday for its own publicity. The Casino de Paris, for example, placed a banner advertisement on the front page of the *Wiener Allgemeine Zeitung* on 20 March, wishing Altenberg a happy birthday.[67] The identity of the Kärntner Bar was thus partly shaped by its prominent participation in the popular fugitive advertising opportunity presented by Altenberg's birthday.

The Kärntner Bar also engaged with the vagaries of fashion in another significant respect. Loos's promotion of English and American culture has been discussed almost exclusively in terms of a masculine ideal, which has, of course, impacted on the interpretation of the Kärntner Bar. However, it must also be seen in the context of the fashionability of all things English and American in Vienna in the early twentieth century. This fashion was not confined to masculine spaces and pursuits; in fact it was most evident in the feminine realm. The Kärntner Bar was just doors away from an 'English and American Manicure and Hair Salon',[68] and a Fashion House that advertised itself as 'patronised by English and American Ladies'.[69] The fact that these businesses, and others (including Victor Tepser, the firm that supplied Loos's upholstery fabrics), chose to publicise their English and American credentials in advertisements placed in Adolf Kronfeld's 1904 *Masterpieces of Painting: Vienna Galleries* – a guidebook to artworks in Vienna written in German, English and French – demonstrates the relationship of the fashion for English and American culture with tourism and the popularisation of high culture. The Kärntner Bar is thus embedded in a nexus of commerce, celebrity and culture. Formal links with Secessionist aesthetics, the portrait of Vienna's renowned coffeehouse habitué, opportunistic advertising, and riding the tide of a current fad for English and American culture, bring feminine elements into the Kärntner Bar, which compromise a reading of it as an unproblematic masculine space.

If the architectural language of the Kärntner Bar is fraught with instabilities that undermine fixed binary oppositions, the idea in the edited history that the bar successfully gendered the social function as strictly male is also unsustainable – in practice, the initial restriction to men was immediately contested. Claire Loos's account of women gaining admittance after five weeks of the bar's opening is corroborated by evidence from the *Wiener Allgemeine Zeitung*. Altenberg's review appeared on 22 February 1909, and the first known advertisement for the bar was a banner beneath the masthead of the 22 March 1909 edition. Two days later, occupying the same position as the previous advertisement, a new notice for the bar announced that, due to popular demand, women's hours were to be introduced – mornings, between 10 a.m. and 11.30 a.m., and afternoons, between 2 p.m. and 5 p.m. – but that 'for the remaining hours the principle of the American bar will be upheld'.[70] The feminine thus entered the bar in a multitude of guises, from intersections with the Secession, popular culture and consumerism, to the physical presence of women customers. The Kärntner Bar, as it is figured in the historiography, is therefore a chimera.

Resituating the Kärntner Bar

In this study, I have traced a reception history of the Kärntner Bar from its reproduction in Trinity College, Dublin in the 1980s, through a body of literature, back to the bar's origins in Vienna in the first decade of the twentieth century. In examining the Kärntner Bar back in its own time and place – the vibrant intellectual and cultural world of fin-de-siècle Vienna – the picture of the bar that emerged was not that of the strictly masculine space that had been 'faithfully' reproduced in Trinity College Dublin, but a much more problematic space, both architecturally and ideologically. In particular, the strict binary oppositions that Loos made such successful use of in his polemical writings – ornament versus plain, feminine versus masculine, high versus low culture – were in much freer play in the Kärntner Bar at the time of its establishment. It remains to be asked, what are the implications of these complexities for where we position Loos and his architecture in Vienna 1900?

One of the main ramifications is that Loos's position on the gendering of social space through architectural means did not necessitate a radical opposition with the Secession at the practical level, even if he assumed this theoretical stance in his writings and lectures. The fact that Loos toyed with the idea of calling the bar the 'Klimt Bar' also shows how he may have wished to maintain links with the Secession at a personal or professional level. Furthermore, Loos, despite being so vociferous in his attacks on the Secession, never publicly attacked Klimt, a conundrum that has been explored by Beatriz Colomina.[71] However, while Colomina suggests that Loos's silence against Klimt may have been a mask, which hid similar, if not stronger feelings, than those Loos had against Hoffmann,[72] my exploration of the Kärntner Bar has presented an alternative view. I would argue that Vienna's cultural scene – at least at the time of the bar's design and opening – was not as strongly divided into opposing factions as it has been characterised in the historiography.

The confrontational artistic climate that Elana Shapira has described – 'Loos's and Kokoschka's "Expressionist team" opposed "the Secessionist team" of Josef Hoffmann and Gustav Klimt'[73] – cannot be applied to the situation in 1907, when Loos was designing the Kärntner Bar. At this time there was no 'Loos and Kokoschka team', as Loos had not yet met the young artist Oskar Kokoschka who he was later to patronise – a move that has been characterised as Loos's recruitment of Kokoschka in his battle against the Secession.[74] In 1907, Kokoschka was studying under Löffler at the Kunstgewerbeschule, and through him receiving commissions from the Wiener Werkstätte. It was in fact Klimt who facilitated Kokoschka's exhibition debut at the Kunstschau of 1908, and thought him 'the outstanding talent among the younger generation'.[75] As Robert Jensen has demonstrated, the 1908 Kunstschau coincided with the collapse of the utopian ideals of the Secession and a radical transformation of Vienna's art institutions.[76] However, at the time of the design of the Kärntner Bar, Klimt was at the head of 'an extraordinary centralisation of power over Vienna's artistic affairs',[77] of which Loos would have been all too aware. At this time, Loos, who had yet to receive a major architectural commission, may not have wanted to completely alienate himself from the centre of power. The reproduction of the Kärntner Bar in Trinity College, Dublin, makes manifest the idea that pervades the reception history of the original – namely, that Loos's identity, shaped in opposition to ornament and to the Secession, was fully realised by 1909, with the Kärntner Bar as its most perfect expression. The reproduction thus acts like a reverse distorting mirror, smoothing out all inconsistencies that would disturb the image of the Kärntner Bar as the exemplar of Loos's masculine modernist architecture. In delving into the history of the Kärntner Bar beyond that which is reproduced in the mirror, I have shown how the bar did not represent a battle won, but the more tentative moves made by Loos in the brokering of his position within the Viennese cultural scene at the beginning of the twentieth century. The Kärntner Bar, far from presenting a fixed artistic, intellectual, gender and social identity for Loos and his architecture, demonstrates just how complex the negotiations of these various identities were in Vienna 1900.

Acknowledgements

I would like to thank Jeremy Aynsley, Tag Gronberg and Simon Shaw-Miller for inviting me to participate in the conference 'The Viennese Café as an Urban Site of Cultural Exchange'; Kenneth McKenzie for alerting me to the existence of the Trinity Bar in the first instance; Shane de Blacam and Edward McParland for meeting me at the bar to discuss the Dining Hall project; Declan Cusack for his photography; and Gemma Blackshaw and Gilbert Carr for their helpful comments on earlier drafts of this chapter.

Notes

1. Anna-Marie Wallner, 'Ein Bar-Geburstag und andere Feste', *Die Presse*, 9 May 2007, http://diepresse.com/home/leben/mensch/382936/index.do?from=simarchiv (accessed on 14 June 2009).
2. Ibid.
3. There are inconsistencies in the published sources as to exactly when the Kärntner Bar opened. In a retrospective account, Oskar Kokoschka writes that it opened in 1907 (Oskar Kokoschka, *My Life*, London 1974, 37), but there is no other evidence to support such an early date. Heinrich Nowak, in another retrospective account, says that it opened in either 1908 or 1909 (Heinrich Nowak, 'Adolf Loos – Der Feind Des Ornaments "Die Sonnenseuche", 1909–1920', in Adolf Opel (ed.), *Konfrontationen: Schriften von und über Adolf Loos*, Vienna 1988, 40). The first published review of the bar appeared in March 1909 (Peter

Altenberg, 'Eine neue "Bar" in Wien', in Opel, *Konfrontationen*, 35–37; first published in *Wiener Allgemeine Zeitung*, 22 February 1909), and its first listing in the telephone directory (*Verzeichnis der Abonnenten und öffentlichen Sprechstellen des Telephonnetzes in Wien und der übrigen Telephonnetze Niederösterreichs*) was in the second volume for 1909, published in June. Combined with Nowak's recollection that the bar opened around Christmas time, these facts suggest an opening date sometime in winter 1908–1909.

4. For the trajectory of the interest in Vienna 1900 see Steven Beller, 'Introduction', in Steven Beller (ed.), *Rethinking Vienna 1900*, New York 2001, 1–5.

5. An exception is John Olley, 'Rebuilding in a Classical Tradition', *Architects' Journal*, 185(24), 1987, 50. Olley places his discussion of the Trinity Bar within a larger consideration of the relevance of Loos's architecture to the restoration project as a whole, which he considers on purely formal terms.

6. Altenberg, 'Eine neue "Bar"', 35–36.

7. Ibid., 35.

8. Ludwig Münz and Gustav Künstler, *Adolf Loos: Pioneer of Modern Architecture*, London 1966. First published in German as Ludwig Münz and Gustav Künstler, *Der Architekt Adolf Loos*, Vienna 1964.

9. Münz and Künstler, *Adolf Loos*, 58.

10. Kokoschka, *My Life*, 37.

11. 'In the coffee-houses we read the newspapers and heard, or sensed, political conflict disturbing the air where once one had been able to drink a cup of coffee in peace and quiet'. Ibid., 23.

12. On the general exclusion of women from the coffeehouses in the nineteenth century, see Gilbert C. Carr, 'Austrian Literature and the Coffee-House before 1890', *Austrian Studies*, 16(1), 2008, 165 and *Das Wiener Kaffeehaus Von den Anfängen bis zur Zwischenkriegszeit*, Vienna 1980, 32.

13. Susan R. Henderson, 'Bachelor Culture in the Work of Adolf Loos', *Journal of Architectural Education*, 55(3), 2002, 125–135.

14. Irish artist Alice Hanratty reproduced the original portrait of Peter Altenberg by Gustav Jagerspacher.

15. On the restoration project, see Olley, 'Rebuilding', 37–51, and Ann Reihill, 'The Restoration of the Dining Hall, Trinity College, Dublin', *Irish Arts Review*, 3(1), 1986, 26–37. Shane de Blacam discusses the project in Shane O'Toole, 'Mirror Image', *Sunday Times* (*Culture*), 21 January 2001, 16–17, and in conversation with the author, June 2008.

16. Olley, 'Rebuilding', 39.

17. O'Toole, 'Mirror Image', 17.

18. On the early history of Trinity, see *The Book of Trinity College, Dublin, 1591–1891*, Belfast 1892.

19. Scholars are elected annually from the student body on the result of an examination held in the second year of undergraduate study. Fellows are academics who have demonstrated scholarship or research achievement of a high order, together with a significant contribution to the academic life of the College.

20. Olley, 'Rebuilding', 42.

21. The only exception is a portrait of Queen Elizabeth I on the landing outside the Senior Common Room.

22. On the history of women in Trinity, see Susan M. Parkes (ed.), *A Danger to the Men? A History of Women in Trinity College Dublin, 1904–2004*, Dublin 2004.

23. 'Extract from the Statement of the Board Regarding Women's Education, July 1895', reproduced in Parkes, *A Danger to the Men?*, 304.

24. John V. Luce, *Trinity College Dublin, The First Four Hundred Years*, Dublin 1992, 175.

25. Susan M. Parkes, 'The 1950s: Breaking the Mould', in Parkes, *A Danger to the Men?*, 199.
26. Report supplied by the Equality Office, Trinity College, based on data collected in November 2008. The figures show, however, that women are under-represented at senior level: the proportion of female professors is just 12 per cent.
27. In the period 1984–1985, women made up only 17 per cent of all academic staff, and were little represented at the higher levels. In 1988, when there were only five female Fellows to 128 male Fellows, a review of the position of women in Trinity was undertaken following a petition by 49 women academics. The findings revealed substantial gender imbalances, and recommendations were made to make Trinity more of a meritocracy. See Maryann Valiulis, 'Putting Women at the Centre: The Establishment of the Centre for Gender and Women's Studies', in Parkes, *A Danger to the Men?*, 222–226.
28. Ibid., 224.
29. Edward McParland, 'The Apollo Portrait: Anne Crookshank', *Apollo*, 126, October 1987, 272–273.
30. Valiulis, 'Putting Women at the Centre', 226–227.
31. Quoted in ibid., 227.
32. From 1897 onwards, Loos wrote articles for a number of Viennese newspapers, including the *Neue Freie Presse*, articles which were later published in collected volumes. He also published his own journal *Das Andere* (The Other) in 1903. He gave public lectures in Vienna and other major European cities from 1910 onwards. See Janet Stewart, *Fashioning Vienna: Adolf Loos's Cultural Criticism*, London 2000, 10–41.
33. Loos's journal, *Das Andere*, was subtitled *Ein Blatt zur Einführung abendländischer Kultur in Österreich* (A Journal for the Introduction of Western Culture into Austria).
34. Adolf Loos, 'Ornament and Crime (1929)', in Adolf Opel (ed.), *Ornament and Crime. Selected Essays,* translated by M. Mitchell, Riverside 1998, 167–176.
35. Ibid., 169, 171, 173.
36. For a discussion of the dating of 'Ornament and Crime', see Stewart, *Fashioning Vienna*, 173 [n. 5].
37. Otakar Máčel, 'American Bar (Kärntnerbar), Vienna (1907–8)', in Christoph Grafe and Franciska Bollerey (eds), *Cafes and Bars: The Architecture of Public Display*, London 2007, 140–144.
38. Ibid., 144.
39. Henderson, 'Bachelor Culture', 132.
40. Claire Loos, *Adolf Loos Privat*, Vienna 1936, 13.
41. Henderson, 'Bachelor Culture', 132.
42. Jan Otakar Fischer, 'White Walls in the Golden City: The Return of the Villa Müller', *Harvard Design Magazine,* 15, 2001, 20.
43. See Beatriz Colomina, 'The Split Wall: Domestic Voyeurism', in Beatriz Colomina (ed.), *Sexuality & Space*, New York 1992, 73–128, and Charles Rice, *The Emergence of the Interior: Architecture, Modernity, Domesticity*, London 2007, 100–104.
44. Franz Glück, *Adolf Loos*, Paris 1931, Plate 8 [unpaginated].
45. Both exhibitions were held in December 1930, Loos's at the Hagenbund and Hoffmann's at the Österreichischen Museum.
46. *Adolf Loos – Ausstellung zu seinem 60. Geburtstag*, Vienna 1930.
47. Münz and Künstler, *Adolf Loos*, 55.
48. Elsie Altmann Loos, quoted in Stewart, *Fashioning Vienna*, 16.
49. Tag Gronberg, *Vienna, City of Modernity, 1890–1914*, Oxford 2007.
50. Ibid.

51. Adolf Loos, 'The Poor Little Rich Man', in Adolf Loos, *Spoken into the Void. Collected Essays 1897–1900*, translated by J.O. Newman and J.H. Smith, Cambridge, Mass. 1982, 125–127. First published in *Neues Wiener Tagblatt*, 26 April 1900.

52. Ibid., 127.

53. In 1903, both the Knips and Henneberg families commissioned Hoffmann in the wake of having portraits painted by Klimt.

54. Eduard F. Sekler, 'Hoffmann, Loos and Britain: Selective Perspectives', *9H* (6), 1983, 2–8.

55. Ludwig Hevesi, 'Eine American Bar', *Kunst und Kunsthandwerk*, 12, 1909, 215.

56. The design is similar to some designs produced by the Silver Studio between 1903 and 1905, but does not correspond to an exact design in the Silver Studio archive. The fabric may have been produced by the English manufacturers Warners, but it has not been possible to pursue this avenue of research as the Warners archive was closed to researchers at the time of writing this chapter.

57. Stewart, *Fashioning Vienna*, 179.

58. Adolf Loos, 'Review of the Arts and Crafts, II', in Adolf Loos, *Spoken into the Void*, 137. First published in *Die Wage*, 26 November 1898.

59. Löffler's drawing is usefully reproduced alongside a copy of the Jagerspacher portrait in Patrick Werkner, 'Altenberg-Portraits', in Heinz Lunzer and Victoria Lunzer-Talos (eds), *Peter Altenberg, Extracte des Lebens: einem Schriftsteller auf der Spur*, Salzburg 2003, 128–129.

60. The Cabaret Fledermaus, a club, theatre and bar, was founded by the Wiener Werkstätte in 1907. Josef Hoffmann designed the interior and Berthold Löffler the ceramic decoration.

61. Reproduced in Burkhardt Rukschcio and Roland Schachel, *Adolf Loos: Leben und Werk*, Salzburg 1982, 86.

62. Altenberg was considered by contemporaries to be an androgynous figure. A full consideration of Altenberg's complex gender identity is beyond the scope of this essay, but has been discussed in Gronberg, *Vienna*, 51–53.

63. Harold B. Segel (ed.), *The Vienna Coffeehouse Wits, 1890–1938*, West Lafayette 1993, 111–112.

64. Letter from Peter Altenberg to Alfred Kerr, reprinted in Egon Friedell (ed.), *Das Altenbergbuch*, Vienna 1921, 97.

65. Reproduced in Lunzer and Lunzer-Talos, *Peter Altenberg*, 151.

66. The copies are located in the Neue Galerie, New York, and in the Wien Museum, Vienna.

67. *Wiener Allgemeine Zeitung*, 20 March 1909, 1.

68. Adolf Kronfeld, *Masterpieces of Painting: Vienna Galleries*, Vienna 1904, iv.

69. Ibid., xx.

70. *Wiener Allgemeine Zeitung*, 24 March 1909, 1.

71. Beatriz Colomina, 'Sex, Lies and Decoration: Adolf Loos and Gustav Klimt', in Tobias G. Natter and Christoph Grunenberg (eds), *Gustav Klimt: Painting, Design and Modern Life*, London 2008, 43–52.

72. Ibid., 50.

73. Elana Shapira, 'The Pioneers: Loos, Kokoschka and Their Shared Clients', in Tobias G. Natter (ed.), *Oskar Kokoschka: Early Portraits from Vienna and Berlin, 1909–1914*, New York 2002, 58.

74. Claude Cernuschi, *Re/casting Kokoschka: Ethics and Aesthetics, Epistemology and Poetics in Fin-de-Siècle Vienna*, Madison and London 2002, 25.

75. Quoted in Tobias G. Natter, '"Portraits of Characters, Not Portraits of Faces": An Introduction to Kokoschka's Early Portraits', in Natter, *Kokoschka*, 88.

76. Robert Jensen, 'A Matter of Professionalism: Marketing Identity in Fin-de-Siècle Vienna', in Beller, *Rethinking Vienna*, 199.

77. Ibid., 201.

Chapter 9

GRAPHIC AND INTERIOR DESIGN IN THE VIENNESE COFFEEHOUSE AROUND 1900

Experience and Identity

Jeremy Aynsley

Introduction: Word and Image in the Café Environment

Representations of people reading became a familiar trope in the history of the Viennese coffeehouse. Whether featuring an older man under the guise of a philosopher or member of the literati, as in Reinhold Völkel's famous painting of Café Griensteidl of 1896, or a fashionably-dressed younger woman participating in a vibrant part of modern life, as in Moriz Jung's equally renowned Wiener Werkstätte postcard of Café Heinrichhof of 1910, popular and familiar forms of visual culture linked the pleasures of coffee drinking and reading in the coffeehouse interior. These images appeared in magazines that offered commentary on the phenomenon of the coffeehouse, and also in the advertisements and other forms of visual promotion for these establishments. This chapter explores the various ways in which print culture intersected with the Viennese coffeehouse. Taking four kinds of graphic representation as its focus – the magazine, the poster, the design and the shop sign – it draws attention to the relationship between the coffeehouse as depicted in graphic form and in terms of its actual interiors. I argue that the two fields were inextricably linked in the everyday experience and identity of the coffeehouse. Furthermore, I suggest that to re-unite these fields in an interpretation that attributes significance to 'designing' as an important activity may offer a fresh perspective for our thinking about the social practice of graphic and interior design, both in turn-of-the-century Vienna and beyond. This chapter will build on the ideas of the café as a site of cultural exchange already explored in other chapters in this volume by examining the particular character of print culture in the coffeehouses of Vienna around 1900.

In the history of print and the graphic arts, it has been suggested that a heightened engagement with the possibilities of word and image often comes to the fore at times of political, social and artistic urgency.[1] Such was the case in turn-of-the-century Vienna, when profound changes in human understanding were occurring, with the advent of psychology and psychoanalysis, together with the impact of urban modernity.[2] Something as apparently straightforward as reading was inevitably implicated in this. Reading, it could be argued, is both an interior activity, a symptom of the processes of the mind and its emblematic interiority, and also an expression of exteriority. Engagement with text takes the reader from a private terrain of individual thought to the public world of shared signs, where it becomes a socialised, group activity. Moreover, to read in public spaces such as the café stresses this paradox: it makes known what a subject is experiencing and thinking. The graphic signs of a book-cover, a newspaper masthead or magazine cover can expose, even betray, the interests and identity of the reader. As depictions of reading have shown, it can also involve a level of performance: the way a certain title is selected, the turning of its pages, the level of concentration or distractedness at each stage, these all offer information about the reader. The coffeehouse was a space where the expectation was for a large number of visitors to participate in a ritualised behaviour in what might be considered a distilled form of modernity, in which they were no doubt conscious and, at times, self-conscious of the ambiguities and nuances of their actions.

To pay attention to graphic culture entails taking account of both word and image. This can involve drawing on distinct interpretative traditions which often function separately. In the case of literary modernism in turn-of-the-century Vienna, the emphasis has been on the café as a site of intellectual exchange, with priority given to the distinguished literary culture of a metropolitan élite: the recognised authors, poets, playwrights, novelists, and journalists of Jung Wien.[3] As such, the literature on the coffeehouse has tended to see the physical environment as an important location for literary production and exchange between protagonists which has rarely been an object of attention in its own right. Less consideration has been given to how words – in various forms – contributed to the social atmosphere and identity of the coffeehouse through their material being.

In contrast with the approaches to literature commented on above, interpretations of the visual arts in turn-of-the-century Vienna have concentrated attention on the contribution of Viennese graphic designers to the Secession style.[4] While no doubt they presented a major contribution to the possibilities of experimental visual culture, to view Secessionist designs solely in these terms can also underestimate their impact, in this case, privileging aesthetic innovation and design reform. By implication, and in parallel with my comments on literary method above, little has been done to return designs to their original contexts, to recover their currency and agency as artefacts in a wider world of consumption. By taking an historical approach to graphic design in the coffeehouse, I hope to draw attention to the form of signage encountered before and on entering a venue, to the various kinds of graphic information, as well as to the range of newspapers, magazines and books that people read during their visit to these sites.[5]

Vienna: Graphic and Publishing Trades – a Context

Like so many other cities during the period of industrialisation and migration to urban centres, Vienna experienced a period of rapid change in the late nineteenth century. The population grew from 607,510 in 1869 to 1,364,548 in 1890, when the over-arching administration of Greater Vienna unified the suburbs, incorporating the eleventh to the nineteenth districts.[6] Part of this urban development saw the consolidation of the city's print industries in a wave of commercial and cultural expansion. Bernhard Denscher describes this period (around 1900) as follows:

> The field of publicity became one of singular importance in and of itself; its separation from the sphere of political power granting it even greater significance. A unique culture of advertising, the press announcement, the poster, the publicity campaign, emerged. A series of publications established themselves, giving serious attention to the new phenomenon of advertising.[7]

The role of Vienna was important in this development. As the fourth largest city in Europe and capital of the Austrian half of the Dual Monarchy of Austria-Hungary, its reputation as a city of cultural significance was long established, while its contribution to artistic innovation and avant-garde culture grew from the 1890s onwards, a period that coincided with the flowering of coffeehouse culture. Vienna was a German-speaking city, but included inhabitants from across Austria-Hungary who spoke many other languages as their mother tongue. In the years before 1918, Austria-Hungary encompassed territories from what are now the Czech Republic, Slovakia, Hungary, Slovenia, Croatia, Italy, Poland, the Ukraine, Serbia and Romania.

As historical commentaries on the newly emergent graphic design and poster movement suggested, Austrian graphic trades, paper manufacture, printing houses and publishing industries also had a long and distinguished history.[8] In most respects, the paradigm for graphic culture was Germany, and Austria was always keen to maintain business and industrial relations with her new nation neighbour state. Many type-foundries, paper manufacturers and publishers operated branches in Berlin, Leipzig and Offenbach am Main, for example, as well as Vienna, and there was constant interchange with other cities. Vienna's role as a key urban centre for Austria-Hungary also gave the city a unique position in terms of its geographical and cultural realm, and this contributed to the particular nature of print culture as played out in the wider public sphere, including the coffeehouses.

A useful reference to gauge Austrian and Viennese achievements in the field of publishing came in 1914, with the important *Internationale Ausstellung für Buchgewerbe und Graphik* (known as BUGRA), an exhibition held in Leipzig in 1914. In many respects this marked the culmination of the previous thirty years of commercial and technical growth in the field of the book trade and graphic design in Europe.[9] The *Oesterreichisches Haus* (Austrian house), which received the highest medal, displayed the rewards of years of progressive moves to make the paper, printing and book publishing industry one of the most important for Austria-Hungary and across central Europe. Friedrich Jasper, the renowned Viennese publisher, was responsible for the catalogue which provided a synopsis of Vienna's modern publishing prowess.[10] The accompanying commentaries constantly stressed how Vienna's sphere of influence extended across the whole of Austria-Hungary.

The foundations of the industry can be traced to the period following the 1848 revolution, when a relative relaxation of press censorship led to the growth of a liberal press, of which the daily newspaper the *Neue Freie Presse,* founded in 1864, was the most important. The commentary in the catalogue laid great emphasis on the central body for the organisation of book-related trades, the *Wiener Korporation der Buchkunst- und Musikalienhändler,* which was proud to be the oldest such body in Europe, with branches in Prague, Graz, Lemberg and Kraków. In 1889, this became the *Verein österreichisch – ungarischen Buchhändler.* The encouragement of reading in Austria-Hungary was also advanced by the public libraries movement, which began in the 1840s and continued throughout the period. Compulsory elementary education, established in 1869, played an important role in increasing literacy in Austria-Hungary. Another important step was the promotion of centralised provision of schoolbooks by the court and state publishing houses from the 1860s. One point of controversy came to a head in the 1890s when the relative costs of postal tariffs in Austria-Hungary and Germany meant that it was cheaper to distribute German newspapers within Austria than the financially challenged home titles. This led to a preponderance of German rather than Austrian titles in the space of the coffeehouse.

At the 'hard' or commercial end of the printing industry, the Austrian sphere of influence spread to cities such as Budapest, Prague, Kraków and Zagreb, producing an interesting correspondence between the linguistic map and the sphere of café culture, too complex to investigate here in any detail. Strong connections at the level of manufacture were echoed in artistic circles between the arts and crafts schools, where great exchanges occurred through shared ideas for the curriculum, along with exhibitions and art publishing initiatives. This 'soft' or cultural end also led to an engagement across national borders within Austria-Hungary in the fields of book design, illustration, poster design, typography and letter arts, the so-called *Freie Graphik* which were displayed as part of the Austrian house at BUGRA.[11]

The work of these graphic artists was known through publications, as communication between the cities of central Europe led to a flourishing of literary and cultural magazines in Vienna, among the most prominent *Die Fackel* (1899–1936) edited by Karl Kraus, *Ver Sacrum* (1899–1903) and *Hohe Warte* (1904–1908). The latter two periodicals shared aesthetic principles with *Pan* (1895–1900) and *Jugend* (1896–1909), published from an earlier date respectively from Berlin and Munich.[12] But more popular titles and consumer magazines also circulated beyond national borders. The first magazines in Vienna had appeared as early as 1725 and after the revolutionary years the numbers escalated significantly. As in other developed European centres, the proliferation of popular weekly magazines took place in the 1870s through a combination of growing literacy among the increasing urban populations, the formation of new kinds of publisher, an innovative style of journalism based on graphic satire and wit, and a desire from the public to be kept informed of the political and current affairs in city life. Cheaper printing and paper also facilitated the growth of the industry.

To link this well-established print culture, celebrated at BUGRA, directly to the coffeehouse, we can turn to the front fascia of Café Betti Riedl in Vienna in 1900 where the sign writer inscribed the newspapers the visitor could expect to find within this one establishment. They included *Le Figaro*, *Journal des Débats*, *Gil Blas*, *Le Journal Amusant*, *L'Illustration*, *The Illustrated London News*, *The Times*, *The New York Herald*, *Pester Lloyd*, *Egyetértés*, *Budapesti Hírlap*, *L'Indipendente*, *L'Illustrazione Italiana*, *Djabel*, *Tygodnik Illustrowany*, *Nowa Reforma*, *Slowo Polski*, *Zycie*, *Kurjer Warszawski*, *Clos Narodu*, *Dziennik Polski*, *Czas* and *Hoboe Bpemr* (and two with Cyrillic titles). The list served to show how international the city was at the time, or, at least, that it wished to present itself as such to the wider world. It was also testimony to how central literacy and languages were to the city's identity and for the experience of its particular urban character, as well as its coffeehouses.[13]

Das Interieur: the magazine

In cafés, popular magazines were more likely to be circulated together with newspapers than more specialist titles. Nevertheless, significant commentary on the coffeehouses also appeared within the art and design press, and such magazines subsequently became an important source for understanding the coffeehouse. It was by no means a coincidence that in 1900 the magazine *Das Interieur,* a title dedicated to the subject of the interior, was launched, for by then, both at a mundane, physical level and within design debates, the interior had definitely entered public awareness. This was a few years after equivalent magazines had begun publication in other cities, as revealed by *Art et Décoration* in Paris, *Innendekoration* and *Deutsche Kunst und Dekoration* in Darmstadt, *Dekorative Kunst* in Munich, and *The Studio* in London.[14] Vienna's reputation as a centre for the decorative arts was confirmed by the acclaim it received at the international exhibitions in Paris in 1900 and Turin in 1902. *Das Interieur*

Figure 9.1 Main view of the Café Lurion designed by Sandor Jaray, *Das Interieur*, May 1904.

was an important ingredient in an enhanced and accelerated cultural movement of the *Wiener Moderne*. The magazine came from the house of Anton Schroll, a leading art and architectural publisher, whose establishment, founded in 1884 on the Graben, published many of the art catalogues for the national museums and made available Viennese art historical scholarship through high-quality, illustrated publications.[15] Schroll published many major monographs together with *Das Interieur* and another significant periodical, *Der Architekt*, from 1895 (Figure 9.1).

The coffeehouse featured as a subject in the very first issue of *Das Interieur* in January 1900. The issue profiled the designs of architect Franz Freiherr von Krauss, as executed by H. Seifert and sons for the Café Lebmann.[16] A short commentary was accompanied by a series of large-format, black and white photographs. The interiors were designed in the Secessionist style, with an emphasis of a total and coherent conception, following the well-understood notion of the *Gesamtkunstwerk*. The photographic presentation of the café drew attention to the overall impact of carved ornament. It illustrated the importance of wood panelling, for instance, in adding unity of decoration to an interior by acting as a framing device for the various spaces, in this case from the cloakroom to billiard room, as well as the distinctive design of the main salon. The wall paintings in Café Lebmann by Josef Maria Auchentaller (1865–1949) were commented on by journalist Paul Althof: 'one must dream a little and fantasise in lines and figures, one must understand the soul of things, and give even the smallest ornament, the least significant leaves, the feel of the whole'.[17] This publication of an interior of a coffeehouse in photographic form inevitably rendered the actual three-dimensional space in two dimensions. An intriguing aspect of the process is how it may have also informed or instructed the eye. Developing his ideas from the writings of Benjamin and Barthes, Jonathan Crary has written of 'techniques of the observer' and how these were altered by mechanised images and their ready availability in the nineteenth century.[18] Rather than offering an interpretation of a photograph as static or fixed, this point of view allows the photograph to assert agency on the viewer, changing behaviour in response to having seen an image. Although such specialisation of viewing was far from unique to the space of the coffeehouse, it would appear that the circulation of images like those in *Das Interieur* and the increasing familiarity with their pictorial conventions informed the 'techniques' or habits and customs of looking, which extended to the experience of being in the café interior. Beyond the professional discourse of interior design, it could be suggested that photographs raised possibilities for performing and socialising within these spaces.

Until 1914, the coffeehouse was to become a regular topic in *Das Interieur*. Interestingly, at a time when the lobby for design reform and the assertion of *Jugendstil* ideas was at its height, the magazine appeared not to be overly partisan in its editorial agenda. Instead, it covered both Secessionist and more traditional, historicist interiors. An intriguing juxtaposition of images, superficially bearing little connection to each other, occurred in May 1904 when two black and white editorial photographs appeared above a panel of small press advertisements[19] (Figure 9.2).

Figure 9.2 A page from *Das Interieur*, May 1904 with photographs of the entrance and newspaper stand at Café Lurion and small advertisements including an announcement for *Beispiele künstlerischer Schrift* by Rudolf von Larisch.

The photographs record the newly designed interior of the Café Lurion, their rhetoric professional and formal. In the sequence, the first image shows the foyer with a bell-boy. Turning the page reveals a photograph of the buffet with the *Kassiererin* (female cashier) *in situ,* and then a view of the central room, where six waiting staff hover self-consciously in the background (see Figure 9.1). The photograph acted as a confirmation for the viewer that this new café space, with its impressive expanse of furniture and lighting, offered all that could be expected from the latest and most modern of establishments. As part of the well-recognised convention of providing aesthetic continuity across the total range of furniture types, the specialised credenza or sideboard was decorated with a running carved Secessionist floral motif border, an abstraction of a rose or thistle, with the decoration carrying over to the purpose-designed coat stand, with its integral mirror, hat rack and umbrella stand, as well as an item of furniture that relates most to the theme of the circulation of the printed word within the café space, the *Zeitungsständer* (newspaper rack).

This piece of specialist furniture took the form of a unit with lockable lower cupboards, a surface for magazines to be arranged for browsing, while both above and below were horizontal shelves with many hooks. From the lower rack, over thirty newspapers were suspended and a similar number hung from the upper shelf. On the top surface, beyond the reach of the average-height person, a set of what appeared to be encyclopaedias was lodged. On first impressions, their arrangement might have been more suited to a home library, or the drawing room of a well-to-do middle-class family, rather than a public café. Although not all newspapers could be individually identified from the photograph, it was significant that among those titles which could be deciphered were *Le Figaro, Corriere della Serra* and *Levant* – a European, and for the time, international mix. The entire arrangement suggested a condensed and efficient reference library, a resource for all those who wished to enter and enjoy the Café Lurion.

The commentaries conveyed a strong sense that such specialist pieces of furniture were in part inspired by American precedents. As is well known from the literature, within Modernist architectural circles both Adolf Loos and Le Corbusier turned in fascination to the advertisements and images in the trade catalogues of office equipment companies, being particularly drawn to those from the United States.[20] Loos's interests, informed by his years in America, were made known in his little journal *Das Andere: ein Blatt zur Einführung abendländischer Kultur in Österreich* (The Other: a journal for the introduction of Western culture into Austria) from 1903 and echoed in the Viennese context by other writings. For example, *Hohe Warte*, a magazine dedicated to promoting urban culture in Vienna, began in 1904 by Joseph Aug. Lux, Joseph Hoffmann and their circle also turned their attention to a related topic in the series of articles on living in the *Mietwohnung* (rented apartment). One in particular examined *Maschinenmöbel* (machine furniture) and was illustrated with several examples of American mass production.[21]

Such articles help us to understand the interest in specialised furniture for the home or office at the time. The illustrations in *Hohe Warte* revealed a preoccupation with the practicality of the designs, depicting interiors of particular items, revealing how doors opened or drawers worked. The appreciation of the newspaper rack derived from a similar recognition of how it met the specific requirements of the café as a designed space. In *Das Interieur*, coffeehouse fittings were considered alongside designs for banks, insurance offices and shops, as well as the domestic decorative schemes aimed at upper-middle-class fashionable Viennese society. In other articles, schemes for gardens, restaurants and hotels, all part of the wider public sphere of the fabricated city, found parallels with the design decisions for the coffeehouse. We might ask which criteria were used to judge these spaces. Often admiration was expressed for the attention given to principles of system and the varied needs of the waiting staff. Before the study of ergonomics was fully developed, this meant recognising elements of order and efficiency involving the circulation of both staff and guests. Another factor that was increasingly mentioned was the heightened awareness of hygiene, in particular the attention given to surfaces.

With this specialisation of commercial environments, there was a growing expectation that similar systems should be applied to the coffeehouse as to other public spaces, with a stress on order, quantity and accountability marking a symbolic move from the domestic to commercial. Yet at the same time, aesthetic effects were needed to reassure the coffeehouse regulars that their individual comforts, habits, tastes and even quirks could be accommodated within such spaces. As has already been remarked, the boundary between the domestic interior or 'home' and the public sphere, such as the coffeehouse, was permeable at both a physical and experiential level, and features of design were often interchangeable.[22] At the level of experience, spending time at the table, *am Tisch*, reading for leisure or edification, consuming food and drink, playing games, taking part in conversations, all these activities could take place in either location, and each informed the other in its practice. The semblance of the rational could therefore be disguised for the comfort of the guest, fusing the subjective with the objective.

Below the photograph of the newspaper stand appeared a group of advertisements, among them, a panel in stylised script announcing a new publication from Anton Schroll. The title was *Beispiele künstlerischer Schrift* (Examples of Artistic Lettering) and it was edited by Rudolf von Larisch. Among the significant designers included in the volume were Georges Auriol (Paris), H.P. Berlage (Amsterdam), Emil Doepler (Berlin), Max Klinger (Leipzig), Richard Riemerschmid (Munich), Heinrich Vogeler (Worpswede), and Charles Rennie Mackintosh (Glasgow) – an impressive list of international designers who were all in sympathy with the movement to 'reform' lettering and the graphic arts. I will return to the significance of its announcement in the pages of *Das Interieur* and the argument put forward by von Larisch for the Viennese coffeehouse in the final section of this chapter.

Advertising and a Poster for Café Lurion

Although the peak of the poster movement coincided with the flourishing of the Viennese coffeehouse, connections between the institution and this particular graphic form are more tenuous than might initially be expected. In retrospect it is easy to assume that posters and coffeehouses were part of the general *mélange* of fin-de-siècle Viennese culture, yet surprisingly little evidence exists to suggest that coffeehouse proprietors commissioned the city's poster artists to any great extent, or that, in turn, posters for coffeehouses populated the city's streets on any significant scale. In many respects, the particular graphic register of the poster, it would appear, did not suit the requirements of the coffeehouse.

The poster movement was at its height between 1890 and 1914 in many European cities, resulting from developments in lithographic printing techniques, changes in taxes for displaying posters, and a general willingness to embrace the artistic possibilities of the medium. A distinctive Viennese style came to the fore with the foundation of the Secession in 1897 and the Wiener Werkstätte in 1903.[23] As important elements of street furniture and decoration, posters featured on purpose-designed columns, *Litfaßsäule*, on the city's Ringstrasse and other key routes, as design reformers and city authorities became increasingly concerned about the widespread use of posters on hoardings, whereby size and quantity, rather than aesthetic quality, were emphasised. Posters were certainly used to establish the identity of a particular brand name of patent foodstuffs and drinks, theatre and musical performances, hotels and other tourist destinations. In the Viennese context, for example, the coffee importer Julius Meinl, founded in 1862 and a major retailer of the drink for consumption at home, became associated with advertising campaigns of visually striking posters. Full-colour lithographic posters of this kind for the Viennese coffeehouse, however, were rare.

A printed poster was no doubt a major investment; its circulation and impact had to be known to be financially worthwhile before a commission was undertaken. In most cases, residents of Vienna would have been familiar with the whereabouts of a particular café and would have understood its presence within the topography of the city. Other forms of graphic announcement therefore possibly served the coffeehouse better. Instead of poster advertising, for example, a prominent café might use the pages of the illustrated press to make its presence felt. Accordingly, during the 1870s café establishments advertised their attractions in the many varied weekly, illustrated magazines. Such was the case for Café de l'Europe, the 'most beloved rendezvous for all foreigners' on St Stephan's Square, which was featured in a full-page drawing which depicted a street scene with fashionable passers-by, an awning over a ground-floor café terrace and cut-away scenes of the fantastic interiors to be found within.[24] In this illustration, the entire façade of the building functioned like a poster.

No doubt aimed towards the local reader of the magazine rather than the outside visitor, other kinds of announcement for coffeehouses appeared for the opening of new establishments (Figure 9.3). These were placed in the back pages of the illustrated papers and competed with advertisements in all variety of typefaces, often incorporating stock engraved images. In such a setting, the coffeehouse found itself in the company of a wide array of commodity culture: patent cures, men's shirts, pianos, Christmas decorations, summer excursions, exotic drinks, billiard tables, the services of tailors, hair colour and tonics, and clock- and watchmakers. For example, Café Mahler, run by Rudolf Mahler on Franz Josefs Kai, welcomed guests to its newly-opened 'tasteful and comfortable'

Figure 9.3 Press announcements for coffeehouses.

premises in October 1875 with an advertisement that depended on the singular visual power of its letterpress name. More effusively, during 1880 one Herr Bauer announced his testimony to quality through a panel advertisement placed in several issues of *Die Bombe*:

Opening Announcement:

I have the honour hereby to bring to your attention that on Sunday 16th July I opened a Café in the 2nd district, Mühlfeldgasse Nr 5. This will enable me to invite numerous visitors, and to ensure that I may endeavour to win the respect of my revered guests through the provision of journals, through good drinks and attentive service.

Yours most respectfully, Bauer.[25]

An exception to this reliance on press advertisements was the case of the opening of the new Café Lurion, a modern, elegant coffeehouse opened by Maxime Lurion in 1903, which we have already mentioned in relation to its interior design[26] (Figure 9.4). In the poster designed for this event by Emil Ranzenhofer, a fashionably dressed woman, recognisably of the Parisian figurative tradition of Jules Chéret and Toulouse-Lautrec, was depicted wearing a dress in the reform style, loose fitting and with a Jugendstil decorative border; she is taking a rest from reading a magazine, the exact title of which we cannot identify. The magazine is supported by a bentwood holder matching the furniture typical of those produced by the Gebrüder Thonet firm for use in cafés throughout the city and beyond. The lettering of the poster is in a soft, organic Jugendstil, rather than the geometricised form preferred by many Viennese artists, designers and architects.

In its overall conception, this poster conformed to the prescription in writings on the artistic poster found in dedicated publications. For example, Rudolf von Larisch wrote:

There recently appeared a small booklet with the title 'The Mirror of the Poster' by Ernst Growald. I take from him the following guiding principles: The poster must work as a unity. The worst quality of a poster is boredom. Lettering and representation must be inseparable. Good posters do not need to be read – they must be seen. A well-chosen slogan says more than a thousand-page brochure.[27]

In all probability the full circulation of the poster in the café space occurred later in the century, with its revival as a central form of communication for cultural events in the 1960s as the pattern became established to display them in the corridors of cafés. Here one must draw attention to a methodological difficulty. The professional interests of architects and designers generally meant that formal photographs, destined for publication and overseen by photographic studios, were staged. They often featured no people, as this was undoubtedly thought to

Figure 9.4 Poster by Emil Ranzenhofer for Café Lurion, 1903, 125 x 94 cm. Courtesy of the Wienbibliothek im Rathaus/Vienna City Library, Poster Collection, P 13296.

bring the reader closer to the original conception of the space. Most photographs of the coffeehouses obeyed this convention and more impromptu arrangements of graphic ephemera, if they did exist, escaped record.

The Published Design Drawing

We now turn to consider the representation of the Viennese café in professional architectural and design drawings. The following example appeared in *Das Interieur*, within the pictorial supplement of volume 3 in 1904; its designer was Vincenz Jerabek (Figure 9.5). Two main views of the coffeehouse interior gave a sense of its major compositional features. The first showed the buffet and newspaper stand with an assortment of tables. Through this, individual characteristics of the chair, seating unit, panelling, frieze and chandeliers could all be identified. The second view indicated the fittings for the billiard room, with a unit incorporating a clock and rack for cues, and panelling with the same repeated ornamental frieze based on the motif of the coffee bean and leaf. This square ornamental device was even repeated on the legs of the billiard table. The window framed the view of the street outside, showing shop façades and fascias with lettering, thereby conveying a general sense of life beyond the coffeehouse. In the Austro-Hungarian context, conventions of presentation drawings of an interior scheme went back at least to the period of Biedermeier. This period has been characterised by decorative arts historian Christian Witt-Dörring as follows: 'The Vormärz period (1815–1848), restricted by political constraints and the forcible intervention of government censorship in all areas of daily life, led to the middle classes turning their backs almost totally on public life'. And he continued: 'The living room, the focal point of the family, was accorded such a degree of significance and importance that it now became an independent theme in painting'.[28]

This convention of pictorial representation found parallels in design drawings of real and imagined interiors in which an interest in establishing a connection between the earlier style and contemporary design prevailed. For example, in the first volume of *Hohe Warte* in 1904–1905, Josef Aug. Lux published the essay, 'Biedermeier als Erzieher' (Biedermeier as Educator).[29] This took up the theme of the exemplary character of the Biedermeier style for contemporary designers. The article was illustrated with scenes of interiors, watercolours and drawings of a variety of Biedermeier rooms by two artists, Aug. Heymann and Jos. Wünsch. A further indication of the contemporary interest in the lasting

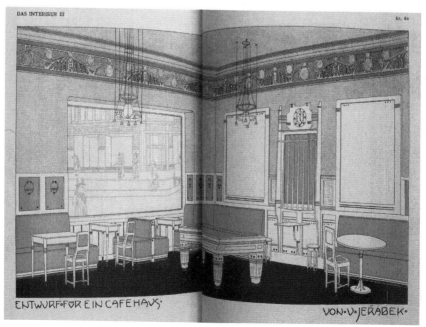

Figure 9.5 Vincenz Jerabek, 'Illustration of Design for a Café', *Das Interieur*, 1904.

historical significance of the Biedermeier style could be seen in the publications of Josef Folnesics, whose important book *Innenräume und Hausrat der Empire- und Biedermeierzeit in Österreich-Ungarn* (The Interior and the Furniture of the Empire and Biedermeier Periods in Austro-Hungary), illustrated with sixty photographs of extant interiors, also appeared in 1904.[30] The pictorial convention in these drawings of Biedermeier schemes that proved so influential took the form of a view on to a room, most often three-sided, and incorporating a window wall. Furniture tended to be arranged near or against the walls, which, even if not a record of the actual disposition of the furniture, gave the illusion of depth of field for pictorial purposes. Attention was often drawn to the parquetry flooring, to give an enhanced sense of measurement, proportion and scale. A typical Heymann line drawing of a *bürgerlich* (middle-class) room from around 1820 was more than just a sketch. It was possible to use such drawings to identify individual pieces of furniture and their style, the nature of the ornamental sculptures and the hanging of pictures on the wall, as well as the general decorative effect. For instance, Heymann paid great attention to the *Kachelofen* (cylindrical ceramic stove) with its neo-classical decoration and figurine surmounting it. As such, the presentation drawing could function simultaneously as a form of information design, an evocation, and a piece of self-promotion.

These principles carried over to the 1904 volumes of *Das Interieur*. By this time, if an existing interior under discussion required illustration, this would most likely involve a high-quality photograph. The choice to continue to present interiors as presentation drawings, we must assume, reflected an editorial preference based on experience and understanding of their aesthetic appeal, or the relative costs of photogravure and lithography and their technical implications. If we return to the Jerabek sequence, simply entitled 'Design for a Café', the drawings appeared modern in their apparent bareness and linearity, yet also quietly traditional in their pictorial conventions, no doubt evoking their Biedermeier precedents in the minds of many viewers. Such associations added to the identity of the Viennese coffeehouse as both a site of important continuity in social as well as aesthetic values and a locus of innovation in design.

The Coffeehouse as Sign

I conclude by asking how the coffeehouse contributed to the changing understanding of commercial signs in the wider context of the historical and modern city of Vienna. To what extent did the coffeehouse operate within a system of signs found elsewhere in commercial spaces, and where, if at all, did its distinctiveness lie? My final source of evidence for how the coffeehouse depended on graphic representation took the form of a prestigious volume, assembled by the specialist art and architectural publisher Anton Schroll under the title of *Firmaschilder – Ladenaufschriften* (Company Signs – Shop Inscriptions, 1900).[31] The book was testimony to the recognition that Viennese shop fronts and sign lettering were worthy of attention and formal appreciation. Comprising thirty sheets with eighty-three photographic records of lettering, the book offered a way of gauging the place of the coffeehouse within the larger setting of the street and other forms of commercial graphic arrangement. Of the total number of pictures, seven specifically depicted various aspects of the frontage of cafés, while other photographs showed related buildings such as restaurants, beer halls and cellars, and in one case, the shop fascia of Julius Meinl, the aforementioned coffee importer.

The majority of those selected were designated 'Café' rather than 'Kaffeehaus'. Within the range of styles shown it is possible to say that the frontages of the cafés were restrained when compared with those of other establishments. The techniques for signs included inscriptions on marble and other polished hard stones, three-dimensional lettering superimposed on architectural façades, and signs made from behind-glass painting, a method particularly popular in Southern Germany and Austria (Figure 9.6). The latter technique was used for designs that depended on calligraphic flourishes and a much more exuberant form of letter art than could usually be accommodated by letter cutting. They also incorporated designs with heraldry or depictions of allegorical scenes related to the goods on sale. The images that were incorporated often echoed those found in the printed advertising of a company, as trademarks and press announcements. Graphic clichés such as the pointing hand frequently appeared, also lifted from the printer's repertoire, whereas medallions from the great

Figure 9.6 Signage for coffeehouses as illustrated in Anton Schroll, *Firma Schilder – Ladenaufschriften*, 1900.

expositions and royal charters were shown as endorsements on the more notable establishments; their formal entrances, with glass signs framed like paintings, added a great sense of propriety and order.

In all of this, coffeehouses retained what might be described as a high register. This level of respectability, when translated into speech, could be considered as equivalent to *Hochdeutsch* (high German), particularly if compared with the vernacular register of the signage of the *Wirtshaus, Weinstube* and *Bierhalle*. In the coffeehouse neo-classical scripts prevailed, while in these other spaces a greater variety of Fraktur (blackletter or Gothic) scripts appeared, along with historicist decorations and a visual conviviality of garlands of fruit and flowers, in particular hops and vines.[32]

One way to understand the implications of the coffeehouse signs and place them in context would be to return to the figure of Rudolf von Larisch. As already mentioned, he was widely recognised as leading the revival and reform of artistic lettering in Vienna. Von Larisch taught at the *kaiserlich und königlich Graphische Lehr und Versuchsanstalt* (Royal and Imperial Graphics Teaching and Research Institute) of the Vienna *Kunstgewerbeschule* during these years. His numerous essays, lectures and publications promoted the teaching of lettering according to his own system to art and design students and art teachers, as well as pupils at elementary schools. An important foundation of von Larisch's approach was his stress on the appearance of a letterform. More than any other figure, he was responsible for the growing awareness of the contribution that script of various kinds could make to modern design. Von Larisch emphasised the total outline, suggesting that the overall impression 'must speak to the viewer'. A distinctive characteristic of the Austrian printing tradition was the use of both Fraktur script and Antiqua (Roman) typefaces in published works as well as in the wider graphic environment. Von Larisch was against what he called 'die Brillenpest' (eye sore) of Fraktur.[33] In this respect, as a moderniser, he argued in his commentary on the situation in Germany:

> With the overthrow of Fraktur type in Germany, we can speak in terms of significant savings to the typographic industries. The step to the sole use of 'world lettering' would be of extraordinary benefit in relation to eye-hygiene and would bring with it the main advantage ... that of approaching nearer to an international consistency in lettering.[34]

As we see, von Larisch spoke out against Fraktur because, in his view, it could not be used as an international type. Typefaces, he argued, should not be chosen for 'pure' aesthetic reasons alone, but also for business reasons. One particular publication did engage with the commercial implications of lettering: *Die ornamentale Schrift im Verkehrsleben* (Ornamental Lettering in the Life of Exchange), developed from an address that von Larisch first made to the Niederösterreichisches Gewerbeverein (Lower Austria Trade Association) and published a year later in 1906. Significantly, for this he drew on the example of Koloman Moser's distinctive trademark for the Wiener Werkstätte as well as the designs of Charles Rennie Mackintosh to indicate what he believed to be the importance of lettering in giving an identity to an organisation or a company. Von Larisch suggested that individual decorative details should be subordinated to the overall effect, and emphasised harmony and unity of design. He also stressed the need to find appropriate letterforms for different kinds of building.[35]

Von Larisch was among the first Viennese commentators to cross the boundary of type as an artistic field to articulate the significance that effective design could give to the commercial identity of a company. In this respect, the coffeehouses fulfilled what von Larisch argued would be the most appropriate form of modern signage. By implication, the decision of Viennese coffeehouse proprietors, no doubt in liaison with the skilled craftsmen of the city, to announce their establishments with the modern, formal rhetoric of neo-classical lettering was grounded in sound business sense and conformed to a growing tendency to think internationally.

Notes

1. Johanna Drucker, *The Visible World: Experimental Typography and Modern Art, 1909–1923*, Chicago 1994.
2. Gemma Blackshaw and Leslie Topp (eds), *Madness and Modernity: Mental Illness and the Visual Arts in Vienna 1900*, London 2009, and Bruno Bettelheim, *Freud's Vienna and Other Essays*, New York 1990.
3. Harold B. Segel, *The Vienna Coffeehouse Wits, 1890–1978*, West Lafayette, Indiana 1993.
4. Werner Schweiger, *Aufbruch und Erfüllung: Gebrauchsgraphik der Wiener Moderne 1897–1918*, Vienna 1988.
5. Among the exceptions to this are the catalogues *Das Wiener Kaffeehaus: von den Anfängen bis zur Zwischenkriegszeit,* Historisches Museum der Stadt Wien, Vienna 1980, and *Traum und Wirklichkeit: Wien 1870–1930*, Historisches Museum der Stadt Wien, Vienna 1985, which give a broader cultural historical interpretation.
6. Stephen Beller, *Vienna and the Jews, 1867–1938: A Cultural History*, Cambridge 1991, 44.
7. Bernhard Denscher, *Tagebuch der Strasse: Geschichte in Plakaten: Ausstellung der Wiener Stadt- und Landesbibliothek*, Vienna 1981, 53.
8. Otto Mazal, 'Oesterreich', in *Lexicon des Gesamte Buchwesens*, Stuttgart 1987, 417–422.
9. Christoph Reisser, Rudolf Larish and Adolf Vetter, *Internationale Ausstellung für Buchgewerbe und Graphik, Leipzig: Österreichisches Haus*, Vienna 1914.
10. Carl Junker, *Ein Wiener Buchdrucker. Friedrich Jasper zu Seinem Achtzigsten Geburtstage am Jänner 1927*, Vienna 1927.
11. Among the artists represented were O.C. Czeschka, Emil Orlik, Moriz Jung and Walter Klemm: see *Internationale Ausstellung für Buchgewerbe und Graphik*, op cit.
12. Catalogue, *Europäische Moderne Buch und Graphik aus Berliner Kunstverlagen 1890 bis 1933*, Berlin 1989.
13. The café was illustrated in Anton Schroll, *Firmaschilder. Ladenaufschriften Wien 1899–1900*, Vienna 1900.

14. For a discussion of the specialist press dedicated to interiors, see Stefan Muthesius, *The Poetic Home: Designing the 19ᵗʰ-Century Domestic Interior*, London 2009.
15. Anton Schroll, *Die Bücher des Verlages Anton Schroll & Co*, Vienna 1927.
16. *Das Interieur*, 1(1), 1900, 8–9 and 40.
17. Paul Althof, *Das Interieur*, 1(1), 1900, 40.
18. Jonathan Crary, *Techniques of the Observer: On Vision and Modernity in the Nineteenth Century*, Cambridge Mass. and London 1992.
19. *Das Interieur*, 5(5), May 1904.
20. Beatriz Colomina, *Privacy and Publicity. Modern Architecture as Media*, Cambridge Mass. and London 1996, and Tag Gronberg, *Vienna. City of Modernity, 1890–1914*, Oxford 2007.
21. 'Die Mietswohnung VI Maschinenmöbel', in *Hohe Warte Halbsmonatschrift zur Pflege der künstlerischen Bildung und der Städtischen Kultur*, Vienna and Leipzig 1906–1907, 335–342.
22. Penny Sparke, *The Modern Interior*, London 2007. See also Richard Kurdiovsky, 'The Cliché of the Viennese Café as an Extended Living-Room: Formal Parallels and Differences', in this volume.
23. Schweiger, *Aufbruch und Erfüllung*.
24. 'Die Bombe', in the ephemera collection *Reklame für Kaffeehäuser, Industrieerzeugnisse und Ausstellungen*, Wiener Stadtbibliothek L 181746L, 38, 1876, 236.
25. Advertisement in the ephemera collection *Reklame für Kaffeehäuser, Industrieerzeugnisse und Ausstellungen*, Wiener Stadtbibliothek L 181746L.
26. The Café Lurion was reviewed in the *Neue Wiener Tageblatt*, 25(12), 1903, 20.
27. Rudolf von Larisch, *Die ornamentale Schrift im Verkehrsleben*, Vienna 1906, 12.
28. Christian Witt-Dörring, in the catalogue *Vienna in the Age of Schubert. The Biedermeier Interior 1815–1848*, London 1979.
29. *Hohe Warte*, 1, 1904/05, 145–155.
30. Josef Folnesics' book was reviewed in *Das Interieur*, 5(5), May 1904.
31. Anton Schroll, *Firmaschilder – Ladenaufschriften Wien 1899–1900*, Vienna 1900.
32. Catalogue, *Im Wirtshaus. Eine Geschichte der Wiener Geselligkeit*, Wien Museum, Vienna 2007.
33. Von Larisch, *Die ornamentale Schrift im Verkehrsleben*, 13.
34. Ibid., 13.
35. Ibid., 10.

Chapter 10

THE CLICHÉ OF THE VIENNESE CAFÉ AS AN EXTENDED LIVING ROOM
Formal Parallels and Differences

Richard Kurdiovsky

The brightly upholstered booths of the typical Viennese café are comfortable and inviting. The high back-rests und softly upholstered arm-rests invite the visitor to sit, to talk and even to stretch out in a relaxed and casual way – as illustrated in the conspicuously casual posture of 'Der Litterat' by Moriz Jung (Figure 10.1).[1] This seating helps to form the special homely character of a Viennese coffeehouse. This furniture type is comparable to that found in middle-class living rooms. It is not merely coincidence that Carl Witzmann, who designed many comfortable and 'refined bourgeois' apartments, is considered as *the* coffeehouse architect of Vienna of the early twentieth century.[2]

The conceptual connection between the home and the coffeehouse is well established. Peter Altenberg advised a visit to the coffeehouse as an appropriate response to whatever fortune or misfortune had occurred.[3] Alfred Polgar did not speak of the guests of the Café Central but of its 'inhabitants',[4] and Gustav Grüner consistently presented the coffeehouse as a permanent domicile from early morning till late at night by characterising the true coffeehouse-guest as somebody who when leaving puts his chair on the table by himself.[5] To these 'inhabitants', Friedrich Torberg just needed to add that they used their apartments for nothing else but sleeping.[6] Since you are 'literally and really at home' in a coffeehouse, according to Helmut Burgert,[7] Egon Erwin Kisch's advice needs no more explanation: 'The coffeehouse saves us from owning an apartment'.[8] The idea of the coffeehouse as an 'extended living room' appears not only in

Figure 10.1 Moriz Jung, *Wiener Cafe: Der Litterat* (postcard produced by the Wiener Werkstätte) [Wien Museum, Inv. No. 165.065]. Courtesy of the Museum.

WIENER CAFE: DER LITTERAT.

fiction but is also used for example as the evocative title of a coffee-table book from 1990 in which Milo d'Or states in an essay that there is no single Viennese coffeehouse where he would not have been at home.[9] Hence this tradition seems to be unbroken. This chapter will explore this association by examining the extent to which the design of Viennese coffeehouses and living rooms related to one another in the late nineteenth and early twentieth centuries.

I will delimit my field of research topographically to the area of the Inner City where around the turn of the century, the neo-classical appearance of the old Biedermeier cafés was superseded by the splendid Ringstrasse cafés. This narrowing of the field automatically means I will be looking at a certain part of the social structure of Vienna only, namely higher-middle and upper classes. This restriction seems justified, because all the famous Viennese coffeehouses were situated in this area and because these grand city cafés served as the model for the smaller and more modest coffeehouses of the inner suburbs where, according to Stefan Zweig, the lower-middle classes used to reside,[10] and also the coffeehouses of the outer suburbs where the living quarters of the proletariat were located. This chapter does not claim to be exhaustive nor does it aim to develop a specific typology of the Viennese coffeehouse systematically. Instead, I will highlight several aspects of the formal appearance of coffeehouses in Vienna, their design and their development, and thus investigate how far the clichéd parallel between the coffeehouse and the living room corresponds to reality. The formal appearance of an interior is characterised by the shape of the room in general, by the treatment and decoration of the walls and by the types, designs and arrangement of the chosen furniture. This chapter will therefore proceed through an analysis of these three areas.

The Spatial Arrangement of the Coffeehouse and the Living Room

The spatial shape of the interior of a coffeehouse differs from that of an apartment substantially. Though Friedrich Uhl stated in 1900 that the Viennese coffeehouse was not primarily characterised by its decoration and formal appearance, but only by the Viennese who frequented it,[11] we can nevertheless find an entry on the Viennese coffeehouse in the highly influential *Handbook of Architecture*.[12] The coffeehouse is intended to accommodate a great number of people who wish to read and sip their drinks, to gossip or converse, to play chess, billiards or to otherwise spend their leisure time.[13] It therefore requires one big unified space or a series of 'high and beautiful halls', as stated in contemporary descriptions in architectural magazines,[14] while the apartment consists of a number of smaller rooms serving a variety of different functions (from receiving guests and dining to working and sleeping) and intended for the comparatively small group of a family.[15] The layout of a typical Viennese apartment consisted of two rows of rooms running parallel to each other, comparable to the French *appartement double*, with the higher status spaces like the reception rooms looking onto the street.[16] The coffeehouse would often be situated on ground floor of such apartment buildings, and similarly orientated towards the street. The floor area of a high-status apartment, especially if located in the district of the Ringstrasse, could easily be of the same size as that of a coffeehouse and the width of the rooms in particular would be identical and therefore substantial. But even in such cases, an apartment was always made up of a sequence of distinct rooms while the coffeehouse more usually consisted of just a single large space or spaces opening on to one another.

One point of similarity between the coffeehouse and the Viennese apartment was the desirability of being located on the corner of a block because this facilitated light from two different sides. The corner apartments of Viennese apartment blocks were usually the biggest and the most attractive, while a situation on the corner allowed a café to attract footfall from two different thoroughfares. This issue of cross lighting is also the logic behind the well-known L-shape plan said to be characteristic of Viennese coffeehouses, still found for instance at the Café Museum or the Café Sperl. This L-shape is so typically associated with the café that, although there would have been enough space for almost any layout, it was even used for the Café Meinl that was temporarily erected on Maria Theresien-Platz during the European football championship in 2008 as an exemplary Viennese coffeehouse. It is striking therefore that when looking up Viennese examples of the building type 'coffeehouse' in the *Handbook of Architecture*, one finds hardly any L-shaped coffeehouses, although the majority of the examples presented, such as the Café Zum Reichsrat or the Arcaden-Café, are situated in the corner of a building.[17] Instead, they consist of individual adjoining rooms of rectangular shape, where the bigger rooms serve as reading or conversation rooms and the smaller ones as games rooms.

While an apartment needs solid walls to provide privacy and sufficient space for the necessary furniture, the coffeehouse was illuminated by as many windows as possible. These windows were also as wide as possible, the *Handbook of Architecture* explains, because 'in the rooms of a coffeehouse one demands to see and to be seen'.[18] To a certain extent, the Viennese coffeehouse seems to have functioned as a weather-independent indoor equivalent to the Italian corso: 'strolling is moved there from the street'.[19] From travel guide books we can even learn that it would have been common to keep your hat on when sitting in a coffeehouse, which is further suggestive of a perceived parallel with being on the street.[20] Windows as big as those of public buildings or shops allowed light to stream in and a quantity of large mirrors further enlarged the interior with their endless reflections. The handbook advises that the coffeehouse should always be situated on the same level as the street to allow immediate entry from it. According to Adolph G. Th. Glassbrenner, already in Biedermeier period coffeehouses were customarily situated on the ground floor.[21] Thus, you could look out and look in without any barrier and there was no obstruction for sight or for access. Interestingly, this is in contrast to the situation in Prague where coffeehouses were commonly situated on the first or mezzanine floors, while the street level was occupied by shops, thus making the guests of the coffeehouse largely invisible from the street.[22] One explanation for the preference of a ground floor location in Vienna was the importance of the *Schanigärten*, the open terraces in front of Viennese coffeehouses where tables are literally set up in the street.

At this point I would like, if not to reject, then at least to qualify the general assertion that the lack of sufficient living-space was responsible for the Viennese coffeehouse becoming a second living room.[23] If we look at how famous representatives of literary circles used to live around the turn of the century this assertion seems rather inaccurate. Admittedly, Peter Altenberg chose a hotel room as a substitute for his own apartment: he chose the

Grabenhotel in the Inner City, a district that never lost its rank as the most noble living quarter. The hotel was close to the most elegant shopping street of Vienna, the Graben, which has been *the* socially accepted meeting place since the Biedermeier period. His choice of residence was therefore determined to a large extent by his desire to live so centrally. We also know that Karl Kraus, a frequent visitor to coffeehouses, owned an apartment in Lothringerstrasse, a very respectable address, and that this apartment consisted of a two-window room as his study and a separate bedroom, thus being of the average size of an apartment for a middle-class household. Adolf Loos owned an apartment with two principle rooms, a small side-chamber and kitchen and bathroom. This was an above-average sized apartment by middle-class standards. Writers like Hermann Bahr, Hugo von Hoffmannsthal or Richard Schaukal owned suburban houses in the exclusive residential areas of Vienna,[24] and by the 1920s were noted as having become unwilling to 'leave the comfort of their villas in the "Cottage"' to visit the café.[25] These famous coffeehouse-goers at least did not belong to a social group that had to frequent coffeehouses out of a desperate need for space.

The Walls of the Coffeehouse and the Living Room

The treatment of the walls shows a stronger relationship between coffeehouse interiors and those of private apartments. The wall decoration of elegant coffeehouses like the Café Habsburg on Rotenturmstrasse (Figure 10.2), which stylistically belong to the historicism of the so-called *Gründerzeit* of the second half of the nineteenth century, consisted of grandiose elements. Following Venetian models for structuring interior walls, the room was adorned with large paintings of complex, multi-figured scenes covering the upper part of the wall from the panelling to the ceiling cornice. A comparable way of using large-size paintings with similar subject matter can be seen in the study of Heinrich Dumba in his palace on the Ringstrasse opposite the Stadtpark by Hans Makart. In the lower half of these interiors, the panelled area of the walls enclose Dumba's personal working and living sphere (the panelling contained bookshelves and other storage facilities), while in the case of the Café Habsburg, we can see the apparatus of the café – tables and chairs and so on – was also contained in this panelled zone.

Living rooms with walls or ceilings decorated with large paintings, reminiscent of the splendour of aristocratic palaces, only formed a small and very exclusive group within the artistically decorated apartments of prosperous Viennese people. Wealthy people like Otto Wagner could afford to live in exquisitely designed interiors, but even there, paintings only appeared as framed pictures and not as the central piece of a ceiling decoration or as a wall-covering as in Dumba's study

Figure 10.2 Kleiner Saal of the Café Habsburg (24, Rotenturmstrasse) in 1910. Collection of Daniel M. Schmid. Courtesy of Archiv Album Verlag, Wien.

or in other Ringstrasse palaces. In the smaller apartments of the middle classes, the use of pictures was restricted to small-scale works in frames. Coffeehouses on the other hand were public spaces and, like theatres, operas and concert-halls, they seem to have served for the broad middle classes as a substitute for the private possession of palatial splendour: 'These local [cafés], conceived as meeting places for families and alternatives to the common living conditions, were given especially splendid decoration (electric lighting, most modern furniture, mirror-glasses, exquisite carpets)'.[26] As such, they served a portion of the public that was distinguished by the relatively high 'rank and resources of the guests'[27] in contrast to the simple pub or inn. In relation to such cafés, therefore, 'In general, the interior decoration shows the character of brilliance and solemnity rather than of comfortableness and cosiness'.[28] Large mirrors often covered the walls, alternating with more or less lavishly decorated panelling, thus evoking the idealised picture of an aristocratic palace. Historicist modes were invoked. Stuccoed vaulting recalled Italianate High Renaissance architecture and heavy coffered ceilings were reminiscent of central European castles. A café, next to the New Town Hall, is an example of this display: 'The vaulted arcade ceilings are richly painted, the walls of true material, ceiling painting with rich gilding, oaken wainscoting, beautiful chandeliers of bronze embellish the rooms'.[29] These pompously decorated coffeehouses served as substitutes for palatial interiors that would not have been achievable in the majority of homes, even if these homes were relatively large.

Figure 10.3 Josef Hoffmann, Design for a coffeehouse interior, *Das Interieur*, I, 1900, pl. 7.

When Art Nouveau became fashionable shortly before the turn of the century, the impact of this new style was so strong that its influence was felt across interiors of diverse sorts. In designs by Josef Hoffmann for instance, obvious analogies can now be found between apartments and coffeehouse interiors. With their room-spanning arches and niches framing sideboards or benches, his designs for coffeehouses published in the art magazine *Das Interieur* in 1900 (Figure 10.3) used the identical repertoire of motifs as in his designs for living rooms such as the hunting lodge of Paul Wittgenstein from 1899, and even shop interiors such as the candle-shop Apollo on the square Am Hof from the same year. All these designs followed the idea of structuring the whole room under one single design concept in the spirit of the *Gesamtkunstwerk*.[30] This special mode of interior design, where wall and ceiling surfaces are covered with ornamental panelling including elements of integrated furniture, can be found in coffeehouses like the Café Eiles[31] or the Café Lebmann,[32] as well as in the anterooms and living rooms of contemporary apartments, such as Richard Hirschl's design for an anteroom,[33] a design for a bourgeois drawing room by Otto Wytrlik[34] (Figure 10.4) or an alcove for playing cards in a gentleman's room.[35]

As a newly introduced style that was not based on historical precedents, Art Nouveau could easily be used for different types of architecture. Because it was free from historical associations, Art Nouveau was especially popular with the rich bourgeoisie and hardly any notable commissions in this new style were executed for the high aristocracy.[36] Applying this new style could thus be interpreted as a shift away from the palatial towards a more bourgeois appearance in the interior decoration of public places such as coffeehouses without detracting from their artistically exquisite or luxurious atmosphere.

Figure 10.4 Otto Wytrlik, Design for a bourgeois drawing room, around 1900, *Das Interieur*, II, 1901, pl. 30.

Just ten years later, when stylistic development tended towards a more pared down appearance, two designers, whose careers stood in opposition to one another and who were both influential in the development of modern architecture, presented their ideas for designing coffeehouse interiors. Adolf Loos and Josef Hoffmann both designed living rooms and coffeehouses according to their personal stylistic concepts and we can detect similarities between the two types of interiors. Stylistically, little distinction is made in this period between design for coffeehouses and for domestic interiors. Adolf Loos, for example, used marble panelling for covering the walls of his Café Capua of 1913, and also often covered the walls of dining rooms, anterooms or halls, all of which need easy cleaning due to their functions, with stone panelling, such as in the dining room of Victor Ritter von Bauer's castle in Brno from 1925.[37] In this interior he even reused the neo-classical frieze from his Café Capua as an upper border of the wall. The use of marble cladding is justified by arguments of functionality: metaphorically speaking, the marble table tops are transferred onto the wall. The aesthetic effect is based on the lively veining of the marble and the sensuous contrast between the cold, gloss polished surface and the dull, matt effect of the plush upholstery of the benches.

Josef Hoffmann used schemes of stone cladding to different effect, for different room types. For example, in his Palais Stoclet in Brussels the use of marble panelling was not restricted to the dining room, but could be found in reception rooms all over the house. He also treated the cladding in a more ornamental or at least atectonic way by framing the slabs with border-like frames.[38] The impact of colours, patterns and materials (some portions look like semi-precious stones) heightens the exclusive value of the *Gesamtkunstwerk*. While Hoffmann's earlier Art Nouveau designs for coffeehouses were only published, but never executed, in 1912 he actually designed and executed the interior of the Graben Café (Figure 10.5) which included stone panelling. In line with his personal style, this coffeehouse shows the strong impact of different materials due to the contrast between the richly patterned fabric of the upholstery and the sober wall panelling. Loos's Café Capua of 1913 seems to be a direct response to Hoffmann's 'over-decorated' Graben Café. Loos acknowledged the points of similarity between the designs with the observation, when he visited the Graben Café in 1928, that finally Hoffmann had arrived where he, Loos, had already been thirty years ago![39]

The Furniture of the Coffeehouse and the Living Room

While the treatment of the walls shows several parallels and correspondences between designs for living rooms and coffeehouses, the way in which the furniture is spatially arranged in the coffeehouse reflects the quite different

Figure 10.5 Josef Hoffmann, Grabencafé (29a, Graben), 1912, *Das Interieur*, XIV, 1913, pl. 36.

needs of the space compared to an apartment. In spite of the desirability of cosiness, for economic reasons a coffeehouse had to be equipped with maximum seating. In an apartment on the other hand, it was more important to arrange the furniture multi-functionally, comfortably and aesthetically by forming individual, island-like seating groups. This arrangement of a 'quantity of smaller and larger seating units', to quote the famous Viennese salonnière Karoline Pichler,[40] tended to be loosely distributed throughout the room. In a coffeehouse, there was a multitude of identical chairs and small tables with durable tops made of marble that could easily be cleaned. All these furniture pieces could be purchased at a reasonable price due to mass production. The arrangement of the furniture was repetitive and two main arrangements were used: in the middle of the room, there were usually free-standing tables mostly with four chairs around them, and a sequence of tables in booths along the inner and the window wall. Unlike in the Parisian café, wall-side seating ran not only parallel to the walls, but projected out at right angles into the room, thus creating separate booth-like seating units – a special feature of Viennese coffeehouse interiors that will be discussed later.

One of the smallest units of furniture nevertheless counts among the most recognisable and important for a Viennese coffeehouse: the chair, in particular the Thonet chair. Model No. 14 is a bentwood chair with a seat made of wickerwork, slightly flared legs and the characteristic curved back-rest in two parallel lines. In the category 'Classics' on the official homepage of the German company Thonet, this model appears as the first in a row of bentwood chairs that can still be purchased and typically enough, it is called 'coffeehouse-chair 214'.[41] The reputation of this chair nowadays obscures the extent to which a range of Thonet chairs were used in Viennese cafés. The famous Café Griensteidl opposite the Hofburg (Figure 2.3) was furnished with the model No. 4 that is somewhat older and, in terms of the shape of the back-rest, much more elaborate. The Arkaden Café behind the New University was equipped with the more complex variant No. 13[42] and nearby in the Café Hoffellner the model No. 19 was used, which is structurally much clearer and more lavish. It seems as if the model No. 56 had the widest distribution of all since we find it in a large number of historical photographs of Viennese coffeehouses such as the Café Reklame in the Nestroyhof[43] in Praterstraße by Oskar Marmorek or the Café Schönbrunn[44] near the Meidling-gate of Schönbrunn Castle. This type of chair was even used in the elegant Café Siller on the Donaukanal in a lavish version that was obviously turned on the lathe.[45]

The classic Thonet chair is a fly-chair, a type of occasional furniture, which in contrast to heavy, carved pieces of massive wood furniture which could only be pushed with the help of casters, was easily picked up and quickly moved somewhere else. Part of its attraction was that without difficulty, one could quickly rearrange seating groups. Fly-chairs made of bentwood were very popular due to their light weight, their cheapness and their flexible use. In many watercolours of the mid-nineteenth century depicting contemporary interiors they appear as a nearly indispensable element of a well-fitted salon.[46] As such and because of its practical flexibility it formed part of the furnishing of the upper-class living culture of the nineteenth century as well as becoming a major indispensable element of the coffeehouse furnishing. When Michael Thonet, who started his Viennese production with a commission for Prince Liechtenstein,[47] showed his products at the Great Exhibition in 1851 his chairs were highly praised for their 'small costs', for their 'strength' despite their 'lightness' in construction, and finally for their shape which was characterised as 'graceful and good'.[48]

Contemporaries reacted in a positive, but not uncritical way to the new chair design. On one hand Thonet's bentwood furniture was highly esteemed: although mass produced, the Thonet chair fulfilled the call of Gottfried Semper, that any product should be designed in such a way that it would harmoniously fit into any surroundings, because as a designer you do not know the person who will buy your product nor the place where it would be used.[49] On the other hand it was stressed that the consumer's eye must get used to the Thonet chair's dainty shape and its strong resemblance to garden furniture.[50] Jakob Falke, the famous Viennese theorist for arts and crafts, stated that although bentwood chairs combined solidity with lightness and could therefore be used advantageously under certain circumstances, for example in coffeehouses, they should not be used in an apartment that has been designed artistically, where they would only appear as flimsy because the eye would demand a more substantial object.[51] Here, Falke reveals himself to be an exemplary member of his generation who disapproved of the lightly coloured ceilings and daintily patterned ornamentation of recent decades.[52]

Adolf Loos assessed the Thonet chair differently. For him it was the only really exemplary seating furniture in production, which he held up for praise in 1898 as *the* prime example.[53] 'Look at the Thonet chair! Isn't it born of the same spirit that developed the Greek chair with the bent legs and back, unadorned embodying the sitting of a time?'[54] Loos's call for truthfulness is recognisable in his design for the Café Museum. There, the bentwood chairs 'are supposed to be, and want to be, bent wood' and they 'avoid … all cabinetmaking or joining'.[55] In this context the fact that Loos – as far as I know – never used bentwood chairs for his interior designs of apartments becomes ever more striking. Of the interiors published in the magazine *Das Interieur*, very few featured bentwood furniture in living rooms or other domestic interiors. Rudolf Frass' dining room interior, illustrated in 1907, is one of the very few exceptions.[56] One of the rare instances of the appearance of a bentwood chair in a domestic setting presented in the pages of *Das Interieur* occurs in a design for a girl's room by the coffeehouse architect Carl Witzmann in 1913.[57] When in the last years before the First

World War, the companies Thonet and Kohn advertised in *Das Interieur*, they either showed bentwood furniture which, according to the text, was intended for hotels, coffeehouses, restaurants, theatres and concert-halls, or they did not feature bentwood furniture at all but rather Windsor chairs. In a coffeehouse the bentwood chair, as an inexpensive type of furniture characterised by mass production, was a dominant feature of the interior, while in an apartment, we can only find it in a subordinate position – if at all.

The situation is different when we look at another characteristic piece of furniture of a Viennese coffeehouse: the upholstered seating booth, placed in the window niches or along the opposite inner wall.[58] Such booths offered a certain character of shelter and a way of avoiding the necessity 'to sit with strangers, a necessity the Viennese do not particularly care for'.[59] This arrangement of seats is comparable to the inglenook, which was one of many elements of English Arts and Crafts design that became popular across Europe at the turn of the century.

To support 'intellectual communication', Adolf Loos is said to have devised the Café Museum interior, not as a typical coffeehouse with comfortable and cosy seating booths, but as a clearly laid out room consisting of only one unified space.[60] Indeed, comfortable, upholstered benches are completely absent and the furnishing is made up of only one type of bentwood chair manufactured to Loos's design by the company Kohn. Loos's coffeehouse aimed to stimulate the 'intellectual' concentration of its customers by means of sparse furnishing and by reduction to indispensable necessities, thus earning the nickname 'Café Nihilismus'.[61] What Loos obviously did not want in his coffeehouse was to seclude the groups of guests gathered around their tables in cosy, sheltered bays. In the tavern Fürstenkeller by Josef Zotti, the separate booths could even be completely closed off from one another by drawing curtains and occupants could thus be hidden from sight like the famous *chambres séparées*.[62]

When designing the interiors of apartments, however, Loos acted differently. In fact, his interiors contained elements that correspond to our idea of a coffeehouse, with cosy seating booths. In the Turnovsky apartment from 1900, for instance, Loos put two glass cabinets at both ends of an L-shaped bench thus creating a sheltered seating area. In his own apartment, furnished in 1903, a U-shaped upholstered bench, again reminiscent of a coffeehouse booth, was placed directly underneath the window. In both cases, these benches created an air of cosy seclusion and were set up against a wall, being thus shielded, as was common in coffeehouses.

While Loos avoided cosiness and a living room-like character in his Café Museum, this special character was obviously sought by other designers for other coffeehouses. Fragile things like lace-covers for the top of the back-rests that necessitated intensive maintenance were commonly associated primarily with domestic spaces, such as those we can see in Loos's interiors for the opera-singer Selma Kurz in her apartment behind the Burgtheater. In particular cases they were included in the furnishing of a coffeehouse on the Ringstrasse, as they were in the Café Lurion, today's Café Prückel (Figure 9.1). This, together with the upholstered chairs, reflects the aim of that coffeehouse to offer a very extravagant service for its customers and to promote itself as a first-class establishment. The Café Lurion was in many ways the absolute antithesis of the Café Museum because its sumptuously adorned furnishings accentuated the decorative appearance. Other details of design that Loos would have used only for apartment interiors can be found in several coffeehouses. Again in the Turnovsky apartment, he put an upholstered chaise longue in front of a kind of folding screen, consisting of a solid part at the bottom crowned by a transparent part with glass insets, with the intention of isolating a certain space on one hand and at the same time of re-connecting this space optically. This design motif can be found in many coffeehouses such as the Café Lurion or the Café Tuchlaubenhof[63] where the individual booths were separated without producing obstacles for the uniform continuity of the whole interior. As has already been mentioned people often wanted to see and to be seen in a coffeehouse, so considerations of privacy had to be finely balanced. In conclusion, we can say that Loos used furniture in his apartment interiors that can be compared to the comfortably upholstered benches of Viennese coffeehouses and their special arrangement forming cosy corners, while his actual coffeehouse interior for the Café Museum was equipped in a completely different way.

Another remarkable piece of furniture that was well established within the Viennese coffeehouse was the billiard table and these can only rarely be found in private apartments due to lack of space.[64] We have records for the existence of billiard tables in Viennese coffeehouses from the eighteenth century[65] and the great popularity of billiards during the Biedermeier period brings us to a final topic that affects our understanding of the coffeehouse: Vienna's highly developed nostalgia for the past.[66] Alongside the triumphant impact of some of the masterpieces of modern Viennese architecture, such as Otto Wagner's Post Office Savings Bank and his church Am Steinhof and Josef Hoffmann's pioneering Sanatorium in Purkersdorf, not to mention the Secession Building by Joseph Maria Olbrich, a certain conservative or at least retrospective trend could also be detected in the early years of the twentieth century. Arthur Scala's 1896 exhibition on the 1815 Viennese Congress, one of the foundation stones for a new interest in the Biedermeier period, was followed by events such as the winter exhibition of the Austrian Museum for Art and Industry in 1901 where exact copies of historic interiors of this period were on display. It became a widely held opinion that the exemplary stylistic traditions of the Biedermeier period, especially in relation to interior decoration, had been negatively interrupted in the 1830s by the historicism of the *Gründerzeit*, and should be taken up again in contemporary interior design. Wagner's views on this matter are as well known, as are those of Adolf Loos for whom the Biedermeier period was also important. It was not without reason that Loos wanted his Café Museum to be seen as a coffeehouse of the early nineteenth century. If we compare this interior with the neighbouring Café Dobner (Figure 1.4), the architecture of which had been designed by the leading Viennese architect of the Biedermeier period, Joseph Kornhäusel,[67] we can see that Loos adopted the simple furnishing scheme of just tables and chairs. Even the design of the table that Loos chose for his Café Museum seems to be the same as in the Café Dobner, and Ludwig Hevesi thought that stylistically, the billiard tables in Loos's coffeehouse also corresponded to the 'Empire' style, as French Neoclassicism under Napoleon is called in German.[68] With the stone wall panelling of his Café Capua, Loos could also be seen to be evoking another element of traditional Viennese coffeehouse furnishing. In 1856, the walls of the Café Gabesam on Mariahilferstraße were covered with white stucco lustro, the marble-like white painting of the walls of the Café Eichhorn on Tuchlauben dated from 1847,[69] and, after alterations in 1837, the walls of the Café Leibenfrost on the corner of Plankengasse and Neuer Markt looked as white as Carrara marble.[70]

Other cultural phenomena corresponded with this nostalgic attitude in Vienna. From the period of the razing of the bastions in 1857/58 and the construction of the Ringstrasse, the traditional old townscape of the city had been altered.[71] The call for a return to the 'good, old days' was repeatedly voiced. A series of publications came out with such emotive titles as *Alt- und Neu-Wien* (Old and New Vienna, 1904)[72] or *Alt-Wien. Monatsschrift für Wiener Art und Sprache* (Old-Vienna: Monthly Paper for Viennese Nature and Language, 1892).[73] Analogously, the disappearence of the Old-Viennese coffeehouse was also mourned. For example, Friedrich Uhl wrote in 1900: 'Once upon a time there was … the Viennese coffeehouse. Even nowadays, there are still coffeehouses in abundance in Vienna, but the old, the true Viennese coffeehouse does not exist any more. It has become the modern Café, a hermaphrodite, that is not any more only a coffeehouse and still not yet a Café-restaurant'.[74] Others maintained that, although the typical Viennese coffeehouse had changed, it had changed only superficially: from the Café Griensteidl in a baroque palace to the Café Sperl in a newly erected building near the Ringstrasse. Its core, its character was not lost: literary as well as artistic circles found new homes in newly erected buildings: 'despite the far-reaching turn towards the mundane that took hold of the metropolitan character, especially in relation to the Ringstrasse-style, the very particular atmosphere of this Viennese institution survived'.[75] In memory and reception the coffeehouse was built up into the site of an irretrievable past and of a transfigured history, it became the encapsulation of the 'good, old days'. A coffeehouse interior like that of the Café Casa Piccola shows the influence of this vogue for the Biedermeier period, not least in the dainty lines of the ceiling decoration (Figure 10.6).

Figure 10.6 Th. Bach, Café Casa Piccola (1b, Mariahilferstraße) around 1900 (before the 1928 alteration by Carl Witzmann), *Der Architekt*, IX, 1903, pl. 60.

Conclusion

By starting our analysis of the coffeehouse with the biggest component, the spatial arrangement, and advancing towards the smaller items like the seating facilities, we find that analogies and correspondences become stronger: the more we examine such details the closer the relationship between coffeehouse and living room interiors becomes. But it remained the case that an object like the bentwood chair would be appraised differently when used for one or the other room type and only single objects and items obviously show formal connections between living rooms and coffeehouses. Coffeehouses are institutions which attempt to meet the public's demands for more prestigious surroundings that could not be satisfied by personal, domestic means. Stylistically, the design does not necessarily need to follow aristocratic models; furthermore, artistic decisions always depend on the designing architect. Functional continuity can be found in both room types in relation to issues such as the need to clean surfaces and the need for easily-handled pieces of furniture like Thonet chairs. We can discern different patterns of arranging the furnishings, patterns that – in the case of the coffeehouse – correspond to the proportionally higher number of occupants, while in relation to certain features, like the function of the booth in a coffeehouse as a cosy seating facility, close analogies can be found to seating arrangements in private living rooms.

Coming back to the question of how the design of living rooms and of coffeehouses relate to each other formally and to the postulated 'cosiness' of home-like coffeehouse interiors, we may ask ourselves if the depiction of the 'Litterat' introduced in the opening lines really illustrates the typical behaviour of customers in a coffeehouse? Of course, it does not. The text informs us that the image represents a person belonging to a special group of coffeehouse customers and their 'characteristic' habits. Indeed, it would be difficult to imagine an elegant lady from the bourgeois middle and upper class sitting in such an undignified manner – neither in the privacy of her home nor in a public space like the coffeehouse. The coffeehouse was, as we have shown, in part a place to see and to be seen, a place of prestigious public performance, with large windows opening into the street on ground-floor level, with large mirrors reflecting the public life on the street and with seating accommodation in the windows or in the *Schanigärten* on the pavement that ostentatiously belonged to the public sphere. We can therefore expect the bourgeois customer to behave in a way that is accordingly polite: as one wishes to be seen by the public. Reinforced by the medium of the caricature, the casual posture of our 'Litterat', recalling in our eyes the private sphere of the home, clarifies the way in which he wants to be seen by the public, in opposition to the usual more private posture of the bourgeoisie. But the interior depicted on this postcard, the upholstered window booth, was not restricted to special 'literary' coffeehouses, but was common across nearly all coffeehouse. Therefore we should not conclude from such illustrations that the living room-like character, the relaxed 'homeliness' that we think we see depicted, would be interpreted or even recognised in the same way by customers of the day. Writers form a distinct sub-group of coffeehouse users, who by virtue of their professions and habits of self-representation, produced a substantial body of texts in which they associated the coffeehouse with the private home.[76] These texts are highly influential nowadays when we consider the nature of the Viennese café around the turn of the century,[77] and they have such a determining authority that one can even raise the following question: 'Or has it perhaps never been anything else than the invention of the literati?'[78]

Notes

1. Wien Museum Inv.-No. 165.065.
2. Margit Claire Bauer, *Die Kaffeehäuser von Carl Witzmann*, Salzburg 1989, 42.

3. Peter Altenberg, 'Kaffeehaus', in Ludwig Plakolb (ed.), *Kaffeehaus: Literarische Spezialitäten und Amouröse Gusto-Stückln aus Wien*, Munich 1959, 5.
4. Alfred Polgar, 'Theorie des Café Central', in Plakolb (ed.), *Kaffeehaus*, 6.
5. Ernst Castelliz, *Formen der Geselligkeit in Wien zu Beginn des 20. Jahrhunderts*, Vienna 1998, 130.
6. Friedrich Torberg, 'Das Kaffeehaus', in *Das Wiener Kaffeehaus: Von den Anfängen bis zur Zwischenkriegszeit*, Vienna 1963, 16.
7. Helmuth Burgert, *Das Wiener Kaffeehaus*, Brixlegg 1937, 20.
8. Daniel M. Schmid, 'Wien ist um einige Kaffeehäuser herum gebaut', in Helfried Seemann and Christian Lunzer (eds), *Kaffeehaus-Album 1860–1930*, Vienna 1993, 15.
9. Michael Horvath, Thomas Lehmann, Fritz Panzer and Nathalie Schüller, *Das Erweiterte Wohnzimmer: Leben im Wiener Kaffeehaus*, Vienna 1990, 12. The epithet 'erweitertes Wohnzimmer' is also used in current previews of publishing houses such as the Viennese Christian Brandstätter Verlag (Verlagsprogramm Christian Brandstätter-Verlag for Autumn 2009, 19: *Erweitertes Wohnzimmer*, Announcement of Barbara Sternthal and Harald Eisenberger, *Coffee to Stay: Die schönsten Cafés in Europa*, Vienna 2009).
10. Stefan Zweig, *Die Welt von Gestern: Erinnerungen eines Europäers*, Vienna 1948, 38.
11. Friedrich Uhl, 'Wiener Kaffeehäuser', in *Wiener Zeitung*, 31 May 1900, 3.
12. Josef Durm, Hermann Ende, Eduard Schmitt and Heinrich Wagner, *Handbuch der Architektur: Vierter Theil: Entwerfen, Anlage und Einrichtung der Gebäude. 4. Halb-Band: Gebäude für Erholungs-, Beherbergungs- und Vereinszwecke etc.*, Darmstadt 1885 (2nd edn 1894).
13. In contrast to the restaurant with which it is related typologically (compare the chapter headings in Durm, Ende, Schmitt and Wagner, *Handbuch der Architektur*, 44), the Viennese coffeehouse does not serve food, but offers a range of hot and cold beverages and small snacks. (Bruno Bucher and Karl Weiss, Wiener Baedeker, *Wanderungen durch Wien und Umgebung*, 2nd edn, Vienna 1870, 16–17). Therefore going to a coffeehouse is not restricted to the times of the day when meals are generally taken. According to the source quoted above, coffeehouses did not keep to the official closing hours and were even kept open the whole night, for instance during carnival.
14. August Köstlin, 'Die Arkadenhäuser neben dem Rathause in Wien', in *Allgemeine Bauzeitung*, 50, 1885, 55.
15. On domestic interiors see most recently Stefan Muthesius, *The Poetic Home. Designing the 19th-Century Domestic Interior*, London 2009. (On the differentiation of room types and functions see in particular p.16 and footnote 16, p.321 with further reading.)
16. On Viennese apartments see also Donald J. Olson, *The City as a Work of Art: London, Paris, Vienna*, New Haven and London 1986, 125–131.
17. Durm, Ende, Schmitt and Wagner, *Handbuch der Architektur*, ill. 90 and 92.
18. Durm, Ende, Schmitt and Wagner, *Handbuch der Architektur*, 47.
19. Durm, Ende, Schmitt and Wagner, *Handbuch der Architektur*, 62.
20. Bucher and Weiss, *Wiener Baedeker*, 17.
21. Adolf Glassbrenner, *Bilder und Träume aus Wien*, 1st vol, Leipzig 1836, 130. See also Ludwig Hirschfeld, 'Kaffeehauskultur', in *Das Buch von Wien*, Munich 1927, 33.
22. Hartmut Binder, *Wo Kafka und seine Freund zu Gast waren: Eine Typologie des Prager Kaffeehauses*, Dortmund 1991, 18.
23. See for example Johannes Spalt, 'Das Wiener Kaffeehaus – Seine Entwicklung und Gestaltung', in *Das Wiener Kaffeehaus: Von den Anfängen bis zur Zwischenkriegszeit*, Historisches Museum der Stadt Wien, Vienna 1980, 46. To verify this hypothesis, statistical data capture concerning the amount of living space that would have been at the disposal of specific coffeehouse customers or of certain groups of them would surely be helpful.

24. Baar's villa designed by Joseph Olbrich is situated in Ober St. Veit, Hofmannsthal lived in the so-called Fuchs-Schlössel in Rodaun and Richard Schaukal's house can still be found in Grinzing.

25. Thomas W. MacCallum, *The Vienna That's Not in the Baedeker*, Munich 1929, 41.

26. Franz Baltzarek, Alfred Hoffmann and Hannes Stekl, *Wirtschaft und Gesellschaft der Wiener Stadterweiterung*, Wiesbaden 1975, 338. In an advertisement of the Arkaden Café from 1882, the particular size and the luxurious decoration are specifically mentioned, together with the electric lightning (*Neue Freie Presse* from 2 October 1882, 6).

27. Durm, Ende, Schmitt and Wagner, *Handbuch der Architektur*, 44.

28. Durm, Ende, Schmitt and Wagner, *Handbuch der Architektur*, 64.

29. Köstlin, 'Die Arkadenhäuser neben dem Rathause in Wien', in *Allgemeine Bauzeitung*, 50, 56.

30. On Hoffmann's highly sophisticated formal concept of connecting furniture objects and interior space by employing these undulated motifs, see Christian Witt-Dörring, 'On the Path to Modernism: The Ambiguity of Space and Plane', in Christian Witt-Dörring (ed.), *Josef Hoffmann: Interiors 1902–1913*, Munich, Berlin, London and New York 2006, 55–57.

31. Seemann and Lunzer, *Kaffeehaus Album*, ills on p.54.

32. *Das Interieur*, 1, 1900, 8–9.

33. *Das Interieur*, 1, 1900, pl. 48.

34. *Das Interieur*, 2, 1901, pl. 30.

35. *Das Interieur*, 2, 1901, 46–47.

36. Joseph Urban's designs for the Esterházy Castle in Abrahám near Galanta (in Hungarian, Szent Abraham near Galánta), east of Bratislava, is one of the rare exemptions. Markus Kristan, *Joseph Urban: Die Wiener Jahre des Jugendstilarchitekten und Illustrators 1872–1911*, Vienna, Cologne and Weimar 2000, 213–219.

37. Burkhard Rukschcio and Roland Stachel, *Adolf Loos. Leben und Werk*, 2nd edn, Salzburg and Vienna 1987, 594 (or catalogue no. 181).

38. For further examples and their formal interpretation, see Witt-Dörring, *Josef Hoffmann: Interiors 1902–1913*, 46.

39. E.F. Sekler, *Josef Hoffmann. Das architektonische Werk. Monographie und Werkverzeichnis*, 2nd edn, Salzburg-Vienna 1986, 206–207.

40. Karoline Pichler, *Denkwürdigkeiten aus meinem Leben 1*, Munich 1914, 322 (quoted in Christian Witt-Dörring, 'Der differenzierte Konsum. Das Wiener Möbel 1815–1848', in *Bürgersinn und Aufbegehren. Biedermeier und Vormärz in Wien 1815–1848*, Vienna 1987–1988, 368–387 (esp. 381 and footnote 60).

41. http://www.thonet.de/index.php?option=com_products&did=143&kat=145&lang=en&suc hsec=133&task=details (accessed on 13 June 2012).

42. Seemann and Lunzer, *Kaffeehaus-Album*, ill. on p.65.

43. Seemann and Lunzer, *Kaffeehaus-Album*, ill. on p.69.

44. Seemann and Lunzer, *Kaffeehaus-Album*, ill. on p.99.

45. The models No. 14 and 56 seem to have been used for inexpensive and therefore less prestigious inns and cafés in the suburbs. The Café Schönbrunn is then a remarkable exception since it was located in close proximity to the imperial summer residence and thus in one of the much sought-after and accordingly expensive living quarters. These models would also have been used throughout Austria-Hungary as examples from Prague, such as in the inn Zum grünen Adler (To the green eagle) show (Binder, *Wo Kafka und seine Freunde zu Gast waren*, ill. 79).

46. Eva B. Ottillinger, 'Die Aktualität des Interieurs. Wiener Wohnkultur vom Biedermeier zum "Zweiten Rokoko"', in *Zeugen der Intimität. Privaträume der kaiserlichen Familie und des böhmischen Adels. Aquarelle und Interieurs des 19. Jahrhunderts*, Schallaburg 1997, 20.

47. Michael C. Huey, *Peter Hubert Desvignes und die Neo-Rokoko-Neugestaltung des Stadtpalais Liechtenstein 1837–1849*, Vienna 1997; Eva B. Ottillinger and Lieselotte Hanzl, *Kaiserliche Interieurs. Die Wohnkultur des Wiener Hofes im 19. Jahrhundert*, Vienna, Cologne and Weimar 1997, 281–302; Eva B. Ottillinger (ed.), *Gebrüder Thonet. Möbel aus gebogenem Holz* (Publikationsreihe Museen des Mobiliendepots: 16), Vienna, Cologne and Weimar 2003.

48. *The 'Art Journal' Illustrated Catalogue of the International Exhibition*, London and New York 1862, 291 (quote after Eva B. Ottillinger, 'Thonet macht Geschichte', in Ottillinger (ed.), *Gebrüder Thonet*, 25.

49. Gottfried Semper, *Wissenschaft, Kunst und Industrie*, Braunschweig 1852, 40 (quote after Ottillinger, 'Thonet macht Geschichte', 25).

50. *Illustrirter Catalog der Londoner Industrie-Ausstellung von 1862*, Leipzig 1863, 106 (quote after Ottillinger, 'Thonet macht Geschichte', 25).

51. Jacob von Falke, *Die Kunst im Hause*, Vienna 1871, 287–288 (quote after Ottillinger, 'Thonet macht Geschichte', 26).

52. Falke, *Die Kunst im Hause*, 247–249.

53. Undated concept for a letter to Felix Salten by Adolf Loos (quote after Burkhardt Rukschcio and Roland Schachel, *Adolf Loos. Leben und Werk*, 2nd edn, Salzburg and Vienna 1987, 53).

54. Adolf Loos, 'Kunstgewerbliche Rundschau 1', in Adolf Loos, *Ins Leere Gesprochen 1897–1900*, Vienna 1981, 36 (1st edn, Paris 1921).

55. Quote after Rukschcio and Schachel, *Adolf Loos*, 418–419.

56. *Das Interieur*, 8, 1907, pl. 102.

57. *Das Interieur*, 14, 1913, pl. 104.

58. Durm, Ende, Schmitt and Wagner, *Handbuch der Architektur*, 52 and ill. 51 and 52.

59. MacCallum, *The Vienna That's Not In The Baedeker*, 37.

60. Rukschcio and Schachel, *Adolf Loos*, 67.

61. Ludwig Hevesi, 'Kunst auf der Straße', in *Fremden-Blatt (Morgen-Blatt)*, 30 May 1899, 14, column 2.

62. *Das Interieur*, 14, 1913, pl. 13.

63. Seemann and Lunzer, *Kaffeehaus-Album*, ill. p.62.

64. One of the few examples is Josef Hoffmann's card room at the Biach House in Wieden (Christian Witt-Dörring [ed.], *Josef Hoffmann*, 157). Billiard tables could often be found in club houses like the Viennese Künstlerhaus.

65. Reingard Witzmann, 'Das Wiener Kaffeehaus als Ort städtischer Geselligkeit und Kultur', in *Das Wiener Kaffeehaus: Von den Anfängen bis zur Zwischenkriegszeit*, 30.

66. Concerning the problem of modernity and tradition in the context of Vienna, see Monika Sommer and Heidemarie Uhl (eds), *Mythos Alt-Wien: Spannungsfelder urbaner Identitäten*, Innsbruck, Vienna and Bozen 2009.

67. *Das Wiener Kaffeehaus: Von den Anfängen bis zur Zwischenkriegszeit*, Cat.No. 159; Felix Czeike, *Historisches Lexikon Wien*, 1st vol, Vienna 2004, 534.

68. Rukschcio and Schachel, *Adolf Loos*, 67.

69. Gustav Gugitz, *Das Wiener Kaffeehaus*, Vienna 1940, 194 and 198–199.

70. Ilse Prehsler, *Das Kaffeehaus als kulturelle Einrichtung im Europa des 18. und 19. Jahrhunderts – Herkunft, Entstehung, Entwicklung und Bedeutung*, Vienna 1985, 93.

71. The extent to which the historic city was subject to alteration can exemplarily be observed in the exhibition catalogue, *Das ungebaute Wien. Projekte für die Metropole 1800 bis 2000*, Historisches Museum der Stadt Wien, Vienna 1999/2000.

72. Karl E. Schimmer, *Alt- und Neu-Wien: Geschichte der Österreichischen Kaiserstadt*, Vienna and Leipzig 1904.

73. Leopold Stieböck, *Alt-Wien: Monatsschrift für Wiener Art und Sprache*, Vienna 1892–.

74. Uhl, 'Wiener Kaffeehäuser', 3.

75. Prehsler, *Das Kaffeehaus als kulturelle Einrichtung*, 89 and 92.
76. See the examples given in the opening section of this chapter.
77. See Harald Schume, *50 einfache Dinge, die Sie über Österreich und die Österreicher wissen sollten*, Frankfurt and Main 2009, 34–38.
78. Robert Waissenberger, 'Vorwort', in *Das Wiener Kaffeehaus. Von den Anfängen bis zur Zwischenkriegszeit*, 5.

Chapter 11

COFFEEHOUSES AND TEA PARTIES
Conversational Spaces as a Stimulus to Creativity in Sigmund Freud's Vienna and Virginia Woolf's London

Edward Timms

The worlds of Sigmund Freud and Virginia Woolf appear to be poles apart, but there are also – as this chapter will show – striking parallels and surprising convergences. The most obvious contrast is that between the public and the private sphere – between coffeehouses and tea parties. In Freud's Vienna around the year 1910, avant-garde intellectuals, artists and musicians enjoyed the benefits of uniquely productive public spaces such as the Café Central and the Café Griensteidl (Figures 2.2 and 2.3). These prestigious coffeehouses are celebrated in the literature of the period and have attracted sustained attention from cultural historians.[1] However, it is important to remember that coffeehouses were not confined to the city centre, but could also be found in less fashionable suburbs. A typical example is the Café Eckl, situated at Neubaugasse 38 in the Seventh District in a building constructed at the end of the eighteenth century. This coffeehouse flourished for over a hundred years, from 1802 until its demolition in 1911. The interior (Figure 11.1) may appear unassuming, but the coffeehouse was large enough to accommodate six billiard tables. Successive owners enhanced its prestige by having frescoes painted on the ceiling and adding a spacious garden room. Its significance in the eyes of contemporaries is reflected in the fact that the Municipality of Vienna arranged for a series of fine photographs to be taken before the coffeehouse disappeared.[2]

Figure 11.1 Café Eckl, 1911, photograph by Siegfried Schramm. Courtesy of the Wien Museum.

This interior may appear rather austere, but coffeehouses were largely accessible public spaces for anyone who was seeking sociability and could afford a drink.[3] Café Eckl was situated in a prosperous manufacturing district to the west of the city centre. It attracted its clientele from businessmen with artistic aspirations, the community whose gradual erosion was so evocatively portrayed by Otto Stoessl in his novel *Das Haus Erath* (The House of Erath, 1928).[4] Habermas assigns special significance to the coffeehouses of the eighteenth century as fora for the emergence of a bourgeois public dedicated to enlightened discussion.[5] Of course, in conservative Austria there were police informants and government spies who ensured that the politics of the coffeehouse did not become overheated. A striking example is recorded from the life of the celebrated author Friedrich Schlegel, editor of the government-sponsored *Österreichischer Beobachter* at the time of the Congress of Vienna. His movements were observed by a police spy who, on 20 November 1814, followed him from the Kaffeehaus in the Herrengasse to the Café Benko on the Stefansplatz and the Rose Wine Bar in the Graben.[6]

In Freud's Vienna at the beginning of the twentieth century there was a concentration of cafés in the city centre – the area of the parliament and city hall, the ministries and banks, the theatres and concert halls. Freud would take a regular weekly stroll along the Ringstrasse to join his friends at the Café Landtmann next to the Burgtheater. Such coffeehouses acquired a central position within an increasingly influential public sphere, interacting with other sectors of political and cultural life. This becomes clear if we construct a diagram of the public sphere in late Hapsburg Vienna and place the institution of the coffeehouse circles within it (Figure 11.2). This diagram has a top-down axis, reflecting the authoritarian political structure. Control in the Dual Monarchy of Austria-Hungary was exerted from above in a traditional and rather autocratic manner: not by parliament (which was virtually paralysed by the nationalities conflict) but by the cabinet and the imperial bureaucracy, acting under the authority of the Emperor. However, this anachronistic system was by no means moribund. For the traditional political structure coexisted with dynamically modern social institutions: commercial (on the left-hand side) and cultural (on the right). Hence the arrows in the diagram run in both directions: top-down, as the traditional hierarchy of autocrats and mandarins attempted to maintain political control; but also bottom-up, as journalists, authors and lawyers, stockbrokers and entrepreneurs, theatre directors and publishers competed to extend their spheres of influence and increase their market share.

Figure 11.2 Diagram of the public sphere in late Hapsburg Vienna (by the author).

On the one hand, given the lack of an effective parliament, newspaper editors exerted a disproportionately powerful influence. On the other, the exceptional prestige enjoyed by culture and the arts meant that theatre directors could make significant public interventions.

This model could doubtless be applied, with variations, to other societies in the throes of modernisation. But the centrality of the coffeehouse is a specifically Viennese feature. It constituted the forum where opinion-makers could meet, what I would call the 'integrative nexus'. Traditionalists might claim that the nexus was formed by the Catholic Church or the Austro-Hungarian Army, both of which exerted a disproportionate influence on public affairs. In a diagram of the traditional power structure, both the Army and the Church certainly would have their place, alongside the state bureaucracy. But my model does not foreground those closed and autocratic institutions. It focuses on the more open public spaces of modernity. If there was one civilisation in which coffeehouses undoubtedly played a defining role, it was that of Central Europe – and especially Vienna – around 1900. This was the space where people from all segments of educated society could meet and exchange ideas. And this discursive space created the potential for the emergence of new forms of anti-establishment culture, especially in music and visual art, literature and psychology.

The contrast with Virginia Woolf's London could hardly be greater. London had certainly in the past enjoyed a flourishing coffeehouse culture. The coffeehouses of the early eighteenth century frequented by Addison and Steele, Pope and Swift generated an exceptionally dynamic culture of debate. This was a phenomenon that, well before Habermas, generated a rich culture of reflection – think of William Hazlitt's essay on 'On Coffee-house Politicians'.[7] However, in the London of 1900 this dynamic public sphere was in decline, for a number of reasons. In part, it had been displaced by gentlemen's clubs, such as the Athenaeum and the Carlton, the Garrick and the United Services Club. Only a self-perpetuating elite was admitted to those exclusive clubs, if you could afford the fees – and if you were male. During the heyday of British imperialism, the links between politicians and intellectuals were no longer forged in the public space of the coffeehouse, but behind closed doors – in clubland. There was no place in the gentlemen's clubs for sensitive young men who did not share the macho values of British imperialism, nor for emancipated women who were claiming the right to participate in public life. Further down the social scale, the urban landscape was transformed by the opening of new chains of teashops designed to appeal to the less privileged – the ABC Teashops and the Lyons Corner Houses. Drinking tea may have sustained the British Empire, but there is little evidence that it inspired artistic or literary innovation.

Where were the writers, artists and intellectuals of the English avant-garde to meet? This question is explored by Peter Brooker in his informative study

Bohemia in London. 'Where is your Montmartre, where is your Quartier Latin?' visitors from Paris would ask. 'We have none,' answered the symbolist poet Arthur Symons in 1908, 'for the café is responsible for a good part of the Bohemianism of Paris and we have no cafés'.[8] Of course, there was the sumptuously decorated Café Royal, notorious since the 1890s for the effete dinner parties hosted by Oscar Wilde. But Wilde's trial and conviction for homosexual offences had put an end to that style of flamboyant public display. When a more circumspect form of modernism began to emerge fifteen years later, its protagonists tended to foregather in restaurants rather than cafés. The Imagists famously dined at Dieudonné's, an expensive restaurant in Ryder Street off Piccadilly, the Vorticists at the Restaurant de la Tour Eiffel in Percy Street, near Tottenham Court Road. Editorial meetings for A.R. Orage's journal *New Age* were held on Mondays at the ABC Restaurant in Chancery Lane, while Harriet Weaver's *Egoist* group preferred Belotti's Ristorante Italiono in Old Compton Street. Ford Madox Hueffer recalls that his first meeting with the sculptor Henri Gaudier-Brzeska took place in 'a low teashop'.[9]

While London was certainly not short of restaurants, coffeehouses comparable to those in Vienna were out of favour. The most notable exception, actually named the Café Vienna, was in New Oxford Street, not far from the British Museum. This was the scene of a momentous encounter between Wyndham Lewis and Ezra Pound, as recalled by Lewis in his memoirs: 'How I can possibly convey the atmosphere of the Vienna Café in 1910 I do not know,' Lewis begins. 'On the first floor was a large triangular room with the mirrored ceiling, which reflected all your actions as if in a lake suspended above your head, surface downwards, and at a couple of tables, on the south side, these miscellaneous people would meet. It was a good club, and it was the only club of that sort in London'. Those 'miscellaneous people' included modernists like Pound and Lewis, Amy Lowell and Henri Gaudier-Brzeska, C.R.W. Nevinson and T.E. Hulme, who were trying to launch a continental-style artistic revolt in London. Their efforts were drastically curtailed when the Great War broke out just four years later. Some like Lewis enlisted, some – including Gaudier-Brzeska and Hulme – were killed, and the Vienna Café was forced to close, 'for it was staffed and owned entirely by Germans and Austrians, "alien enemies". It could not have survived under all-British management'.[10]

Given the shortage of coffeehouses of this inspirational kind, the English modernists and their American allies tended to meet either in stylish restaurants or in private houses. Brooker's study contains helpful street plans of central London, identifying the most significant of those private meeting places, including Lady Ottoline Morell's residence in Bedford Square, the Georgian house in Frith Street (off Soho Square) where Hulme presided over his Tuesday evening salon, Pound's bed-sitting room in Church Walk and Ford Maddox Hueffer's home at South Lodge (both in Kensington).[11] Even more significant were the addresses off Tottenham Court Road which formed the nucleus of the most significant – and by far the most long-lasting – modernist circle in London, the Bloomsbury Group. Denied access to the exclusive men's clubs, lacking the coffeehouse facilities that were flourishing on the continent, the Bloomsbury Group created their own conversational spaces – in private.

The writers and artists of Bloomsbury met in the comfort of private houses, starting in 1904 at 46 Gordon Square, the home of Adrian Stephen and his sisters Virginia and Vanessa, better known by their married names, Virginia Woolf and Vanessa Bell. There were half a dozen such houses in central London where they and their friends would foregather – by invitation only – for their genteel tea parties and animated evening conversations. Bloomsbury, of course, literally denotes an area of central London, but as the name for a cohesive artistic and literary group it includes significant locations in the countryside. The most famous, which exists to the present day, is Charleston Farmhouse. The contrast between Café Eckl and Charleston Farmhouse, the austere coffeehouse and the cosy domestic interior with cups ready for a tea party, provides a visual summary of my argument about public and private spheres. The Bloomsbury drawing room, colourful and cluttered, was accessible by invitation only. The Vienna coffeehouse, ranging from the plain to the luxurious, was a public space open to all comers who were prepared to respect its conventions. In addition, there is clearly a gendered dimension. The one space seems predominantly masculine, the other beguilingly feminine. The pivotal figures in Bloomsbury were both female and feminists – Virginia Woolf and Vanessa Bell – while the pivotal figures in Vienna were not only male but in some cases also anti-feminist – think of Sigmund Freud and Karl Kraus.

The contrast becomes even clearer if we place two artistic depictions of those defining interiors side by side (Figure 11.3). The painting by Reinhold Völkel is justly celebrated, not only because the Griensteidl (as Gilbert Carr's contribution in this volume shows) was the centre for literary modernism in the 1890s, but also because the image provides a wealth of suggestive detail. First, it confirms the masculinity of the coffeehouse ambiance (only two female figures can be seen accompanying male guests in the background). It then highlights the function of the café as a place to read and discuss newspapers and magazines, which seem far more important than the tiny coffee cups. Then through the figures in the foreground to the right it dramatises the idea of discussion: the figure seated in a hat gesticulating with his hands, sometimes identified as the author Peter Altenberg, is clearly delivering an impassioned tirade, while the table companion next to him sips his coffee thoughtfully. The third person at that table – a humorous touch – seems to have fallen asleep. There are no writing materials depicted, but the tables are clearly spacious and solid enough for writing, and some of the modernists, notably Altenberg, actually composed essays and articles, poems and letters in coffeehouses.

Figure 11.3 Reinhold Völkel, *Café Griensteidl*, 1896. Watercolour. Courtesy of the Wien Museum.

The Bloomsbury ambiance was very different, as we can see from Vanessa Bell's painting of 1912, 'Conversation at Asheham House' (Figure 11.4). Again, our attention is drawn to three figures, each of whom has been identified by researchers on the Bloomsbury group. On the left is the tall figure of Adrian Stephen, the brother of Vanessa and Virginia. The figure on the right has been identified, despite the simplified features, as Leonard Woolf, soon to become Virginia's husband. And just visible in the bottom right-hand corner is the art historian Clive Bell, husband of Vanessa. Again, there is an undercurrent of humour – while most of Clive's body is invisible, his blue socks are clearly displayed. Only in the mirror above the fireplace do we glimpse a reflection of his face.[12]

In short, where the matrix of innovation in Freud's Vienna was the accessible coffeehouse, in Woolf's Bloomsbury it was the intimate house party (Asheham House, which has since been demolished, was situated near Lewes). It is true that the Wednesday evening meetings of the psychoanalysts originally took place in a private house, at Freud's family home in the Berggasse. But he valued these interdisciplinary discussions so highly that he arranged for them to be recorded by a member of the group who was a skilled stenographer, Otto Rank. Published in four volumes, the *Minutes of the Vienna Psychoanalytical Association* provide unique insights into the value of conversational space for the development of European modernism. Moreover, Freud's ideas were immediately projected into the public domain by means of journalistic articles, lectures and book publications.

Figure 11.4 Vanessa Bell, *Conversation at Asheham House*, 1912. Copyright estate of Vanessa Bell. Courtesy of Henrietta Garnett.

There is a marked contrast between Vienna's urban dynamism and Bloomsbury's domestic cosiness. However, one shared feature brings our two images together in a surprising way – the depiction of a conversation. The Asheham House picture is centred on what really mattered for Vanessa Bell, as for her sister Virginia: not realistic details but intimate conversational spaces and the psychological interactions they encourage. Both Freud's Vienna and Woolf's Bloomsbury were committed to uncompromisingly frank discussion. The common ground depicted by the Völkel and Bell paintings introduces the second theme of this paper: the parallels between these discursive worlds. In both cases we have intimate circles relying on intensive oral communication. The question is how did these esoteric coteries become influential modernist movements, challenging received assumptions? A first answer lies with the creative cross-fertilisation between different disciplines which characterises both groups. Their interest in literature and psychology was underscored by a passion for music and theatre, aesthetic theory and the visual arts.

The transition from the private to the public was intensified after each group set up its own publishing house: the Wiener Psychoanalytischer Verlag, created to publicise Freudian psychology, and the Hogarth Press, founded by Leonard and Virginia Woolf and operated first from their south London home in Richmond and then back in the Bloomsbury district at Tavistock Square. This made it possible for the two groups to project their shared dissatisfaction with 'Victorian' values – through influential books and essays – into a public critique: Freud's assault on conventional sexual morality, Lytton Strachey's ironic pen portraits of 'Eminent Victorians', Virginia Woolf's subtle reflections on the oppression of women. These critiques owed their explosive power to the way in which they challenged conventional concepts of gender roles and libidinous attachments.

Above all, we may note the importance of networking as a means of projecting dynamic ideas into the public sphere. My publications on the satirist Karl Kraus have illustrated this process by means of a diagram of creative interactions in Vienna (Figure 11.5). This diagram places Freud and the Psychoanalytical Association in the context of what I have described as a 'condensed system of micro-circuits'.[13] The result was an extraordinary cross-fertilisation between different disciplines through the overlaps between the circles which made the

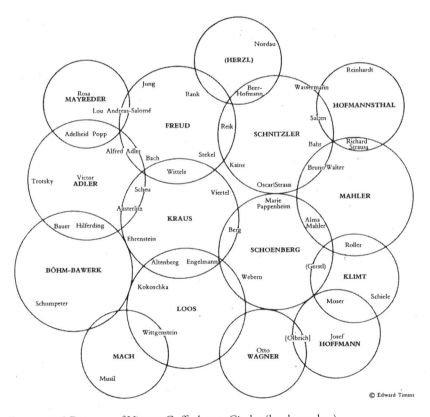

Figure 11.5 Diagram of Vienna Coffeehouse Circles (by the author).

whole system so interactive. Thus the innovations of the Vienna Psychoanalytical Association can be seen as centrifugal. Although it developed into a formal society with a membership list and rules of procedure, it could never be called a closed group. Its members were extraordinarily versatile and cosmopolitan, and they intersected with other groups, generating dynamic spin-offs.

With the Bloomsbury Group in London the situation was reversed. It was never a formally constituted society and there were no explicit rules governing membership or procedure. The group made a cult of informality, but it was socially exclusive. It was a relatively closed society, perceived – and often resented – by contemporaries as a clique. Moreover, it did not form part of a whole network of avant-garde activity. There were tenuous links with Fabianism and the Labour movement (through Leonard Woolf), but no real connections with Bernard Shaw and the political theatre. Indeed, the group was sealed off from the other pioneers of Anglo-American modernism, Wyndham Lewis and Ford Madox Hueffer, Ezra Pound and T.S. Eliot, James Joyce and D.H. Lawrence.

In the fine account of the Bloomsbury Group by one of its younger members, Quentin Bell, the membership is pictured as follows (Figure 11.6). Introducing this schematic representation of the group around the year 1913, Quentin Bell emphasises the 'high degree of confident intimacy' that obtained among them.[14] The core members are placed near the centre, clustered around the artists Vanessa Bell and Duncan Grant and the authors Virginia and Leonard Woolf and Lytton Strachey. More peripheral figures, like the novelist E.M. Forster and the editor and translator James Strachey, are placed nearer to the margins. Clearly, given the amorphousness of the group, such a diagram can never be complete. But one

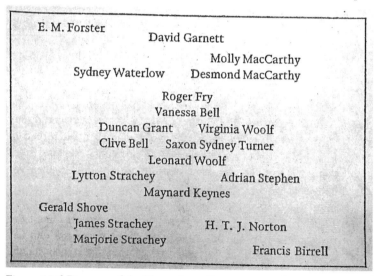

Figure 11.6 Diagram of the Bloomsbury Group in 1913 (by Quentin Bell). Courtesy of the Society of Authors as the literary representative of the estate of Quentin Bell.

of the most striking features of the diagram is the way in which the figures seem 'boxed in'. The diagram suggests strong boundaries that exclude outsiders – a striking contrast to the fluid and interactive model of creativity represented by my Vienna Circles.

There is thus a fundamental contrast between the dynamic outreach of the Psychoanalytic Association in Vienna and the more esoteric Bloomsbury Group. This becomes clearer if we focus on a subject that was crucial to both groups – sexuality. The relationship between London and Vienna cannot be summed up by the conventional view that creative spirits on the continent were uninhibited in the pursuit of wine, women and song, while the educated British middle classes were life-denying puritans. The Imagists, the Vorticists and the Bloomsbury Group were just as radical in their personal lives as any group in Vienna, breaking down the barriers of conventional morality. Bloomsbury, in particular, rejoiced in transgressive sexuality, including homosexuality, lesbianism and partner-swapping (regardless of gender). But their sexual experiments took place within a closed space, and they failed to develop a public discourse of sexuality.

By contrast, the Viennese avant-garde succeeded in creating a new discourse of sexuality, quite distinct from the technical medical jargon of the nineteenth century, but equally distinct from the sub-culture of pornography. Freud's achievement was to show that one can speak publicly about sex, and explore all its ramifications, in a language accessible to any educated person. Freud's *Three Essays on the Theory of Sexuality* (1905) has a breath-taking originality. In this and other early writings he brought the subject of sex out into the open. The discussions of the Psychoanalytic Association – for example, about masturbation or homosexuality – were not merely conducted behind closed doors; they published their findings as pamphlets designed for the general public. Moreover, these developments took place within a context, within what is now recognised as the context of fin-de-siècle Vienna: the erotic sub-culture. Through the writings of Karl Kraus and Arthur Schnitzler, through the paintings of Gustav Klimt and Egon Schiele, the sexual drive was emphatically affirmed. What would earlier have been denounced as perversion or pornography rather suddenly came out of the closet and laid claim to the status of artistic sophistication and emotional maturity. What was it that held those predominantly male coffeehouse circles together? It was obviously not ideas alone. Libidinal energies of attraction and rivalry infused the whole network, driving that explosion of creativity which we associate with the coffeehouse culture of Vienna.

Homosexuality, one of the themes of Freud's *Three Essays*, began to be seen as part of the spectrum of normal experience, more openly discussed and practised in Vienna and Berlin than in London. A recent exhibition in Vienna explored this phenomenon under the title *Geheimsache: Leben – Schwule und Lesben im Wien des 20. Jahrhunderts* (Top Secret: Life – Gays and Lesbians in Twentieth-century Vienna, 2005). The catalogue cites a series of articles that appeared in 1907 in the *Illustrierte Österreichische Kriminalzeitung*, a newspaper whose readership was by no means restricted to the police force. This identified coffeehouses and wine bars that were well known as meeting places for homosexuals: the Weinstube Dipauli, the Bodega on the Ringstrasse, the Café Scheidl on the Kärntnerstrasse and the Café Tirolerhof, then in the Herrengasse. A letter published in the *Kriminal-Zeitung* on 2 September 1907 complains that the Tirolerhof has become a notorious meeting place for lesbians.[15] 'Was this widely known at the time?' you may wonder. An answer can be found in the 1905 edition of Baedeker's *Austria-Hungary*. Studying the small print, we see that after the list of leading coffeehouses there is a note saying 'Also many Coffee and Milk rooms, which ladies may visit'.[16] Respectable women may have been rare birds in the mainstream coffeehouses, but among the milk rooms recommended for ladies we find the Tirolerhof (Baedeker catered for all tastes).

Meanwhile, back in London, the Bloomsbury Group was also passionately interested in both avant-garde art and sexual liberation, but it cannot be said that they succeeded in bringing the two together. In the domain of sexuality, there is a strangely inhibited quality in both the artistic and literary work of the Group. In private, as we know from numerous biographies, memoirs and letters, they talked about sex with remarkable frankness. It was the fashion to sprinkle your letters and conversations with words like 'buggers', 'copulation' and 'semen'. But in public, in their literary work? The novels of Virginia Woolf and E.M. Forster, the two finest writers associated with the Group, explore every nuance of feeling except one – sexual passion. The difficulty, for leading figures in the Bloomsbury Group, was how to represent homosexuality. In this sphere, London was just as 'advanced' as Vienna, but there is a striking lack of correlation between public artistic expression and private homoerotic experience. Male homosexuals were haunted by the threat of criminal prosecution, which had destroyed the career of Oscar Wilde. Thus Forster's novel about homosexual love, *Maurice*, was never published in his lifetime, and Virginia Woolf's *Orlando* transformed the concept of gender change into a historical romp. It is hard to find any convincing representation of homosexuality in the published writings of the group. The same is true of the Bloomsbury artists. The paintings of Duncan Grant, Vanessa Bell and Roger Fry abound in subtle portraits and homely interiors, but there was an almost complete failure to develop a visual language commensurate with the erotic pursuits of their private lives. Duncan Grant felt obliged to hide his paintings of sexually excited male nudes under the bed, though he would take them out to show to intimate friends when they came for tea.[17]

Would the writers of Bloomsbury have been less inhibited if they had been familiar with the more open expression of homoeroticism in Berlin and Vienna? An answer is provided by two younger members of the group who were to bring the worlds of Freud's Vienna and Woolf's London together – James and Alix Strachey. In the summer of 1920 the newly married Stracheys travelled to

Vienna, on the recommendation of Ernest Jones, to consult Sigmund Freud. The momentous consequences are documented in a selection of letters published under the title *Bloomsbury/Freud*.[18] James Strachey had an extended analysis with the master, who agreed to see him for a fee of one guinea an hour, but Alix fell ill with pneumonia and had to be nursed by friends. For several years she had been suffering from depressions, which may have been associated with her bisexual disposition. Whether she visited the Café Tirolerhof in the Herrengasse we do not know.

Since Alix's analysis was incomplete, Freud arranged for her to undergo a more systematic analysis with Karl Abraham in Berlin. The letters she wrote to James from Berlin during the years 1924–1925 offer a wonderfully vivid picture of the encounter between Freud's most distinguished German follower and a woman regarded by Virginia Woolf as one of the 'Bloomsbury Bunnies'.[19] Having studied Modern Languages at Cambridge, Alix was fluent in German and thrived in the cosmopolitan atmosphere of Berlin, meeting leading German analysts and attending Otto Fenichel's weekly gathering of young radicals, the *Kinderseminar*. But the experiences she describes with greatest passion took place in the city's restaurants and coffeehouses, especially those that played the dance music broadcast by Berlin radio. 'Dear James,' she wrote from the Café Schilling on Friday 5 December 1924, 'I'm sitting in my favourite Rundfunk Konditorei listening to a succession of Strauss waltzes'. The Romanisches Café, meeting place of the literary avant-garde, was another favourite haunt, but Alix's greatest passion was for dancing, with both male and female partners. An exuberant letter, dated 2 February 1925, describes the thrill of attending a masked ball with Melanie Klein, who was 'elaborately got up as a kind of Cleopatra – terrifically decolletée – & covered with bangles and rouge'.

Alix's response to the coffeehouse culture of Berlin alerts us to a further factor – the link between social class and ethnicity. The Bloomsbury group was predominantly recruited from the English upper (or upper-middle) class, and only one of its leading members was of Jewish origin – Leonard Woolf. But he had pukka British credentials – public school, Cambridge University (where he became a member of the Apostles), foreign service examination and colonial administration. Berlin society was different. Much as Alix enjoyed the intellectual ferment, she was disconcerted to find that her most stimulating conversational and dancing partners often turned out to be Jewish. Whereas in Bloomsbury she had been closeted within a relatively closed society, her beloved Romanisches Café was open to all comers.[20] In Alix's letters, her editors observe, 'a reflex antisemitism typical of her class shows up with distressing frequency'. However, they add that she probably preferred Jewish company to the machismo of German conservatives.[21] She must have formed a similar impression in Austria four years earlier, for the membership of the Vienna Psychoanalytic Association was also predominantly Jewish.

It was James and Alix Strachey who arranged for Melanie Klein to come to London, where she established herself – with the help of Ernest Jones – as a pioneering child analyst. But the Stracheys' greatest claim to fame lies with their achievements as translators. Freud's Vienna and Woolf's London did ultimately converge, through a translation project that was to transform attitudes towards sexual experience and unconscious emotional life: *The Complete Psychological Writings of Sigmund Freud* in 24 volumes. This annotated English edition, which had a worldwide impact, was published under the general editorship of James Strachey, with Alix as one of his most productive co-translators. The project began in Vienna in 1920, when Freud asked James Strachey to translate the Case Histories. It was not until the 1960s that the mammoth task was completed.

The publication first of Freud's *Collected Papers* and then of the *Complete Psychological Writings* was undertaken by the Hogarth Press, directed by Leonard Woolf with the assistance of his wife. This brings us to a final and rather elusive question: was there a meeting of minds between the principals of psychoanalytic Vienna and literary London, Sigmund Freud and Virginia Woolf? If so, when did it occur? Standard accounts of Woolf's reception of psychoanalysis place her reading of Freud right at the end of her life. 'She did not read any of his works until December 1939,' declares Jan Ellen Goldstein in her account of 'The Woolfs' Response to Freud'.[22] This seems to be confirmed by Woolf's own records. A passage about her father Leslie Stephen in 'A Sketch from the Past', written in 1939, reads as follows: 'Rage alternated with love. It was only the other day when I read Freud for the first time that I discovered that this violently disturbing conflict of love and hate is a common feeling; and is called ambivalence'.[23] This appears to be connected with her diary entry for 2 December 1939: 'Began reading Freud last night; to enlarge the circumference, to give my brain wider scope, to make it objective; to get outside'. From her Reading Notebooks, we know that the book concerned was *Group Psychology and the Analysis of the Ego*.[24]

Virginia Woolf, Goldstein concludes, was a 'non-participant in the Freudian revolution' and was indeed 'almost untouched by it'. But she does concede that Woolf was acquainted with psychoanalysis 'in the ordinary way of conversation', citing a comment by the novelist to this effect, which dates from 1931.[25] This view is echoed in more recent studies, including the comprehensive biography by Hermione Lee: 'she finally read Freud in 1939'.[26] There is a consensus that during her most creative period Woolf was sceptical if not actually hostile towards psychoanalysis, and that the use of stream of consciousness technique in her finest novels, *Mrs Dalloway* and *To the Lighthouse*, was not influenced by Freud. But the question comes into sharper focus if, building on our study of avant-garde conversational spaces, we reconstruct the knowledge of psychoanalysis that Woolf is likely to have acquired 'in the ordinary way of conversation'.

When the first English translation of Freud's *Psychopathology of Everyday Life* was published in 1914, it was enthusiastically reviewed in the *New English Weekly* by Leonard Woolf. Are we to suppose that, while writing this review, he made no attempt to share his discovery with Virginia (they had married two years earlier)? Surely, they must have discussed the book over tea, and wouldn't he have encouraged her to read the review? In the absence of reliable evidence these must remain open questions. But we may assume that the review copy of *Psychopathology of Everyday Life* was placed in the library, for it is possible that a few years later Virginia took it off the shelf and began to browse.

Around 1914, Virginia Woolf's knowledge of psychoanalysis was indeed only 'conversational', but we must remember that her circle included people who were becoming passionately interested in the subject, including not only James and Alix Strachey, but also James's more famous older brother, Lytton Strachey. If only we could reconstruct those early conversations about Freud among members of the Bloomsbury group! Well, in a sense we can. Shortly after the publication of the English edition of *Psychopathology of Everyday Life*, Lytton Strachey wrote an amusing dialogue entitled 'According to Freud'. It portrays a flirtation between an advanced young woman named Rosamund and a rather conventional young man named Arthur.

The scene is set in one of those typical Bloomsbury country house gardens. Arthur is writing a letter with his fountain pen when Rosamund suddenly appears from inside the summer-house, where she has been reading a book. Assuming their meeting is 'just one of those lucky accidents', he is taken aback by her response:

Rosamund: Accidents? According to Freud there are no such things.

Arthur: According to *who*?

Rosamund: According to Freud. [...]

Arthur: So that was what you were reading? Freud: and what is Freud?

Rosamund: What is he? He's a doctor. But you'd better find out the rest for yourself, for no doubt you'll be shocked if I were to explain him to you. You'll find the book in there – on top of one of the six cushions. *The Psychopathology of Everyday Life*. I'll leave you with it, and before dinner you will have learnt all about the impossibility of accidents, and the unconscious self, and the sexual symbolism of fountain-pens [she takes his up], and – but I see you're blushing already.

After further exchanges, they decide they are 'incompatible' and Arthur walks away, only to return – because he has forgotten his fountain pen. 'There may be rather more in Dr Freud than I'd supposed,' he says – and they disappear into the summer-house.[27]

This amusing glimpse of Bloomsbury conversation prompts us to look for more firmly documented evidence of Virginia Woolf's knowledge of psychoanalysis. This was the period when the adjective 'Freudian' entered common parlance. A significant early use of the word in print occurred as the heading of a book review in the *Times Literary Supplement* of 25 March 1920, entitled 'Freudian Fiction'. This dealt with *An Imperfect Mother*, a novel about an incestuous mother/son relationship by J.D. Beresford. Reviews were published anonymously, so few people would have guessed at the time that this article was by Virginia Woolf (it is reprinted in her collected essays). The title 'Freudian Fiction' was doubtless supplied by the editorial staff, but the review itself indicates that Woolf had already grasped the basic ideas of psychoanalysis. Her main concern was to draw a line between 'artistic' and 'scientific' conceptions of human character, between the imaginative creations of the novelist and the scientific analyses of the medical man. The psychoanalytic interpretation of character is repudiated, not because it is untrue, but because it leaves the reader with 'cases', not 'people of flesh and blood'.[28]

A further turning point occurred when the Hogarth Press, the small publishing company run jointly by Leonard and Virginia Woolf, took the International Psychoanalytic Library, including the first volume of Freud's collected papers. In a letter of July 1924 Virginia comments on the consequences: 'all the psychoanalytic books have been dumped in a fortress the size of Windsor Castle in ruins upon the floor'.[29] At the end of 1924 the Hogarth Press published the second volume of Freud's collected papers under its own imprint. An even greater impact was made by the third volume, which they brought out the following year. This 600–page publication contained the great case histories, translated by James and Alix Strachey. At that date, Virginia was still very much involved with the everyday work of the Press, including proof-reading, and some of the Freud volumes passed through her hands. She wrote to her friend Molly MacCarthy in October 1924: 'I shall be plunged in publishing affairs at once; we are publishing all Dr Freud, and I glance at the proof and read how Mr A. B. threw a bottle of red ink on the sheets of his marriage bed to excuse his impotence to the housemaid'.[30] Woolf is citing a passage from Freud's discussion of obsessional symptoms in the *Introductory Lectures*.[31] This letter emphasises her scepticism about the psychoanalytic concept of free association – but it also shows that she understood it well enough to make fun of it.

Thus in the period 1920–1925 Virginia Woolf found herself in the midst of a vogue for Freud's writings in which she, Leonard and their Bloomsbury friends played a leading role. Initially seen as a commercial risk, the Freud volumes actually earned a handsome profit, providing a further incentive to take them seriously. The Bloomsbury conversation about Freud continued in their letters. In November 1924 the Press published a pamphlet by Roger

Fry entitled *The Artist and Psycho-Analysis*, a defence of disinterested aesthetic activity which questioned the assumptions of Freud's essay on 'Creative Writers and Daydreaming'. After reading the proofs, Virginia was so excited that she felt she 'must write off at once and say how it fills me with admiration and stirs up in me, as you alone do, all sorts of bats and tadpoles – ideas, I mean' (letter to Roger Fry, 22 September 1924). His pamphlet impressed her far more than the more controversial article entitled 'Dr Freud on Art' by Clive Bell, published in the journal *Nation and Athenaeum*.[32]

A dinner-party conversation on 13 May 1925, as recorded in a letter from James to Alix Strachey, enables us to pinpoint Virginia's evolving attitude: 'Last night I dined with the Wolves [...]. Virginia made a more than usually ferocious onslaught upon psychoanalysis and psychoanalysts, more particularly the latter'.[33] This contains two crucial clues. First, it shows that Virginia's involvement in debates about psychoanalysis was quite a 'usual' feature of her social intercourse. Secondly, it suggests that her hostility related less to Freud's theories than to the practice of psychoanalysis as a treatment for mental illness. Her own mental breakdowns gave her a personal interest in this question. Neither she nor Leonard ever favoured psychoanalysis as a treatment for her depressions, a factor which may help to explain the defensiveness of some of her comments. However, it is questionable whether she really benefited from the more conventional cures prescribed by their chosen British specialist, Sir George Savage.

The dinner-table conversation recorded by James Strachey acted as a trigger for Woolf's creativity. The following morning, 14 May 1925, she sat down at her desk and mapped out the plot of *To the Lighthouse* in her diary:

> This is going to be fairly short; to have father's character done complete in it; and mother's; and St Ives; and childhood; and all the usual things I try to put in – life, death, etc. But the centre is father's character, sitting in a boat, reciting we perished, each alone, while he crushes a dying mackerel.[34]

The plot summarised here echoes the classical oedipal pattern of psychoanalysis, although Woolf does not conceptualise it in those terms. And the exceptional quality of the finished novel lies in its exploration of unconscious ideas and emotions.

It cannot be a coincidence that during the years 1924–1927, a period of intensified publicity for psychoanalysis and heated debates about Freud, Virginia Woolf's writing underwent a paradigm change. This is reflected in the narrative techniques of her novel about post-war London, *Mrs Dalloway* (1925), and the more complex exploration of family dynamics in *To the Lighthouse* (1927). In *Mrs Dalloway* the transformation is still tentative and incomplete, although we encounter obviously Freudian symbolism – Peter Walsh stealthily fingering his pocket-knife as he pursues a strange woman through the streets of London, and the tower of Big Ben as a symbolic centre for the reflections on gender relations that shape the narrative.

If *To the Lighthouse* can be seen as Woolf's finest work, this is because the stimulus received from psychoanalysis becomes so subtly fused with her own memories and preoccupations. The decision she took, so soon after that dinner-table conversation, to rework her own childhood in the form of an autobiographical novel could even be regarded as her alternative to psychotherapy – a form of self-analysis that enabled her to discharge poignant memories in fictional form. She was trying to beat the psychoanalysts at their own game – to go beyond what she had criticised as the reductive elements in Freudian fiction and create a more complex picture, in which patriarchal attitudes are subtly undermined.

The portrayal of the lighthouse, as the symbolic centre of the novel, has implications which are by no means merely phallic, although oedipal tensions are introduced on the very first page. Whether Woolf was fully conscious of this at the time may be doubted. This question was put to her in May 1927 by one of her greatest admirers, the art critic Roger Fry, who wondered whether 'arriving at the Lighthouse has a symbolic meaning that escapes me'. To this she replied:

> I meant nothing by The Lighthouse. One has to have a central line down the middle of the book to hold the design together. I saw that all sorts of feelings would accrue to this, but I refused to think them out, and trusted that people would make it the deposit of their own emotions – which they have done, one thinking it means one thing, another another.[35]

Woolf presupposes active readers who will bring their imagination into play in response to the complexities of the text, but this does not mean that she provides no clues. Her reply that the lighthouse forms a 'central line' echoes the indication in her diary note two years earlier that 'the centre is father's character'. In the process of creation a displacement has taken place from personal memory to symbolic structure.

The lighthouse forms a crystallisation point for a cluster of contradictory feelings about the limitations of the phallic realm. It is identified not simply with the father figure, Mr Ramsay, but also with the barely conscious spiritual aspirations and sensuous desires of his wife, Mrs Ramsay. This becomes explicit in Part One, chapter 11, where Mrs Ramsay, alone at last at nightfall, contemplates the lighthouse through the window as she completes her knitting:

> Losing personality, one lost the fret, the hurry, the stir; and there rose to her lips always some exclamation of triumph over life when things came together in this peace, this rest, this eternity; and pausing there she looked out to meet that stroke of the Lighthouse, the long steady stroke, the last of the three, which was her stroke [...].[36]

This illustrates the way in which a Freudian borrowing may be transformed into something more original. For it seems likely that Woolf was half remembering a passage from the *Psychopathology of Everyday Life*, where Freud highlights the significance of 'the third stroke' in one of his anecdotal examples. This parallel has been analysed by Mary Jacobus in an article entitled '"The Third Stroke": reading Woolf with Freud'. In Freud's anecdote, the 'third stroke' represents the phallus, associated in the mind of his patient with the difference between the letter 'm' and the letter 'n'. The letter 'm' has something that 'n' lacks – 'the third stroke [...] a whole piece more'. In her feminist interpretation of the novel, Jacobus comments: 'This is the stroke that Woolf gives back to Mrs Ramsay in an act of reparation'.[37]

In 1927 Virginia Woolf may not have been fully aware of any debt to Freud. However, a dozen years later, in 'A Sketch of the Past', she explicitly acknowledged the connection in a passage about her obsessive memories of her mother, who had died when Virginia was thirteen:

> Then one day walking round Tavistock Square I made up, as I sometimes make up my books, To the Lighthouse; in a great, apparently involuntary rush. ... I wrote the book very quickly; and when it was written, I ceased to be obsessed by my mother. I no longer hear her voice; I do not see her.

> I suppose I did for myself what psycho-analysts do for their patients. I expressed some very long felt and deeply felt emotion. And in expressing it I explained it and then laid it to rest.[38]

So finally there was a meeting of minds between Freud and Woolf. The story was completed when Freud and his family arrived as refugees from Nazism. Among the first to welcome them to London were Virginia and Leonard Woolf, and by December 1939, as she notes in her diary, she was 'gulping up Freud'.[39]

The war against Hitler's Germany had begun, and bombs were falling on London, destroying much loved locations in Bloomsbury. But Virginia's failing spirits were lifted as she studied Freud's more political writings, including 'Thoughts for the Times on War and Death'. In her own wartime writings, as Hermione Lee has shown, 'she adopted Freud's belief in the essential aggression and destructive instincts of the human species'. Civilisation seemed to be in ruins, but the fault, according to Woolf's feminist reinterpretation of Freud, lay with the specifically male form of aggression that motivated fascism. Hence the faith in a non-patriarchal alternative expressed in her transformation of his 'Thoughts [...] on War' into her own 'Thoughts on Peace in an Air Raid' (1940).[40] Despite the many divergences, the creative dynamics of Vienna and London, of coffeehouse and tea party, did finally coalesce after all.

Notes

1. For an overview, see Gilbert J. Carr, 'Austrian Literature and the Coffee-House before 1890', in J. Beniston and D. Holmes (eds), *From Ausgleich to Jahrhundertwende: Literature and Culture 1867–1890*; *Austrian Studies*, 16, 2008, 154–171. See also the anthology, Kurt-Jürgen Heering (ed.), *Das Wiener Kaffeehaus. Mit zahlreichen Abbildungen und Hinweisen auf Wiener Kaffeehäuser*, Frankfurt 1993. For an attempt to convey the flavour of this writing in English, see Harold B. Segel (ed.), *The Vienna Coffeehouse Wits 1890–1938*, Indiana 1993.

2. See Reingard Witzmann, *Das Wiener Kaffeehaus: von den Anfängen bis zur Zwischenkriegszeit*, Vienna 1980, 33–34 and 87–89.

3. The accessibility of coffeehouses as public spaces is considered in more detail in Charlotte Ashby, 'The Cafés of Vienna: Space and Sociability' in this volume.

4. Otto Stoessl, *Das Haus Erath*, Leipzig 1928, reprinted Graz 1983.

5. See Charlotte Ashby, 'The Cafés of Vienna: Space and Sociability' in this volume.

6. Ernst Behler (ed.), *Kritische Friedrich Schlegel-Ausgabe*, 35 volumes, Munich 1958–, vol. 7, xcviii.

7. William Hazlitt, 'On Coffeehouse Politicians', in *Table Talk, or Original Essay on Men and Manners*, second edition, London 1824.

8. Arthur Symons, *London: A Book of Aspects*, quoted in Peter Brooker, *Bohemia in London: The Social Scene of Early Modernism*, Basingstoke 2007, 31.

9. Ford Madox Ford, 'Henri Gaudier: the Story of a Low Teashop', *English Review*, October 1919, cited in Brooker, *Bohemia in London,* 119. In response to the anti-German hysteria of the First World War, Hueffer changed his surname to Ford.

10. Wyndham Lewis, *Blasting and Bombardiering: An Autobiography*, London 1967, 272 and 280–281 (originally published in 1937).

11. Brooker, *Bohemia in London*, xii and xiii.

12. See Richard Shone, *The Art of Bloomsbury*, London 1999, 84–85.

13. Edward Timms, *Karl Kraus – Apocalyptic Satirist: Culture and Catastrophe in Habsburg Vienna*, New Haven and London 1986, 9.

14. Quentin Bell, *Bloomsbury* (New Edition), London 1990, 14–15.

15. Andreas Brunner (ed.), *Geheimsache: Leben – Schwule und Lesben im Wien des 20. Jahrhunderts*, Vienna 2005, 97.

16. *Baedeker's Austria-Hungary*, Leipzig 1905, 3.

17. For further details, see Douglas Blair Turnbaugh, *Duncan Grant and the Bloomsbury Group*, Secaucus 1987.

18. Perry Meisel and Walter Kendrick (eds), *Bloomsbury/Freud: The Letters of James and Alix Strachey 1924–1925*, London 1986. The details that follow are based on the introduction to this volume as well as the letters themselves.

19. Virginia Woolf, *The Question of Things Happening: Collected Letters II*, Nigel Nicolson (ed.), London 1994, 211.

20. For further information, see Jürgen Schebera, *Damals im Romanischem Café ... Künstler und ihre Lokale im Berlin der zwanziger Jahre*, Leipzig not dated.

21. Introduction to Meisel and Kendrick, *Bloomsbury/Freud*, 38.

22. Jan Ellen Goldstein, 'The Woolfs' Response to Freud', in Edith Kurzweil and William Phillips (eds), *Literature and Psychoanalysis*, New York 1983, 239.

23. Virginia Woolf, *Moments of Being* (Second Edition), Jeanne Schulkind (ed.), London 1985, 108.

24. Anne O. Bell (ed.), *The Diary of Virginia Woolf*, London 1982, V, 248; Brenda R. Silver, *Virginia Woolf's Reading Notebooks*, Princeton 1983, 116.

25. Goldstein, 'The Woolfs' Response to Freud', 240 and 247.
26. Hermione Lee, *Virginia Woolf,* London 1996, 68.
27. Lytton Strachey, 'According to Freud', in Paul Levy (ed.), *The Really Interesting Question and Other Papers,* London 1972, 112–120.
28. Virginia Woolf, *Contemporary Writers,* London 1965, 152–154.
29. Virginia Woolf, *A Change of Perspective: Collected Letters III,* Nigel Nicolson (ed.), London 1994, 119.
30. Woolf, *A Change of Perspective,* 134–135.
31. Sigmund Freud, 'Introductory Lectures on Psycho-Analysis', tr. James Strachey, in *The Complete Psychological Works of Sigmund Freud,* Standard Edition, XVI, 262. For a discussion of Woolf's response to this passage, see Elizabeth Abel, *Virginia Woolf and the Fictions of Psychoanalysis,* Chicago 1993, 18–19.
32. Woolf, *A Change of Perspective,* 132–133. The contrasting attitudes of Roger Fry and Clive Bell to Freud's theory of creativity are noted in Abel, *Virginia Woolf,* 17–18.
33. Meisel and Kendrick, *Bloomsbury/Freud,* 264.
34. Bell, *Diary of Virginia Woolf,* III, 18–19.
35. Woolf, *A Change of Perspective,* 385.
36. Virginia Woolf, *To the Lighthouse,* Susan Dick (ed.), Oxford 1992, 55.
37. Mary Jacobus, '"The Third Stroke": Reading Woolf with Freud', in Rachel Bowlby (ed.), *Virginia Woolf,* London 1992, 106–107.
38. Woolf, *Moments of Being,* 81.
39. Bell, *Diary of Virginia Woolf,* V, 249.
40. See the perceptive discussion of Woolf's wartime writings in Lee, *Virginia Woolf,* 722–731 (esp. 724).

NOTES ON CONTRIBUTORS

Charlotte Ashby was awarded her PhD in 2007 by the University of St Andrews for a thesis examining the intersection of nationalist and modernist aspirations in turn-of-the-century Finnish architecture. She went on to hold the post of Postdoctoral Research Fellow on the Viennese Café Project at the Royal College of Art. In 2008 she curated the exhibition *Vienna Café 1900* at the Royal College of Art and co-ordinated the accompanying programme of events and the conference *The Viennese Café as an Urban Site of Cultural Exchange*. She currently lectures for Birkbeck, University of London and the Courtauld Institute of Art.

Gilbert Carr is Fellow Emeritus of the Department of Germanic Studies, Trinity College Dublin. He has twice been awarded an Alexander von Humboldt Research Fellowship (University of Munich 1980, University of Göttingen 1992) and was awarded the Government of Ireland Senior Research Fellowship 2001/2. He has published extensively on German and Austrian literature and culture of the period 1890–1930, especially the Viennese fin-de-siècle.

Steven Beller is an independent scholar and author of *Vienna and the Jews, 1867–1938: A Cultural History* (Cambridge 1989); *Herzl* (Halban 1991); *Francis Joseph* (Longman, 1996); *A Concise History of Austria* (Cambridge 2007); and *Antisemitism: A Very Short Introduction* (Oxford 2008). He was also the editor of *Rethinking Vienna 1900* (Berghahn, 2001).

Tag Gronberg is Reader in the History of Art and Design and Postgraduate Tutor in the Department of History of Art and Screen Media at Birkbeck, University of London. Her research interests lie in the area of gender and modernism, and in projects that range across art, design and architecture. She was a member of the curatorial team organising the 2006 V&A exhibition "Modernism: Designing a New World 1914–1939". She is author of *Vienna – City of Modernity, 1890–1914* (Peter Lang, 2007) and *Designs on Modernity: Exhibiting the City in 1920s Paris* (Manchester University Press, 1998) (paperback 2003).

Shachar Pinsker is Associate Professor of Hebrew Literature and Culture at the University of Michigan. He is the author of *Literary Passports: The Making of Modernist Hebrew Fiction in Europe* (Stanford University Press, 2010), and the co-editor of *Hebrew, Gender, and Modernity* (University of Maryland Press, 2007). He has published numerous articles and chapters dealing with Hebrew, Jewish and Israeli literature and culture. He is currently working on a book entitled *To Write in a Silent Language: Yiddish as a Double Agent in Israeli Literature and Culture*, and a book on *Urban Cafés and Modern Jewish Culture*.

Katarzyna Murawska-Muthesius teaches at Birkbeck College, University of London. She was Curator and the Deputy Director of the National Museum in Warsaw. Her current research centres on caricature, art of the Cold War, and artistic exchanges between Poland and Britain. Her publications include *Europäische Malereiausdem Nationalmuseum Warschau* (Braunschweig 1988); *Trionfobarocco* (Gorizia 1990); *Borders in Art: Revisiting Kunstgeographie* (Warsaw 2000); *National Museum in Warsaw Guide: Galleries and Study Collections* (Warsaw 2001, 2006); *Kantor was Here: Tadeusz Kantor in Great Britain* (London 2011).

Ines Sabotič is Assistant Professor at the Croatian Catholic University, Zagreb, Croatia. She obtained a PhD in 2002 from the University of Paris I (Pantheon Sorbonne), in history with the thesis, *Les Cafés de Zagreb de 1884 à 1914: Sociabilités, Normes et Identités*. Her thesis was published in Croatian in 2007. Her many published articles focus on the cultural history of Croatia during the nineteenth century and her latest area of interest relates to the urban history of Zagreb around 1900.

Mary Costello is an AHRC-funded PhD candidate at the University of Plymouth, researching the intersection of the visual arts and ethnographic collecting and display in fin-de-siècle Vienna. She gained a Masters degree with distinction in Art History in 2007 and a first class degree in Art History with Gallery and Museum Studies in 2006, both from the University of Plymouth. She won the Art History department's prize for the best undergraduate dissertation in 2006, and in 2005 she won the University of Plymouth's Ede and Ravenscroft Prize for the most outstanding achievement in a pre-final year.

Jeremy Aynsley is Director of Research and Professor of History of Design at the Royal College of Art. His research interests are in late nineteenth- and twentieth-century design in Europe and the United States, with a special focus on design in Germany. His books include *Nationalism and Internationalism*, within the series *Design in the 20th Century* (V&A Publications, 1994), *Graphic Design in Germany 1890–1945* (Thames and Hudson, 2000) and *Designing Modern Germany* (Reaktion, 2010).

Richard Kurdiovsky is a Junior Researcher in the Department of History of Art in the Austrian Academy of Sciences. He was awarded his PhD in 2008 for a thesis on Carl von Hasenauer and Gottfried Semper's stylistic influence on his œuvre. Since 1997 he has been freelance member of staff at the Architecture Collection of the Albertina in Vienna. Since 2005 he has worked for the Commission for the Austrian Academy of Sciences research project on the Viennese Hofburg. He is also an assistant lecturer at the University of Vienna. His special area of research is Central European architecture from the Baroque period to the early twentieth century and he has published extensively within this area.

Edward Timms is a Fellow of the British Academy and Research Professor in History at the Centre for German-Jewish Studies, University of Sussex. His work as founder of the Centre was recognized when he was made an officer of the Order of the British Empire in 2005. In 2002 he was awarded the Austrian State Prize for History of the Social Sciences and in 2008 the Austrian Cross of Honour for Arts and Sciences. He has published widely on German and Austrian culture and politics. Of his numerous publications, he is best known for his book *Karl Kraus – Apocalyptic Satirist*, published in two volumes as *Culture and Catastrophe in Habsburg Vienna* (1986) and *The Post-War Crisis and the Rise of the Swastika* (2005).

Simon Shaw-Miller is Professor of the History of Art at the University of Bristol. He studied at the universities of Brighton and Essex (UK) and previously held positions at the universities of St Andrews and Manchester and was Professor of History of Art & Music at Birkbeck, University of London. In 2005 he was made an Honorary Research Fellow, and in 2007 an Honorary Associate of the Royal Academy of Music, London. He is the author of many essays and articles on the relationships between music and art, including the books *The Last Post: Music after Modernism* (1993) and *Visible Deeds of Music: Art and Music from Wagner to Cage* (2002). His co-edited collection of essays *Samuel Palmer Revisited* was published in 2010 and his new book *Eye hEar: The Visual in Music* will be published by Ashgate in 2013.

SELECTED BIBLIOGRAPHY

Allen, Roy F., *Literary Life in German Expressionism and the Berlin Circles*, Ann Arbor 1983.

Antoine, Eugene, 'Erinnerungen an das Cafe Griensteidl', in *Agathon: Almanach auf das Jahr 1948*, Vienna 1947/48, 41–55.

Baltzarek, Franz, Alfred Hoffmann and Hannes Stekl, *Wirtschaft und Gesellschaft der Wiener Stadterweiterung*, Wiesbaden 1975.

Banta, Martha, *Barbaric Intercourse: Caricature and the Culture of Conduct, 1841–1936*, Chicago and London 2003.

Barker, Andrew W., *Telegrams from the Soul: Peter Altenberg and the Culture of Fin-de-siècle Vienna*, Columbia, S.C. 1996.

Bauer, Margit Claire, *Die Kaffeehäuser von Carl Witzmann*, Salzburg 1989.

Bauschinger, Sigrid, 'The Berlin Moderns: Else Lasker-Schüler and Café Culture', in Emily Bilski (ed.), *Berlin Metropolis: Jews and the New Culture, 1890–1918*, Berkeley 1999.

Beckermann, Ruth and Teifer Hermann, *Die Mazzesinsel Juden in der Wiener Leopoldstadt 1918–1938*, Vienna 1984.

Beller, Steven, *Vienna and the Jews, 1867–1938: A Cultural History*, Cambridge 1991.

——— (ed.), *Rethinking Vienna 1900*, New York 2001.

Binder, Hartmut, *Wo Kafka und seine Freunde zu Gast waren: Eine Typologie des Prager Kaffeehauses*, Dortmund 1991.

———. *Wo Kafka und seine Freunde zu Gast waren: Prager Kaffeehäuser und Vergnügungsstätten in Historischen Bilddokumenten*, Prague 2000.

Bradbury, Malcolm and James McFarlane (eds), *Modernism: A Guide to European Literature 1890–1930*, London and New York 1991.

Brunner, Andreas (ed.), *Geheimsache: Leben – Schwule und Lesben im Wien des 20. Jahrhunderts*, Vienna 2005.

Burgert, Helmuth, *Das Wiener Kaffeehaus*, Brixlegg 1937.

Canetti, Elias, *The Play of the Eye*, New York 1999.

Carr, Gilbert J. 'Austrian Literature and the Coffee-House before 1890', in J. Beniston and D. Holmes (eds), *From Ausgleich to Jahrhundertwende: Literature and Culture 1867–1890*, Austrian Studies, no. 16, 2008, 154–171.

Castelliz, Ernst, *Formen der Geselligkeit in Wien zu Beginn des 20. Jahrhunderts*, Vienna 1998.

Colomina, Beatriz, *Privacy and Publicity: Modern Architecture as Media*, Cambridge, Mass. and London 1996.

Cowan, Brian, *The Social Life of Coffee*, New Haven and London 2005.

Crowley, David, *National Style and Nation-State: Design in Poland from the Vernacular Revival to the International Style*, Manchester and New York 1992.

——, 'Castles, Cabarets and Cartoons: Claims on Polishness in Kraków Around 1905', in Anna Kwilecka and Francis Ames-Lewis (eds), *Art and National Identity in Poland and England*, London 1996, 103–118.

Czeike, Felix, *Historisches Lexikon Wien*, 5 vols, Vienna 1992–1996.

Dubrovic, Milan, *Veruntreute Geschichte*, Berlin 2001.

Durm, Josef, Hermann Ende, Eduard Schmitt and Heinrich Wagner, *Handbuch der Architektur: Vierter Theil: Entwerfen, Anlage und Einrichtung der Gebäude. 4. Halb-Band: Gebäude für Erholungs-, Beherbergungs- und Vereinszwecke etc.*, Darmstadt 1885 (2nd edn 1894).

Ellis, Markman, *The Coffeehouse: A Cultural History*, London 2004.

Gee, Malcolm, Tim Kirk and Jill Steward (eds), *The City in Central Europe: Culture and Society from 1800 to the Present*, Aldershot 1999.

Girhatz, T. 'Das "Café Griensteidl"', in *Alt-Wien*, 5(10), October 1896, 203–207.

Grafe, Christoph and Franziska Bollerey (eds), *Cafés and Bars: The Architecture of Public Display*, London 2007.

Gronberg, Tag, *Vienna, City of Modernity, 1890–1914*, Oxford 2007.

Gugitz, Gustav, *Das Wiener Kaffeehaus: Ein Stück Kultur- und Lokalgeschichte*, Vienna 1940.

Habermas, Jürgen, *The Structural Transformation of the Public Sphere: An Inquiry into a Category of Bourgeois Society*, (1962) trans. Thomas Burger et al., Cambridge 1989.

Haine, W. Scott, *The World of the Paris Cafés: Sociability among the French Working Class, 1789–1914*, Baltimore and London 1996.

Hall, Peter, *Cities in Civilization: Culture, Innovation, and Urban Order*, London 1998.

Heering, Kurt-Jürgen (ed.), *Das Wiener Kaffeehaus: Mit zahlreichen Abbildungen und Hinweisen auf Wiener Kaffeehäuser*, Frankfurt 1993.

Hirschfeld, Ludwig, *Das Buch von Wien: Was nicht im Baedecker Steht*, Munich 1927.

Horvath, Michael, Thomas Lehmann, Fritz Panzer and Nathalie Schüller, *Das Erweiterte Wohnzimmer: Leben im Wiener Kaffeehaus*, Vienna 1990.

Im Wirtshaus. Eine Geschichte der Wiener Gesellligkeit, Wien Museum, Vienna 2007.

Janik, Allan and Hans Veigl, *Wittgenstein in Vienna: A Biographical Excursion Through the City and Its History*, Vienna 1998.

Johnson, Julie M., 'Athena Goes to the Prater: Parodying Ancients and Moderns at the Vienna Secession', *Oxford Art Journal*, 26(2), 2003, 47–70.

Johnston, William M., *The Austrian Mind: An Intellectual and Social History 1848–1938*, Berkeley 1983.

Kos, Wolfgang and Christian Rapp (eds), *Alt-Wien: Die Stadt die Niemals War*, Vienna 2004.

Köstlin, August, 'Die Arkadenhäuser neben dem Rathause in Wien', in *Allgemeine Bauzeitung*, 50, 1885, 54–56.

Kretschmer, Helmut, *Kapuziner, Einspänner, Schalerl Gold.: Zur Geschichte der Wiener Kaffeehäuser*, Vienna 2006.

Liberles, Robert, 'Les Juifs, le Café et le Négoce du Café au XVIIIe Siècle', *Les Cahiers du Judaïsme*, 26, 2009, 4–14.

MacCallum, Thomas W., *The Vienna That's Not in the Baedeker*, Munich 1929.

Mayer, Sigmund, *Die Wiener Juden: Kommerz, Kultur, Politik 1700–1900*, Vienna 1916.

McCracken, Scott, *Masculinities, Modernist Fiction and Urban Public Sphere*, Manchester 2007.

Nautz, Jürgen and Richard Vahrenkamp (eds), *Die Wiener Jahrhundertwende Einflüsse,*

Umwelt, Wirkungen, Vienna 1993.

Ottillinger, Eva B. (ed), *Gebrüder Thonet. Möbel aus gebogenem Holz* (Publikationsreihe Museen des Mobiliendepots 16), Vienna, Cologne, Weimar 2000.

Plakolb, Ludwig (ed.), *Kaffeehaus. Literarische Spezialitäten und amouröse Gusto-Stückln aus Wien*, Munich 1959.

Polgar, Alfred, 'Theorie des "Café Central"', in Alfred Polgar, *Kleine Schriften*, Marcel Reich-Ranicki et al. (eds), Reinbek 1984, vol. 4, 254–259.

Prehsler, Ilse, *Das Kaffeehaus als Kulturelle Einrichtung im Europa des 18. und 19. Jahrhunderts – Herkunft, Entstehung, Entwicklung und Bedeutung*, Vienna 1985.

Rossmeisel, Claudia, *Das Gewerberecht im Wandel der zeit unter besonderer Berücksichtigung des 19. und 20. Jahrunderts dargestellt am Gasthaus-. Kaffeehaus- und Schankgewerbe*, Ph.D dissertation Universität Wien, Vienna 1995.

Rössner, Michael (ed.), *Literarische Kaffeehäuser*, Wien 1999.

Rozenblit, Marsha L., *Jews of Vienna, 1867–1914: Assimilation and Identity*, New York 1984.

Sabotič, Ines, *Les cafés de Zagreb de 1884 à 1914: sociabilités, normes et identités*, Ph.D. dissertation. Paris: Université Paris I Panthéon-Sorbonne, 2002.

Schebera, Jürgen, *Damals im Romanischem Café … Künstler und ihre Lokale im Berlin der zwanziger Jahre*, Leipzig not dated.

Schimmer, Karl E., *Alt- und Neu-Wien: Geschichte der Österreichischen Kaiserstadt*, Vienna and Leipzig 1904.

Schorske, Carl E., *Fin-de-siècle Vienna: Politics and Culture*, London 1980.

Schume, Harald, *50 Einfache Dinge, die Sie über Österreich und die Österreicher Wissen Sollten*, Frankfurt am Main 2009.

Schwaner, Birgit, *Das Wiener Kaffeehaus: Legende, Kultur, Atmosphäre*, Vienna 2007.

Seemann, Helfried und Christian Lunzer (eds), *Das Wiener Kaffeehaus 1870–1930: Das Wiener Kaffeehaus in Zeitgenössischen Photographien*, Vienna 1993, reprint 2000.

Segel, Harold B., *Turn-of-the-Century Cabaret: Paris, Barcelona, Berlin, Munich, Vienna, Cracow, Moscow, St. Petersburg, Zurich*, New York and Oxford 1987.

——— (ed.), *The Vienna Coffeehouse Wits: 1890–1938*, West Lafayette, Indiana 1993.

Soja, Edward, *Thirdspace: Journeys to Los Angeles and Other Real-and-Imagined Places*, Oxford 1996.

Sparke, Penny, *The Modern Interior,* London 2007.

Spiel, Hilde, 'Das Kaffeehaus als Weltanschauung', in *Wien: Spektrum einer Stadt*, Munich 1971.

Sternthal, Barbara and Harald Eisenberger, *Coffee to Stay: Die schönsten Cafés in Europa*, Vienna 2009.

Thiele-Dohrmann, Klaus, *Europäische Kaffeehauskultur*, Düsseldorf 1997.

Timms, Edward, *Karl Kraus, Apocalyptic Satirist: Culture and Catastrophe in Habsburg Vienna*, New Haven and London 1986.

Torberg, Friedrich, *Die Tante Jolesch oder Der Untergang des Abendlandes in Anekdoten*, Munich 1977.

———, *Die Erben der Tante Jolesch*, Munich 1981.

———, *Tante Jolesch or the Decline of the West in Anecdotes*, trans. Maria Poglitsch Bauer, Riverside, Cal. 2008.

Traum und Wirklichkeit: Wien 1870–1930, Historisches Museum der Stadt Wien, Vienna 1985.

Uhl, Friedrich, 'Wiener Kaffeehäuser', in *Wiener Zeitung*, 31 May 1900, 3–5.

Ury, Scott, "'Juste un café ?" Le rôle des cafés juifs à Varsovie au tournant du XXe siècle', *Les Cahiers du Judaïsme*, 26 (2009), 14–23, 26–30.

Weigel, Hans (ed.), *Das Wiener Kaffeehaus*, Vienna 1978.

Weinberg, Bennett Alan and Bonnie K. Bealer, *The World of Caffeine: The Science and Culture of the World's Most Popular Drug*, London 2000.

Das Wiener Kaffeehaus: von den Anfängen bis zur Zwischenkriegszeit, Historisches Museum der Stadt Wien, Vienna 1980.

Wistrich, Robert S., *The Jews of Vienna in the Age of Franz Joseph*, Oxford 1989.

Wobick, Sarah, 'Interdits de café: L'influence de la révolution de Juillet sur la condition des Juifs de Hambourg', Kurt Wolff (trans.), *The Sociology of Georg Simmel*, New York 1950.

Zweig, Stefan, *The World of Yesterday: An Autobiography*, London 1943.

INDEX